Author of The Cleanup Man

Engineered By THE LORD

Authored By G.S.CREWS

www.gscrews.com • crewspublications@yahoo.com

This novel is a work of fiction. Any references to real people, events, establishments, or locales are intended only to give the fiction a sense of reality and authenticity. Other names, characters, and incidents occurring in the work are either the product of the author's imagination or are used fictitiously, as those fictionalized events and incidents that involve real persons. Any character that happens to share the name of a person who is an acquaintance of the author, past or present, is purely coincidental and is in no way intended to be an actual account involving that person.

ISBN 13: 978-0-9795236-3-2
Editor: Windy Goodloe (Email: windy.goodloe@gmail.com)
Typesetting: www.MarionDesigns.com
Library of Congress Cataloging-in-Publication Data; G.S. Crews

Motorcycle supplied by BMW Ducati Husqvarna Motorcycles of Atlanta
1750 Cobb Parkway SE, Marietta, GA 30060 • www.bmwmcoa.com

Gone Missing a novel/by G.S. Crews

www.gscrews.com

Copyright © 2010 by G.S. Crews. All rights reserved. No part of this book may be reproduced in any form without the permission from the publisher, except by reviewer who may quote brief passage to be printed in a newspaper or magazine.

Dedication

This book is dedicated to Ellen Crews: My mother and my inspiration. Thank you for teaching me about true friendship and real love.

Special thanks to my loving and understanding wife, Delicia Crews. Thank you for being there through the tough times.

Thank you to the Crews family: my father (Steve Crews Jr) & my brothers (Charles, Steve III, Reginald, Greg, & Gabriel).

Also, I would like to thank the Richard Family: Mr. Rice, Mrs. Gail, Nikki, & Candace. Thank you all for the support and the love! Thank you all for believing in me and my talent!

Foreword

People go missing every day. They get with the wrong crowd. Then, they are gone. Be careful. Be very careful...*Ellen Crews*

The full moon rose high in the darkening sky as a white seagull soared on a warm breeze.

"Eek! Eek! Eek!" cried the seagull. The bird continued to flap its wings as it ascended higher into the night air. Its cries were heard only by a group of palm trees.

"Eek! Eek! Eek!"

The bird's destination was South Miami Beach, where the most beautiful people congregated because of the beach's promise of an endless nightlife. In this city, beauty was only skin deep. Below the surface of the exciting party scene, lush paradise, and gorgeous people grew a sinister tumor.

Unaware of this impending evil, the seagull continued to fly over the noisy party commotion on the Ocean Drive strip. It veered left, swooping between a set of three-story, white condominiums until it landed on the sidewalk of a gas station, located two blocks from the busy street.

"Eek! Eek! Eek!" cried the seagull again.

There was only one car in the parking lot of the station. Standing outside with church pamphlets in his hands was a white, middle-aged street preacher named Reverend Robinson. The night before, he had folded two hundred pamphlets by hand. He then spent the whole day handing out the fliers and ministering. At the waning of the day, he had passed out all but two. He glanced down at the logo of his church on the pamphlet which was a crown perched atop a cross, and prayed silently. This image symbolized all that was most important to Reverend Robinson. He was passionate about leading this lost earthly flock to their heavenly father.

Reverend Robinson was a simple man. His wrinkled navy suit and ten dollar dusty shoes had come from the Goodwill and were proof that the godly man cared more about salvation than appearance or prestige. He quietly prayed for two more souls to appear to receive his pamphlets. As soon as he finished his prayer, an Asian woman dressed in an orange shirt and skinny jeans exited the store, Reverend Robinson swiftly approached her and offered her one of his pamphlets.

"Hello, my sister in Christ. My name is Reverend Robinson of First Baptist Church. Please take this, miss, for the nourishment of your soul."

"Thanks, but no thanks."

"Excuse me, miss, but Buddha is not going to get you into the kingdom of heaven!"

The young woman smiled sweetly as she slowly raised her middle finger. Then, she turned, used a remote to unlock the doors of her car, and said, "Not all Asians pray to Buddha! For your information, I am Catholic!"

"I am sorry for passing judgment."

"That is fine, but can you do me a favor?" she asked as she opened her car door.

"What may that be, miss?"

"Invest in an iron and dust off your shoes! You look pathetic!"

Satisfied at having had the last word, the woman hopped into her car and drove off, leaving Reverend Robinson alone in the gas station parking lot. As the car disappeared down the street, he stooped down and wiped the dust from his shoes. At that moment, the seagull wobbled towards him and loudly cried, "Eek! Eek! Eek!"

"Greetings, my little friend! You don't care about my dusty shoes or wrinkled pants, do you?"

"Eek! Eek! Eek!"

Reverend Robinson reached into his pocket and dropped some crushed crackers to the ground as he quoted a scripture from the Bible, "'For I was hungry and you gave me something to eat.' Eat, my friend. You do not have to worry about spreading the word of God to people who don't believe."

As Reverend Robinson watched the bird eat the crackers, he became lost in thought. He thought about how the Lord always provided on all levels and how the word of God sustained a person during the most difficult of times.

2

Inside the gas station, Dave Anderson, a young white man dressed in flip-flops, khaki shorts, and a white short-sleeved shirt, walked to the counter with a handful of items. He was spending the weekend in Miami with his wife, Becky.

"Good evening, my friend," the Middle Eastern cashier greeted. "My name is Ahmed."

"Nice to meet you," Dave replied.

"Are you visiting for, how do you say, Valentine's Day?"

"As a matter of fact, yes, we are. The weather in New Hampshire was just too cold to enjoy the holiday."

"Valentine's Day is even more lovely when it falls on the weekend. How often does that happen?"

Dave scratched his head. After quickly adding some figures in his head, he answered, "I think it occurs once every twelve years."

"That is amazing! Only in America! Only in America!"

As Ahmed exuberantly extolled the virtues of America, Dave looked over his shoulder and saw Becky pulling a bottle of water out of the beverage section. Her shoulder length blonde hair fluttered in the wind.

"Becky, did you get everything?" Dave called out.

"Yes. Do you want a bottle of water?"

"Yes, please."

As the couple placed their items on the counter in front of the cash register, Ahmed's cell phone rang. He quickly answered it without paying any regard to his customers. "Hello? Yes. I have one that just came in. Yes. Blonde."

"This is not customer service! This is customer disservice," Dave fussed.

Ahmed overheard Dave and held up the first finger of his hand, indicating it would only be a moment. In that brief moment, Dave noticed a golden ring on Ahmed's finger. It was shiny and polished.

"Nice wedding band, but it's on the wrong finger," Dave said in a condescending voice.

"Okay. Sí, señor," Ahmed said as he concluded his cell phone conversation.

"I hope you are not as committed to your wife as you are committed to customer service. Gee whiz!"

Ahmed gently placed his phone on the counter and responded, "In regards to your comment about my ring, my friend, this is a special ring. It was worn by my father, his father, and his father before that."

"Look, I don't give a crap about your heritage or where you come from! I am ready to check out!"

"Relax, babe," Becky whispered as she put the bottle of water on the countertop. Her voice was just the balm that Dave needed to calm his nerves. He drew her close to him and turned his body to face hers. Then, he looked deeply into her eyes. The two kissed as Ahmed scanned the items.

Ahmed put an item in a bag and muttered under his breath, "May the angels welcome you whether in heaven or hell!"

"What did you say?" Dave asked angrily as he turned to face Ahmed.

"I-I said, 'That will be three-fifty,'" Ahmed fumbled.

"No, you didn't! You told me to go to hell, didn't you?"

"C'mon, babe. Forget about it. Just pay the man, so we can get out of here," Becky said.

Dave pulled out his credit card, but Ahmed blocked the credit card device with his right hand. He dared not allow Dave to use the device for fear of an electronic trail being created for the authorities to follow.

"No! No! You cannot use that, my friend! The machine is broken!"

"But the screen looks—"

"It is broken! It will charge you three times! Three times!"

Dave reached into his pocket and fished around, but there was nothing.

"Um, I don't have any cash. Becky, do you have any cash?"
"Nah, I left it in the room," she answered.
Ahmed put the remaining items in the bag and handed them to Dave.
"Just take it, my friend. It is, as you Americans say, on the house."

"Um, thanks. I won't argue with free!"

As Dave followed his wife out of the store, Ahmed reached under the counter and clicked a button, powering off all of his security cameras. He watched the couple as they walked to the exit, holding hands like lovers on a stroll through a park.

"Enjoy these last moments of happiness. El Hombre Guapo is coming," Ahmed muttered as he kissed his golden ring. Then, he turned and walked into a nearby room where he closed the door. He kneeled down on a mat and put a pair of headphones over his ears. Soon, there would be screams for help, and he did not want to hear them.

3

As the couple neared the exit, the automatic glass doors slid apart. Reverend Robinson immediately approached them with his last pamphlet in his hand.

"Hello, my brother in Christ. I am Reverend Robinson of the First Baptist Church."

"Nice to meet you," Dave said as he shook Reverend Robinson's right hand. "My name is Dave, and this is Becky."

"Nice to meet you, Mr. Dave and Mrs. Becky. All thanks be to our savior in Christ who has all power to do all things!"

"Amen," Dave replied.

"Please take this pamphlet. I hope that it will feed your spirit with the word of God."

"Thanks. Have a blessed Valentine's Day."

"May the Lord bless your day, too, Mr. Dave."

As Dave took the pamphlet from his hand, Reverend Robinson felt an overwhelming burning sensation in his hands. When his hands burned after touching a person, that meant that that person was in immediate danger. This phenomenon began when he was twenty years old. He had been involved in a tragic accident that had taken his girlfriend's life. He had fought hard to save her, but he was unsuccessful. He deeply regretted it and had often prayed for the ability to help others before it was too late. God had answered his prayers. The only catch was that he had to lay hands on that person to find out what kind of danger he or she was in.

"Mr. Dave, wait!" Reverend Robinson shouted.

"Yes?"

"Please come back! I must tell you something important!"

Becky tugged at Dave's arm as she whispered under her breath, "This guy, like, gives me the creeps! Let's go, Dave!"

"I can't walk away from a preacher. For goodness' sakes, he is in South Beach handing out pamphlets on Valentine's Day!"

"Okay, but don't take long. I want to freshen up at the hotel before we go to the club."

"I will be back in two and two. Hold the pamphlet."

Becky smiled as Dave handed her the pamphlet. Dave, then, walked back to the where Reverend Robinson stood. When he was a couple of feet away, Dave addressed the street preacher in a polite manner, "I'm sorry, reverend, but we are here on vacation and—"

Suddenly, Reverend Robinson grabbed Dave by the shoulders. Dave panicked and tried to move away, but the strength of the street preacher was amazing! The seagull flew away as Reverend Robinson closed his eyes and concentrated.

"Let me go! You're hurting me!" Dave shouted.

"Let him go!" Becky cried out.

Reverend Robinson advised, "Shhh! Be still. It will be over soon."

His grip tightened more. In desperation, Dave punched Reverend Robinson's forearm several times, but Reverend Robinson did not feel any of the punches. Dave, however, could feel Reverend Robinson's nails digging into his skin. He felt weak. He felt faint.

"Almost there. Almost," the reverend said.

"Let him go! Let my husband go, you bastard!" Becky cried.

Reverend Robinson's grip tightened even more, causing Dave to drop to one knee. There was a sharp flash of pain as his knee struck the ground.

Dave shouted. "B-becky, y-your purse! The stun gun!"

Becky quickly fished the stun gun out of her purse. Just as she pulled it out, Reverend Robinson let go of Dave's shoulder. Dave collapsed to the ground, grasping his shoulder.

"H-have you lost your mind?" Dave asked.

"No, but I had to lay hands on you to see your future," Reverend Robinson responded.

"Y-you're a loon!" Dave shouted as Becky helped him to his feet.

Reverend Robinson shook his head and said, "Dave, you

misunderstand. You are in grave danger!"

"It is Valentine's Day! The only dangers are these high gas prices, and you putting the holy claw on me!"

"He scratched you, Dave. Your arm is bleeding," Becky said.

"You, bastard! I am going to have to get a tetanus shot! You better not have AIDS!"

"Heed my warning, Dave," Reverend Robinson prophesized. "Beware of the man in the gray suit that wears the golden rings. When you see him, run for your life!"

"I'm going to sue your holy ass. When I am through with you, you won't even be able to preach on the street! Let's get out of here, Becky!"

Reverend Robinson briskly walked away and disappeared into the nearby darkness. Becky shook her head as the man fled away and said, "That guy is as crazy as a bat!"

"He shouldn't be out here on the streets," Dave said. "What if he attacks a little kid like that?"

"I know, right?"

"I need to get to a doctor, so I can get a shot. That guy could have any number of diseases."

"Dave, I think you are overreacting. You just need some peroxide."

Dave gave his wife a sideways look as he stood on the sidewalk near the gas station door. He could not believe what he was hearing, so he responded, "A bum just attacked me, and you are saying that I am overreacting?"

"Dave—"

"A backsliding preacher attacks your husband, and you say he is overreacting? You are so full of it!"

"Dave, I was just saying—"

"What are you saying, Becky?"

"Dave, I'm just saying that you are fine! They're surface scratches for God's sake!"

"Do you have any idea how many people get staph infections from little scratches?" Dave asked angrily.

"Just forget it, Dave. We will find you a hospital, and we will spend all night in the freaking emergency room!"

Dave saw the hurt in his wife's face and quickly apologized, "I'm sorry, Becky. Let's go to the room and get refreshed. I will go to the hospital tomorrow."

Becky did not respond as she looked down at the pamphlet Reverend Robinson had given them. Its cover read:

Who Can Find a Virtuous Woman?
For Her Price is Far Above Rubies

Suddenly, a pearl white Rolls Royce Phantom entered the parking lot of the gas station and parked at a nearby gas pump.

"Becky, take a look at that car! It is amazing!" Dave exclaimed.

"Huh? Wh-where?"

"Over there! Pump number five!"

Becky looked where Dave pointed and saw the luxury vehicle. The white light from the security lights gleamed across its golden grill and gave it an even richer appearance.

"That is so epic!"

"Quick, Becky. Take a picture!"

As Becky reached into her purse and pulled out her digital camera, the pamphlet fell from her hands and fluttered towards the Rolls Royce. At that moment, the driver's side door of the Rolls Royce opened up and out stepped a chauffeur dressed in a black tuxedo. He opened the rear passenger door, and a slim, light complexioned man with dark hair stepped out. He was dressed in a gray suit. Golden rings were on each of his fingers. The man in the gray suit whispered something to the chauffer, and the chauffer stepped back into the car. Becky gasped as she grabbed Dave's arm, "Oh, my God! That man is wearing a gray suit!"

"The who?"

"'Beware of the man in the gray suit with the golden rings.' Reverend Robinson warned us!"

"Quit being superstitious! This guy is probably some record producer or music artist!"

The man in the gray suit coolly walked to them. As he drew closer, he stopped and picked up the pamphlet that had escaped Becky's hands. After reading it, he continued to walk to them, all the while staring at Becky with eyes that were as cold as the back of an arctic cave. It was the look of a predator stalking its prey.

"Becky, come closer," Dave whispered as he noticed the stare.

The man stopped in front of the couple and spoke in an accented voice that was similar to the infamous Tony Montana. He said, "Not 36-24-36, but it will do, mane. Nice headlights on the rack!"

"Quit looking at my wife like that, you bastard!" Dave furiously shouted.

"It's okay! It's okay! You have a beautiful wife, mane!"

"Let's get out of here!" Becky said.

Dave and Becky tried to step to the right, but the man in the gray suit blocked their way.

"What do you think you're doing?" Dave asked.

"I don't want any trouble, mane. I read the title on the sheet of paper the lady dropped. I am always looking for women of her caliber for my magazine Sea Through."

Dave shook his head and said, "I know your kind. You're a pimp or some type of low life thug!"

"Such titles are only words, mane. Let me introduce myself. My name is El Hombre Guapo."

"The handsome man," Dave translated.

"So, you speaka Spanish?" El Hombre Guapo asked.

"No hablo español," Dave rudely replied. "Now, get out of our way!"

"Señor White Bread, you have a smart mouth, but how smart is your wife's mouth?"

Dave balled up his fists at the rude comment and said, "Buddy, you are about to need a partial plate 'cause I am going to knock all your teeth out!"

"Really?"

"Yes, sir! You are about to get last week's lunch kicked out of you!"

"Don't be so hasty. First, I would like for you to meet my shiny friend, Cynthia!"

Dave's body lost its energy as El Hombre Guapo reached beneath his suit jacket and pulled out a chrome pistol.

"Oh, my God!" Becky yelled. "H-he has a gun!"

"You are correct, señora, but do you know what type of gun Cynthia is?" El Hombre Guapo asked. Becky did not respond, so El Hombre Guapo answered, "Cynthia is a .45 Magnum, one the most powerful handguns in the world! Cynthia is made of pure steel. Do you know the mystery of steel?"

Again, there was no response.

"Steel is strong, but the will to live is even stronger!" Then, El Hombre Guapo turned to Dave and said, "Now, Señor White Bread, give me your wife, or I will blow off your freaking head!"

"B-becky, run!" Dave ordered.

"Dave!"

"Becky, run!"

"Dave!"

"Run! Now!"

El Hombre Guapo cocked back the gun and aimed it at Dave's chest.

"Such bravery. Such foolishness! I love it!" El Hombre Guapo said.

"Becky, get the hell out of here!" Dave yelled.

"Señor White Bread, may the angels welcome you whether in heaven or hell," El Hombre Guapo said coldly.

Becky broke out in a mad dash toward the street. Suddenly, there was a thunderous noise. Becky screamed as she tripped over her feet at the sound of the gunshot. The asphalt tore her palms, scraping back the tender skin.

"Dave!"

Becky turned around and saw Dave lying in a pool of his own blood. A wisp of smoke drifted from El Hombre Guapo's gun as he stood over her wounded husband.

"D-Dave! Dave!" Becky cried as she closed her eyes.

"Be patient, señora. I will be with you shortly."

El Hombre Guapo stood over Dave and unloaded three more shots into his chest.

"Dave! No! Dave! Dave!"

Suddenly, a shadow fell over Becky. She opened her eyes and saw El Hombre Guapo standing over her.

"Señora, it's true. Your price is worth more than rubies! Where you're going, blondes are priceless!"

"Bastard!"

"Don't be so angry, señora," El Hombre Guapo said calmly. "You are going to Costa Rica to see a friend of mine named El Ojo, and he will work you to death!"

In the distance, the sound of sirens could be heard.

"Time to go, señora."

The chauffeur popped the trunk as El Hombre Guapo roughly grabbed Becky by her blonde hair and jerked her to her feet.

"H-help! Help!" Becky cried out.

"¡Cállate!" shouted El Hombre Guapo.

He shoved the barrel of the pistol into Becky's right side. She, however, did not stop struggling. As the sirens grew louder, so did Becky's strength.

"Help! Somebody! Help!"

She knew that it would be just a few more seconds before the police arrived.

"Let me go! Let me go! Help! Somebody! Help!"

"¡Señora, cállate!"

In an act of desperation, El Hombre Guapo grabbed her by the waist and dragged her to the Rolls Royce just as the police arrived.

"Ha! Ha! You maniac!" Becky laughed hysterically. "You're going to jail, and they are going to gang rape you in the shower!"

The black Dodge Charger squad car pulled into the parking lot. The officer stepped out of the car with his hand on the pistol at his hip. He stared at the man in the gray suit as he held Becky by the waist with the gun at her back.

"Freeze! Don't move!" the officer ordered.

"Somebody put a fork in this dude because he is done!" Becky screamed. "El Whatever Your Name Is, you are so done!"

The officer pressed the miniature radio that was strapped on his left shoulder and said, "Dispatch. Officer Grayson, on the scene. Over?"

"Officer, what is the status of that report of gunfire at the gas station off Ocean Park?" dispatch asked.

"One white male. Gunshot wounds to the chest. DOA."

"Are there any other victims?" dispatch asked.

"There are no other victims. I repeat. No other victims."

"Signal five. Sending ambulance."

"What...what just happened?" Becky asked, bewildered.

The officer walked over to them and spoke in a low voice, "Hurry! The others will be here soon!"

"W-what just happened?" Becky asked hysterically. "Y-you're the police! The freaking police are supposed to save me!"

El Hombre Guapo replied in a calm voice, "Do you see the ring on his finger, señora?"

"Y-yes."

"It represents a very powerful bond. It represents La Committee."

"La-La Committee?" Becky stuttered.

"We have been around for centuries! My friend there is in the lower level of the organization, but he will get a promotion for this."

"The ring...even the cashier wore a golden ring."

"That is correct, señora. Those who wear the golden ring serve the will of La Committee, and I am their God! I own the local businesses; I own the polícia, the coast guard, and I even own you!"

There was a low popping sound as the trunk door of the Rolls Royce opened. El Hombre Guapo scooped Becky off her feet and carried her to the trunk where he gently placed her inside. Defeated, she curled up in a fetal position and cried, "Th-this can't be happening! This isn't real! It isn't real!"

"What you call real is only a fantasy," El Hombre Guapo

said. "Death is the ultimate reality."

"Th-this isn't real!"

El Hombre dropped a handkerchief inside the trunk and coldly said, "Wipe yourself off, and do not stain the interior. It is from Persia."

The chauffer closed the trunk of the Rolls Royce. Then, he opened the back passenger door for El Hombre Guapo. Once the two men were seated, the chauffer drove off. As the sleek Rolls Royce cruised down the street, an ambulance pulled into the gas station.

Chapter 2
Keysha's Grief

Not too far away from the gas station where Dave was gunned down and Becky was abducted, a light came on in the upstairs bedroom of a luxurious lakeside home. The outside of the home was astounding: terracotta roofing, stucco finish, and magnificent landscaping with coconut trees. However, inside one room, the conditions of the living quarters were well below the poverty level.

A ceiling fan slowly rotated as it hung from a dusty, mildewed ceiling. The walls and floor of the room were a bare brown wood. There was no decoration. In the cracks of the walls, funnel webs had formed, and the black legs of a spider were extended, waiting for a victim.

Down a short hallway was a bathroom and a walk-in closet. From these two rooms, a dank, musty odor— a mixture of urine, mold, and feces— filled the bedroom. In the left corner of the room was a dark colored nightstand. The dull finish was peeled at the edges, and the shelves within were broken. Even when the light was on, roaches scurried in and out of the broken shelves of the nightstand. On top of the broken nightstand rested a black laptop with a webcam, a damaged telephone, and a clock/radio. Positioned between the nightstand and the window was a worn-out, stained mattress. Dried, plum colored stains decorated the surface of the mattress. The stains were blood.

No person should have had to live in such conditions. Yet, one person survived in that filthy room. Sitting on the edge of the mattress, dressed in a pair of filthy gray sweatpants and a long sleeved t-shirt, was a sad woman named Keysha Belle. This sad woman was more than a prisoner. Keysha was near death and had all but given up hope of escaping her terrible existence.
She touched her thighs and cringed, "Ouch! T-They whipped me good. I have bruises from my ankles to my thighs!"

She shivered from the shakes, but it was nothing like it had been weeks before. She was finally getting over the shakes from the heroin they had given her a couple weeks ago. Keysha glanced over at the laptop with the webcam and said, "It is almost time to check in. I-I can't be late anymore."

Two weeks ago, she had checked in two minutes late. Later that night, El Hombre Guapo and one of his henchmen had burst into the room. The henchman held her down as El Hombre Guapo beat her with a bamboo stick.

"My life is ruined. I-I just can't keep living like this!"

Keysha wiped the tears from her face and looked on the floor near the door. She spotted the silver tray.

"That crazy rat bastard! He left me a piece of molded bread, a cup of water, and a syringe of Afghan heroin, strong enough to overdose on!"

Keysha stared at the syringe as she thought about her family.

"Mom, Dad, Nikki, and Candace, you wouldn't want to see me like this. Y'all are never going to find me."

Keysha reached out towards the syringe. Her hand trembled as her mouth went bone dry.

"My faith is gone! My hope is gone! It's time to go to sleep!"

Keysha leaned forward. Just as her fingertips were inches away from the syringe, she glanced to her left. Sitting on the floor was the only friend she had come to know during her six weeks of captivity. Staring at her was a brown teddy bear with black buttons for eyes.

"Teddy!"

Instead of picking up the syringe, Keysha picked up the brown teddy bear.

"T-teddy, how did this happen to me? I should have never gone to that photo shoot! I walked right into their trap! I should have seen it coming!"

She held Teddy close to her chest and sobbed, "Teddy, I remember...I remember how the sun felt on my shoulders as I leaned on the railing of the yacht and looked over the bay. Teddy, I remember how the sun reflected off Von Gretchen's bald head as he greeted me. I remember...I remember..."

Keysha squeezed the teddy bear as her mind flashed back to the photo shoot with Sea Through magazine that had taken place four weeks prior. She could feel the warm sun and the ocean breeze on her shoulders. She thought it was a moment of opportunity, but the moment proved to be something unimaginable, something inhumane.

2

A white seagull skimmed the blue water as Miami's noon sun glared across a private bay where a yacht was docked. Leaning on the white railing of the yacht and watching the bird was a very beautiful young lady dressed in an orange two-piece bathing suit and clear six-inch stiletto heels. The woman was Keysha Belle.

"Eek! Eek!" the white seagull cried out.

"Hi, little birdie!" Keysha joyfully replied.

The white seagull landed on the deck and searched the polished hardwood for something to eat.

"Eek! Eek!"

"I am sorry, little birdie, but I don't have any bread for you. This deck is as clean as a whistle."

As if the bird understood what she was saying, it flew away. Keysha watched as the white seagull flew across the bay and toward a cluster of lush trees. In the distance, purple rain clouds loomed on the horizon.

"Goodbye, birdie," Keisha said gleefully. "This is my first assignment! Wish me luck!"

Keysha tilted her head back, letting the warm sun beam on her face, neck, and bare shoulders.

She sighed, "Ocean breeze, where have you been all my life?" The cool ocean breeze slightly ruffled her long, curly hair. Moments passed. Finally, an accented voice greeted her, "What brings an angel down from heaven to visit us mortals today, yah?"

"Depends on who is asking?" Keysha smiled, turning around.

"My name is Von Gretchen."

He was a thin man with a bald head, dressed in khaki shorts and a tank top with a black camera slung across his shoulder.

"Nice name for a picture man," Keysha said.

"Picture man, yah? I have not heard that one before. What brings you here, today?"

"Opportunity knocked, so I answered. I am going to be the next top model for Sea Through magazine!"

"Very good answer. What is your name?"

"Keysha Belle."

"I am greatly pleased to meet you, yah."

Keysha shook Von Gretchen's hand. As her soft, delicate hand came in contact with his feeble one, a cold shudder ran through her body. However, Keysha kept her composure as she said, "I noticed your accent, Von Gretchen. Are you from Sweden?"

"Yah, that is my birthplace. Keysha, I noticed something different in your voice, too. Are you Italian or Spanish?"

"No. I am black and proud."

"Really? So, where are you from?"

"I am from Lafayette, Louisiana, home of crawfish boils and zydeco dancing!"

"Hmm, so what brings you to Miami, Florida?"

"I got a job transfer, but I was laid off. Then, I got behind on my bills."

"I see. Continue."

"Then, I saw your ad in the paper for a position as the top model with a ten thousand dollar advance."

Von Gretchen raised an eyebrow and asked, "What modeling agency do you represent, Keysha?"

"Me, myself, and I. This is my first shoot."

Von Gretchen rubbed his bald head and exclaimed, "You are an amateur?"

"Y-yes. Is that a problem?"

"This photo shoot is for a person of skill, a person of experience! There is no time for an amateur!"

"Von Gretchen, I can do this! At some point, Whitney Houston was an amateur! All I need is a chance!"

"How can you be so confident, Keysha? You have no experience!"

"I can do this, Von Gretchen. I can do this because I need this! When a person needs something, she uses other experiences to get the job done!"

Von Gretchen ceased rubbing his bald head and took a good look at her. Keysha possessed all the attributes that were required. She had a beautiful face, sexy body, and youthful appearance.

"Very well. We will shoot, but I must warn you. At the first sign of insubordination, we will abandon the shoot!"

"Thank you! Thank you!"

"Thank me later."

Keysha was elated. She hugged Von Gretchen and kissed him on the cheek. Quickly, Von Gretchen gave out the instructions, "Today, Keysha, I will be taking shots of you lying on the deck with your left leg stretched out and your right knee bent."

"Like a number four?"

"Exactly! Lean back on your elbows and arch your head back."

Keysha laid on the hardwood deck and arched her head back, sending her curly hair streaming down like a dark waterfall. She was natural, professional, and sensual.

"Good, Keysha! Now, don't forget to breathe! That is the most common mistake most models make!"

"Would you like for me to smile?"

"No, I want the tone of this cover to be serious. Dead serious, yah!"

He licked his thin lips as he put the high-resolution, professional digital camera to his left eye and zoomed in on Keysha's well-conditioned legs, toned abdominals, and well-proportioned breasts.

"Your almond shaped eyes are like jewels. Your complexion is flawless, and your hourglass figure is timeless."

Keysha kept her serious pose but smiled on the inside. This was the breakthrough she had been waiting for.

"Now, for some Mother Nature! Bosh, bring in the water pole!"

Keysha glanced at the pudgy blonde teenager, Bosh. He had

transported her from the bay to the yacht earlier. Bosh walked up to Keysha carrying a modified shower pole. He extended it over her.

"Let it rain!" Von Gretchen shouted.

Bosh turned on the warm water, creating a light rain shower. Von Gretchen's camera rapidly snapped pictures from various angles.

"Keysha, you are stunning! You are a stunning vixen! No, you are a stormy, stunning vixen!"

Within minutes, Von Gretchen had snapped over one hundred pictures. When the shoot was over and Keysha dried off, Von Gretchen walked over and shook Keysha's hand. He said, "There was nothing amateur about that photo shoot."

"Thanks."

"You are phenomenal! Your talent is going to take you far!"

At that moment, the sun glinted off the numerous stones set in a golden ring on Von Gretchen's right hand. It caught Keysha's attention, so she asked, "That is a nice ring, Von Gretchen. Did you play sports?"

"No, I have two left feet when it comes to the running and the dancing. This ring is a family heirloom."

"Well, that is a very nice ring. Now, Von Gretchen, if you will excuse me, I would like to go to the little girls' room and change clothes."

Von Gretchen pointed at a small bathroom that was located to their right.

"Of course. You can change in there. I am about to make a

phone call to my boss. Meet me back on the deck."

"Okay."

"Congratulations, Keysha. You should be proud of yourself."

"Don't worry. I am."

She walked to the bathroom and changed her clothes. She looked into the mirror with a face filled with excitement.

"Daddy is going to be so proud! His little princess is going to make something out of herself!"

She quickly changed clothes, slipping on a pair of gray sweatpants, a long sleeved white t-shirt, and a pair of tennis shoes that she had brought in a gym bag. She pulled her curly hair back into a ponytail. When she walked out of the bathroom, Von Gretchen was waiting for her with a white rose in his hand.

"Von Gretchen, what is this rose for?"

"Where I am from, Keysha, a person gives another person a white rose to signify the beginning of a relationship."

Keysha put her hands on her hips as she asked, "And what type of relationship would that be?"

"A business relationship, of course."

"Von Gretchen, I want to set the record straight. I am not like other women."

"I—"

"I wasn't finished," Keysha interrupted. "I just want you and your boss to know that I have values. I have no intention of becoming a video vixen or porn star!"

Von Gretchen smiled, revealing his coffee-stained teeth, and said, "It is this innocence that makes you perfect for the job! We are seeking someone for longevity, not a person who is here for a moment."

"Then, I am the woman you need to take your company to new heights."

"When I posted the advertisement, I was searching for a woman exactly like you. Your beautiful face, exciting flare, and amazing body will be the image of this company!"

"Can you repeat that? I am a little hard of hearing sometimes!"

"I said, 'You will be the image of this company.'"

Keysha looked around herself and said, "This is a joke, right? Is there a hidden camera somewhere around here?"

"This is no joke, and this is not a reality show. It gets better," Von Gretchen assured.

"How much better?"

"The boss is eager to meet you right now, yah."

Keysha felt her heart flutter as she asked, "After one photo shoot, I am going to get to meet the owner of the company?"

"Yah, this is a rare occasion."

"I mean this is the equivalent of meeting the president of a Fortune 500 company after your first hour on the job!"

"Yah, this is a once in a lifetime opportunity."

"W-who is the boss?" Keysha nervously asked. "What is his name?"

"His name is El Hombre Guapo."

"My Spanish is a little rusty, but doesn't that mean the handsome man?"

"Yah, they do not make too many men like El Hombre Guapo. He will change your life forever."

"When can we meet?"

"You are in luck. He is in the cabin below."

"Are you serious?"

"Yah, follow me."

Von Gretchen escorted Keysha down a flight of stairs that led to a single white door in the lower deck of the yacht. Von Gretchen opened the door and beckoned for her to enter the foyer of the cabin.

"After you, my darling."

"Von Gretchen, I just wanted to say th—"

"There is no need to thank me. Your destiny awaits you!"

As Keysha entered the well-lit room, Von Gretchen closed the door behind her. Then, he leaned against it. Above him, a rain cloud passed over the sun, and rain began to fall. Von Gretchen fell to his knees, dropped his head in regret, and prayed, "Lord, please have mercy on me in the judgment. Please forgive me for sending your flock into captivity!"

He inserted his key and locked the door. Keysha heard the door lock and wheeled around at the sound to face the door. Her heart pumped both fearfully and joyfully in her chest. Almost as a reflex, she called out, "Von Gretchen? Where are you?"

At that moment, a man with an accented voice called out to her. The voice sounded like the infamous Tony Montana.

"It's okay! It's okay, doll face! Come into the back, so El Hombre Guapo can get a good look at the person who is going to take my business to new heights!"

Keysha straightened her posture and walked into the spacious cabin where she noticed several flat screen televisions with video game consoles, a foosball table, and a pool table. She entered a hallway where an aquarium was imbedded in the walls. It was home to an impressive collection of exotic, glowing fish.

"Marco!" El Hombre Guapo called out.

"Polo!" Keysha joyfully responded.

"You're getting warmer, doll face!"

She walked down the hallway. When it ended, she stepped into a lavish living room with a chaise lounge, a sofa, and a recliner that faced a glass window that overlooked the bay. Near the lounge was a table with a bottle of chilled champagne and two glass flutes.

"You have a nice yacht," Keysha said to the person sitting in the recliner.

"Ahh! You found me!"

"I never play a game to lose."

"Then, you will never know the taste of defeat!"

The recliner rotated to reveal a handsome man with a light complexion and short dark hair. The man was dressed in dark pants with a red shirt that was unbuttoned near the top, exposing a patch of thin chest hair. Gold rings were on each of the man's fingers.

"El Hombre Guapo, I presume."

"Sí, and you must be the lovely Keysha Belle."

"Twenty-four hours a day, seven days a week!"

"Von Gretchen said that you had flare and pizzazz! I like it!"

"Thank you. You know you look like a person on television."

"I was just having a similar thought about you. Pray tell, who do I favor on your television?"

"Your keen nose and chin remind me of a slim version of the wrestler called The Rock."

"That is a first. Most people say I look like God!"

"Huh, okay," Keysha said in an uneasy voice.

"Now, it is my turn. Do you know who you remind me of?"

"A lot of people say I look like Vivica Fox."

El Hombre Guapo shook his head and said, "In the body, but not in the face. This woman was in the polícia movie with Will Smith and Martin Lawrence."

"Oh! You mean Gabrielle Union."

"Sí, you are a lighter version with teddy bear eyes!"

Keysha blushed, "Wow! Now, that's a first! She is beautiful"

"Señorita, please sit. Take a load off," he said as he beckoned her to have a seat on the sofa.

"Thank you," Keysha said as she sat.

"I am about new beginnings. Welcome to one of my humble abodes."

"One of your houses?"

"Sí, my father has many, many mansions."

"I know he is getting killed in taxes," Keysha said as she leaned back and crossed her legs.

"Are you the IRS?" El Hombre Guapo asked in a serious tone.

"No, but I am good with numbers. I was an accountant until I was laid off."

"The economy is bad. Companies are cutting jobs like a hot knife through butter, but guess what?"

"Umm, you saved a lot of money on your car insurance?" Keysha asked humorously.

"Ha! Ha! I love a woman with a sense of humor!"

"My mother always says that laughter is the cure for any sickness."

"Your mama is wise," El Hombre Guapo said as he stood up from his recliner. Then, he changed the subject as he stated, "Your name does not do your beauty justice."

"Thank you for the compliment," Keysha blushed.

"Keysha Belle is a lovely name, but that name isn't good enough for you!"

"You're so silly."

"What do you call those brainiac stooges in college who teach the students?"

"Umm, professors."

"Sí, professors!" El Hombre Guapo exclaimed as he snapped his fingers. "Professors can't even come up with a name for your beauty! Every time they try, it escapes them like a phantom, like a ghost!"

"Then, who can name me?"

El Hombre Guapo proudly placed the palm of his right hand on his chest and said, "You are looking at him in the flesh! Let me get my camera!"

El Hombre Guapo made an 'L' shape with the first finger and thumb on each hand, then turned one in the opposite direction of the other, forming a rectangle.

"W-what are you doing?" Keysha giggled.

"I am making a high-def camera! Almost done!"

"You're nuts!"

"No, I am bananas! Smile!"

"Alright. Go for what you know."

"Let me zoom in. Be still. Be still," El Hombre Guapo said as he moved his hands back and forward, mimicking the movements of a skilled photographer.

"Put this one in your photo album," Keysha said as she posed with one hand on her hip and blew him a kiss with the other.

"Voilà! I have it! The name worthy of your beauty is Bonita Chica!"

"Bonita Chica? Beautiful Girl?" Keysha translated.

"¡Bueno! Your Spanish is good, but I think you could use a few more classes."

"Classes?" Keysha asked.

"Sí, my personal one-on-one classes," El Hombre Guapo answered.

Keysha rolled her eyes. She had known that this was too good to be true, so she said, "El Hombre Guapo, I am not that type of girl! I never have been and never will be!"

"I did not mean to offend you. Accept my apology, por favor?" El Hombre Guapo said as he took her hand and lightly kissed her knuckles. The sensation of his soft lips pressing against her skin was pleasurable and nothing short of charming.

"Your apology is accepted. Just don't make that mistake again! First and foremost, I am a woman."

"Gracias for your mercy. A thousand apologies. It will never happen again."

"I can live with that. Can we proceed to the business at hand?"

"Sí. Did Von Gretchen give you any specifics on your assignment?"

"Um, no. He just informed me that you wanted to meet me."

"Very well. First, let's have a glass of champagne."

"Sí."

Keysha watched as El Hombre Guapo picked up the bottle of champagne and unscrewed the cork.

"This drink is strong," El Hombre Guapo said as he poured champagne into one of the glass flutes.

"Don't worry. I know how to handle my alcohol," Keysha said, turning around and taking in the room in which she now found herself. Then, she asked, "Doesn't it get lonely here?"

"At times. This is my escape from the fake world of political agendas and other things that make the world a bad place."

"I understand. The world can be cruel."

"Yes, it can very cruel. Here, I filter out the bad and relish the good. Your champagne, Bonita Chica."

El Hombre Guapo handed the glass of champagne to Keysha.

"Thank you."

"To the start of a new life, Bonita Chica."

"A new life."

They tapped their glasses together and took a drink. El Hombre Guapo placed his champagne on the nearby end table and began to explain the purpose of their business.

"Three days ago, I placed an ad in the paper that stated we were looking for a top model for Sea Through. In five hours, we received five hundred applicants."

"Wow! There are a lot of aspiring models around here!"

"Sí, it is a lifestyle here in Miami. We took fifty applicants. Of the fifty, you were number one. This opportunity calls for you to have a unique relationship with the company, almost like a marriage."

"I won't have to do the laundry or anything like that?"

El Hombre Guapo let out a hearty laugh and shook his head, saying, "No, Bonita Chica, you will be the model of models. You could have your own servants if you wanted to."

"That's very kind of you, but I won't need any servants. I do want to tell you that Von Gretchen is a great photographer. He made me feel really comfortable."

"He has been with me from the beginning and has always done a great job."

El Hombre Guapo raised his glass again and said, "Cheers to our success!"

He again tapped her glass with his. Then, he drank all of his champagne. Keysha did likewise, draining her glass of the champagne. She touched the left corner of her neck as she felt the tingly sensation of the alcoholic beverage.

"Whoo! That is a strong drink! What kind of champagne was that?"

"It is my own special champagne. It has a special ingredient that cruel kings used to poison their enemies."

"Um, excuse me? El Hombre Guapo, did you just say something about poison?"

"Sí, Bonita Chica, you just drank poison."

"What in the hell do you mean? I just drank poison?"

"Your modeling days and everything that you know are over, Bonita Chica."

"Excuse me? You just switched from Dr. Jekyll to Mr. Hyde!"

El Hombre Guapo leaned forward and spoke in a sinister voice, "Bonita Chica, I am a business man, a drug lord, and a high trader in the Central American female slave market!"

"I-I can't believe this crap."

"Believe it. You should start noticing some of the side effects of the poison very soon."

"You…you tricked me," Keysha said as her breathing became short.

"I gave you what you wanted, Bonita Chica. You are a top model for Sea Through magazine."

"But why? Why did Von Gretchen help you?"

"Von Gretchen is my half-brother. More importantly, he is a gambler who is indebted to me. He repays me by supplying me with beautiful women."

Keysha rubbed her hands on her face as she began to understand the diabolic trap that had ensnared her.

"The fifty…fifty women that you shot are all your prisoners, so Sea Through magazine doesn't exist!"

"Bonita Chica, you are very intelligent. Nothing gets passed you!"

"You…you lied to me!"

"There is truth in every lie, Bonita Chica!"

Keysha leapt to her feet and immediately became dizzy.

"My head…I can't stand up. M-my head is spinning!"

"Fast movements increase blood flow. Fast movements are not good."

Keysha fell back down onto the sofa and glanced at the bottom of her champagne glass. Minute specks of some type of powder were stuck to the sides of the glass.

"You poisoned…me. I feel…like…I'm dying," Keysha moaned.

"You will live, but the poison is potent and attacks the nervous system."

Keysha dropped her glass, and it shattered on the floor.

"Have…to… get… away."

"Bonita Chica, it is useless to struggle."

"Y-you bastard!"

Keysha spat at El Hombre Guapo. The wad of saliva splattered below El Hombre Guapo's left cheek. He calmly pulled out a handkerchief and wiped his face.

"That was rude and nasty, Bonita Chica. Very unpleasant."

Keysha's mouth started to go numb, but she managed to say, "The p-police are going to know that I am missing. T-they will look for me!"

"No one will come looking for you. Yours will be just another unsolved disappearance."

The numbness grew, and her speech slurred, "Dey whill ome! I nuh dey will!"

"Before you lose consciousness, let me show you something."

El Hombre Guapo grabbed Keysha by her arm and jerked her to her feet. He dragged Keysha from the living quarters down another short hallway until they came to a metal sliding door.

"Stand up!"

"I...I can't."

Three hard slaps to the face made Keysha stagger to her feet. El Hombre Guapo slid the door open and forced her to look through the doorway.

"¡Mira, Bonita Chica! Look and be filled with despair!"

"Oh, my God!" she gasped.

She looked into a room that normally housed jet skis or other water crafts. Instead, the room housed pallets of white cocaine bricks, bundles of cash, and numerous cages of battered women of all races.

"I have white, black, Haitian, Cuban...all flavors," El Hombre Guapo said.

"The police will come," Keysha said weakly. "Missing Cubans and white people always get reported missing."

"Um, you are correct, Bonita Chica, but do you see la policía over there?"

Keysha was filled with horror when she saw the uniformed

police officers who were overseeing them. She even noticed that some of the officers were part of the Coast Guard.

"Oh, my God!" Keysha cried aloud.

"Help us! Help us!" one blonde haired woman cried out.

"Shut up!" commanded a police officer. He withdrew his baton and struck the blonde haired woman's knuckles as she held the bars of the cage. She fell on her back screaming and holding her hands. Keysha felt faint at the sight of such cruelty.

"T-this isn't real! How can this be?"

"Bonita Chica, those police officers are a few of my roaches. My roaches are in every house and every building. If someone comes looking for you, they will find it very difficult to find you!"

"W-where are you going to take us?"

El Hombre Guapo ran his fingers through Keysha's curly hair and licked her face with his wet tongue. Keysha so weak that all she could was cringe.

"Bonita Chica, you all are now property of La Committee. Those women will be sent to Costa Rica. However, you will stay with me in Miami and become one of my wives."

"Why-why me?" Keysha sobbed.

"Because you are strong, and I like to break things that are strong!"

After hearing those words, Keysha fainted. When she awoke, Keysha found herself lying on a worn out mattress in this room. A teddy bear was next to her.

"What? Where am I?"

Memories of El Hombre Guapo and the women in cages

swiftly flooded her mind. Immediately, Keysha leaped off of the mattress and rushed to the door. She twisted the door handle, but it would not move.

"Locked!"

She rushed to the window and jerked the blinds up. Nails had been pounded along the frame of the window and a protective sheet of glass covered the window.

"Who would nail a window shut?"

Keysha stepped back and kicked the protective glass as hard as she could. The glass did not break. Its enforced glass propelled her backwards and onto the mattress.

"Aggh! My ankle!"

As Keysha laid there, holding her ankle, a ceiling fan slowly rotated above her, and its light gently fell upon her. Seconds became minutes. Then, minutes became hours as Keysha laid on the floor, passing in and out of time and existence.

3

Keysha kissed the bear and said, "Thank you for listening, Teddy. I have to get out of here or else I am going to die."

Keysha rose from her mattress and walked to the window. She carefully opened the blinds.

"The evening patrol hasn't started his shift yet. I can get in a couple more scratches."

Keysha picked up a nail she had found behind the nightstand a couple of days ago. Ever since then, she had been scratching away at the glass as the patrols ended their shifts.

"If I keep scratching at this rate, it should be able to break soon. The last time I kicked it, I almost broke my ankle!"

As Keysha scratched at the window, a black Impala drove up the street. She quickly closed the blinds and dropped to the floor.

"That was a close call!" Keysha said as her heart skipped a beat.

Suddenly, the radio on her nightstand came on.

"It's ten o'clock. I have two minutes to check in!"

She raced over to the clock radio. As she was about to turn the radio off, a commercial for the grand opening of a new club on Ocean Drive came on.

"Miami! Are you tired of the same ol' DJ playing the same ol' thang?"

"Yeah!" cheered a loud rambunctious crowd.

"Then, come down to the spot so hot that it had to be named Fuego! It is Valentine's Day, and you don't have to be alone! Come and get yo' grown folks on!"

"Yeah!"

"Gas too high for you to get by? Don't worry! If you need a ride, call 555 and Miami Taxi will pick you up free of charge! Brought to you by Rasheed Locke, CEO of Locke Records!"

The commercial ended, leaving Keysha feeling in a daze.

"It's Valentine's Day. I've been here for six weeks."

She glanced at the red numbers on the clock. Immediately, she turned off the radio. Then, she hurriedly opened up her laptop and positioned the web cam.

"I can't be late! I can't be late!"

The password dialog box appeared in the middle of the computer screen. Keysha spelled out the password as she typed it: G-O-D. She pressed enter on the keyboard. Then, a clear digital picture of El Hombre Guapo appeared on the monitor screen. He wore only red swim trunks as he gave instructions to a group of men dressed in gray suits and dark shades.

"Cien Fuegos!" El Hombre Guapo bellowed. "I call on you today because there is a traitor threatening the brotherhood! Cien Muertes, step forward!"

A man with a mullet hairstyle and dressed in a gray suit stepped forward. He held a short chainsaw.

"Sí, El Hombre Guapo."

"You are my right hand man and have never failed me."

"It is my pleasure to serve the will of La Committee."

"¡Bueno! Find this hijo de puta and his crew! When you find his crew, I want you to cut off their feet, their fingers, and pluck out their eyes!"

"What of the traitor?"

"Bring el puto snitch to me! I will deal with him personally!"

The men in gray suits walked away. El Hombre Guapo continued to sit in his chair at a table that was near the edge of an oval shaped swimming pool. After Cien Fuegos left, he snapped his fingers. Suddenly, numerous beautiful women dressed in bikinis gathered around him.

"Papi! Papi! Papi!" cheered the women.

"Shut up and do some work while I think!" El Hombre Guapo

replied.

Some of the women fanned him with large fans; others massaged his feet and hands. Keysha cleared her throat. El Hombre Guapo looked up and saw Keysha's face on his laptop. He glanced at his watch and smiled, saying, "Ahhh! Bonita Chica, I am happy to see that you are on time."

"Yeah, you could say that," Keysha dryly replied.

"When you start acting better, you can come to parties like this and meet my other wives!"

"I am sorry, but that is not my type of crowd."

"Why are you so ungrateful, Bonita Chica?"

"Am I ungrateful because I choose not to be your whore?"

"Bonita Chica, do you know what your problem is?"

"Is it the fact that I was kidnapped, or is it that I live in a roach infested room and eat moldy bread?"

"Bonita Chica, you think you are special!"

"You know what?" Keysha said as she crossed her arms. "I am special! Even with all of those women and killers surrounding you, El Hombre Guapo, you are still a weakling, a shadow of a man!"

El Hombre Guapo's wives stopped what they were doing. They had never heard anyone speak to El Hombre that way. He snapped at the women, "¡Vamos, you ticks! ¡Vamos!"

The women quickly left El Hombre Guapo alone. Then, he turned his attention back to the camera and spoke in a calm voice, "Bonita Chica, this is the last day you will disrespect me! I—"

"El Hombre Guapo," Cien Muertes interrupted as he walked

into the view of the camera.

"Sí," El Hombre Guapo said.

"We found the traitors. They will not be able to walk, see, or touch in the afterlife."

Keysha put her hand over her mouth as she saw bits of flesh clinging to the blade of the chainsaw.

"That is why you are my right hand man, Cien Muertes! You are quick and efficient!"

"Gracias, El Hombre Guapo."

"¿Y el puto snitch?"

"A sleeper caught him on his way to see a private investigator from Atlanta! We have him here!"

"Bring him to me now!"

Cien Muertes walked away. He returned in a matter of seconds, roughly escorting a bald-headed man by the arm. Keysha could hear the man being brought to El Hombre Guapo.

"Let me go! I didn't do anything! You're hurting my arm!"

"¡Cállate!" Cien Muertes shouted.

He shoved the man to his knees in front of the laptop. Keysha cringed at the man's broken nose and bruised face. She could see the white bone jutting from the bridge of his nose.

I know that man, Keysha thought, It can't be him! It can't be!

"Welcome, Von Gretchen," El Hombre Guapo said. "I am glad to see you could stop by."

"I didn't do anything! I promise!" Von Gretchen cried.

Cien Muertes's open palm smashed against Von Gretchen's face and busted his lip. A stream of blood flung from his mouth.

"Thank you for ceasing this dog's barking! Now, crank the chainsaw," El Hombre Guapo ordered.

"My pleasure!" Cien Muertes said.

"Please! Please!" Von Gretchen begged.

"Stretch out your left hand," El Hombre Guapo ordered coldly.

"No! No, I can't!" Von Gretchen cried.

"Do it now, or I will have your face cut off!"

Cien Muertes slid the screaming chainsaw near Von Gretchen's battered face. He could feel the heat of the buzzing blade. Von Gretchen trembled as he stretched out his hand.

"Make it clean," El Hombre Guapo ordered.

Cien Muertes slowly lowered the blade of the chainsaw. Keysha turned her head as the blade cut through the man's flesh and bone.

"This is what happens, Von Gretchen, when you bite the hand that feeds you!" El Guapo angrily shouted.

"E-El Hombre Guapo, I can explain!"

"Ever since I stopped you from kidnapping little boys for your sadistic pleasures, you have been against me!"

"I-I-I was never against you!" Von Gretchen cried.

El Hombre Guapo grabbed Von Gretchen by the collar and said, "If you are against La Committee, then you are against me!"

"I-I am sorry!" Von Gretchen apologized as he wept. "Please forgive me!"

"Your apology is not accepted. I know of your meetings with the private investigator from Atlanta."

Von Gretchen's face exploded with surprise. His lips quivered in fear as he asked, "H-how do you know?"

"Von Gretchen, I am God. I have eyes everywhere! Cut off his ear!"

Without hesitation, Cien Muertes did as he was told.

"Arrgh! My ear! I am sorry! So, so sorry! Please don't cut off anything else!"

"Cien Muertes, put away the chainsaw. It is giving me a headache," El Hombre Guapo commanded. Cien Muertes turned off the chainsaw at El Hombre Guapo's request, and Von Gretchen let out a sigh of relief as he clutched his wounds.

"¡Gracias! ¡Gracias, El Hombre Guapo!"

"Cien Muertes, I have one more request."

"¿Sí?"

"Give me my pistol," El Hombre Guapo ordered.

"With pleasure!"

Cien Muertes cocked a chrome pistol, sending a bullet into the chamber. The audible clicking sound caused goose bumps to form on Keysha's arm.

"Please! Please! Don't do it!" Von Gretchen pleaded.

"The truth will always set you free," El Hombre Guapo replied as he received the gun, "Von Gretchen, I will set you free!"

"El Hombre Guapo, I am sorry!"

"This day has been written since your birth. There will be no alterations!"

"For Christ's sake, I am your brother! We have the same mother!"

"My brothers are the members of La Committee, and my mother is the most sacred code of La Committee: Death before dishonor."

El Hombre Guapo aimed the gun at Von Gretchen's head. Tears streamed down Von Gretchen's bruised face as he helplessly pleaded, "El Hombre Guapo, please. I am your brother!"

"May the angels welcome you, whether in heaven or hell!"

"Please, I beg—"

BLAM!

Von Gretchen's body flew backwards and crashed onto the ground.

BLAM! BLAM! BLAM! BLAM!

El Hombre Guapo fired four more shots into Von Gretchen's chest, making sure he was dead.

"No!" Keysha screamed.

Keysha's scream traveled through the video feed. A cold feeling crept up Keysha's arms as El Hombre Guapo turned his maniacal gaze on her.

"Bonita Chica, you are still with us?"

"I-I didn't see anything," Keysha stuttered.

"Bonita Chica," El Hombre Guapo sighed, "I hate liars. My brother lied to me, and I killed him. So, what do you think I will do to you?"

"El Hombre Guapo, please."

"Bonita Chica, honesty is one of the basic building blocks of a happy relationship. Wouldn't you agree?"

"El Hombre Guapo, please. I am begging you to have mercy

on me."

"Now, I must be completely honest with you. Your services are not needed anymore. You are an ungrateful liar!"

"El Hombre Guapo—"

"Do you remember the women in the cages? Do you remember the terror in the eyes of the women that I sent to Costa Rica?"

"Yes."

"Bonita Chica, you will not experience that! You will experience something shorter but more painful!"

"No, I will not! If you are going to kill me, then kill me; but I will not be afraid anymore!"

El Hombre Guapo smiled, "Bonita Chica, you are strong, strong like Texas leather, but, in Costa Rica, they do not use Texas leather. Look out your window."

"I know that the black car is there to watch me."

"No. No. No, Bonita Chica. That was his old job. His new job is terminator."

Tears slipped from Keysha's eyes.

"That guy is going to leave to get the proper tools to do his work: a gun, plastic bag, and shovel. When he returns, it will be the long buenas noches for you, Bonita Chica!"

"You can't do this!"

"It is done. Prepare to meet the angels whether in heaven or hell."

El Hombre Guapo turned off the laptop, terminating the connection.

The tires of the black Impala squealed as it sped off. Keysha hurried to the window and looked through the blinds just in time to see the black Impala disappear.

"What am I going to do?"

Suddenly, a thought occurred to her.

"Club Fuego!"

She quickly picked up the damaged telephone on the nightstand. El Hombre Guapo had crushed the keypad and removed all of the keys. However, there was a small hole where the five key was once positioned.

"Please work! Please work!" Keysha begged as she used the pointy end of a nail to press the hole.

"Please work! Please work!"

Beep!

"Come on!" Keysha said as she pressed down again.

Beep!

"One more time!"

She pressed, but nothing happened. Keysha bit her bottom lip and pressed again.

"Lord, help me! Please help me!"

She pressed down one last time.

Beep!

"Yes!"

The phone dialed, and a lady with a perky voice answered the phone with an exciting sales pitch, "Vroom! Miami Taxi. One call, and that's all!"

"I need to be picked up at ASAP!"

"No problem," lady with the perky voice replied. "I see you

are calling from 7483 Crane Lane! We have a taxi in your area. Vroom! Thank you for choosing Miami Taxi!"

Keysha dropped the phone and rushed to the closet. There was a pink v-neck tee and a pair of jeans that were exactly her size.

"Whoever wore these before me, I pray that God had mercy on your soul!"

Keysha put on the clothes, laced up her tennis shoes, and jerked the blinds up.

"It's now or never!"

She kicked the damaged glass as hard as she could. Her foot crashed into the scratched glass and shattered it. As a result, a security alarm went off.

"I didn't know about an alarm!"

Quickly, Keysha grabbed a nearby lamp and used it to clear away the jutting glass and debris. Then, she leaped out of the window and rolled onto the ground as the house alarm blared. At that moment, the taxi cab pulled up. She stared at the white driver with blonde dreads. Quickly, Keysha leaped into the cab.

"Ey mon! Antee one call a taxi?" the driver asked in an islander accent.

"Yes, now drive!" Keysha shouted.

"Dey name's Sunshine. Where to, miss?"

"Take me to the bus station as fast as you can!"

"We'll be there in fifteen ticks!"

The taxi drove down the street. Keysha smiled as the large houses passed in a blur. Sunshine glanced in the mirror at Keysha.

"Why is a woman with a pretty smile like yours sneaking out of the house. You look afeared!"

"Sneaking out is an understatement! I ain't never coming back!"

As the taxi exited the lakeside community, a black Impala swerved out from a side road.

"Friend of yours?" Sunshine asked.

Keysha turned around in her seat. Her heart dropped as she saw the black car following closely behind them. How the Impala driver knew that she was in the car was beyond her.

"The opposite of that. Can you drive faster?"

"Are you in some type of trouble?"

"Yes! Can you take me to the nearest bus station?"

"No problem."

"Wait! I can't go there! They may be there!"

"Who are you talking about, miss?"

"They! Them! La Committee!"

Sunshine bit his bottom lip as his eyes lit up with surprise.

"Then, you need to go somewhere new that has not been corrupted yet."

"Yes, can you take me to Club Fuego on Ocean Drive?"

"If we are going there, the ride is free. The club owner has paid all fees."

"Wow, that's unheard of in Miami. Do you know anything about him?"

"He is from Atlanta and a close friend of mine. Do you see

the stack of cards to your left?"

Keysha looked to her left and discovered a set of business cards. She picked one up and read it aloud.

"Private Investigator Sonny Sunshine?"

"That's me."

"You don't look like an investigator."

Sunshine removed the blonde dread wig and revealed his short crew cut. Even his dialect changed from islander to proper.

"How about now?"

"Now, you look like a PI. So, what are you doing in Miami?"

"I was hired to find a woman who disappeared after attending a photo shoot here in Miami. I believe La Committee is responsible."

"So, you are here investigating a kidnapping?" Keysha asked as she leaned forward.

"At the firm, we call it gone missing. Word on the streets is that there is a female slave market that is in full swing!"

"Tell me about it. I have been their prisoner for the last month!"

"You better be thankful that you are alive! We've learned that La Committee often likes to kill for fun!"

"It hasn't been easy."

"I have searched Miami for months and finally found a Swedish lead last week. However, he did not check in today as scheduled."

"Did he have a bald head? Was he a kind of older guy?" Keisha nervously asked as she bit her fingernails.

"Yes! Have you seen him?"

"He is dead. I saw him executed over a live video feed just minutes ago. The guy who is chasing me has been ordered to kill me!"

"Then, you are definitely coming with me!"

"Thanks."

"Fasten your seat belt!"

Sunshine pressed the gas and accelerated toward a busy intersection.

"Um, Sunshine, the light is red," Keysha said.

"Red as Santa's sleigh! Hold on!"

Keysha closed her eyes as the taxi's speed increased and sped through the intersection. Cars swerved and crashed into each other to avoid the speeding taxi cab. Keysha looked out the rearview to see the black Impala being slowed up by the wreck. She relaxed. So far, she had escaped from El Hombre Guapo, but the night was still young. Anything could happen.

Chapter 3
The Compassion of Rasheed Locke

A man stood before a full length mirror, dressed in only a pair of white boxers. He flexed his back, shoulder, and arm muscles. Then, he kneeled down in the middle of the living room of the presidential suite that overlooked South Beach. Not many twenty-one year old men had accomplished as much as this man. He was a star athlete for the Atlanta FireHawks professional basketball team and the CEO of Locke Records. This man was Rasheed Locke, and his cousin, Gwen Harris, had gone missing in Miami two months ago.

As he kneeled down in the middle of the room, he prayed for God to help find his lost cousin, saying, "Father God, please grant me your favor. You said, 'Ask and it will be given; seek and ye shall find; knock and the door will opened.' God, I am knocking! Please help me find my cousin! Amen!"

Rasheed rubbed his head as he stood up and walked over to a closet that held only a few items: a black business suit, a black designer t-shirt with angel wings silkscreened on the back, and a pair of black jeans. Rasheed picked up a nearby remote control and turned on the television. Sandra Gomez of On-Time Anytime News reported the local Miami news.

"Good evening, Miami. This is Sandra Gomez, reporting live from the scene of a fatal shooting at a gas station two blocks from Ocean Drive."

"Dang! That is right around the corner," Rasheed muttered.

He slipped on a pair of black socks as Sandra Gomez continued, "The victim's name will not be released until his family has been notified. There were no witnesses to the incident, and the security cameras were not working."

"Wow," Rasheed said. "The family is going to take that hard. No witnesses and no security video? That is like getting a Reese's with no peanut butter. That ain't right!"

Rasheed slipped a black belt with a silver buckle through the loops of his jeans as his washboard abs tightened. Sandra Gomez continued her live report, "The store owner stated that he just happened to look in the parking lot and see a dead body. The victim's death adds to the increasing murder rate that, so far, has Miami police baffled."

Rasheed pulled the black t-shirt over his sculpted chest and added, "Baffled is an understatement. Wait until they give the family the runaround like they did my family."

"Police are now trying to piece together the clues, if any,

but this is looking more like another unsolved mystery that will plague this beautiful city. This—"

"This is garbage," Rasheed said as he turned the TV off. "Mrs. Gomez, the murders are not the only problem plaguing your city. People are going missing like it is something new to do."

Rasheed laced up a pair of black tennis shoes. Then, he propped a pair of dark shades on his forehead. He reached into his wallet and pulled out a picture of Gwen as she posed, dressed in a pink v-neck shirt and denim jeans. An English ivy tattoo started at her first finger and wound up her wrist.

"I'm going to find you," Rasheed said to the photo. "I am going to find out who runs Sea Through. Just stay alive."

Rasheed tucked the picture safely away and pulled out his cell phone. He accessed his address book and called one of his best friends. Rasheed patiently waited for his friend to answer the phone.

2

Hundreds of miles away, in Georgia, in the thriving suburban area known as Camp Creek, a light was on in a brick house that rested on top of a hill bordered by thin trees. In the bathroom of this house was a bald-headed black man, holding a cool, wet washcloth to his throbbing face. The man moaned, "She got me good. I mean real good. My eye is purple, and my face is swollen. One minute, we were having an adult conversation. Then,— WHAM!— she hits me with a black skillet! This woman is going to kill me if I stay around, but I can't leave. No man walks out on love. I know Aisha loves me. I just know it."

He removed the washcloth from his face and saw a blood stain. He lightly touched his deeply bruised face and winced. He put down the washcloth and slowly took off his white tank top. Several scratches raced along his ribs.

Suddenly, the house phone rang. Before it could ring again, he answered the cordless phone in a concerned voice, "Hello! Hello!"

"Whoa now!" Rasheed replied. "What's up, Gary?"

"W-who is this?"

"It's ya boy."

"Oh, Rasheed, I thought you were someone else. What's up?"

Gary hoped the sound of disappointment was not evident in his voice as he walked back to the bathroom.

"Were you busy?"

"Nah! I was just using the bathroom. I got some type of stomach virus."

"Drink plenty of water. Those things will make you feel like someone beat the hell out of you!"

"That is exactly how I feel right now," Gary said as he glanced in the mirror. "What's going on?"

"I was just calling to let you know the business deal is completed, and I wanted to thank you for helping me find the spot on Ocean Drive."

"It was no problem. I had done some marketing work for the previous owner. The power of networking is real."

Rasheed nodded his head as he replied in an excited voice,

"On Monday, I am going to wire the money to your account for the marketing services you rendered. It was fabulous! No! It was great! Man, let me tell you…"

Gary did not hear anything else Rasheed said. His mind was on the argument that had led to his black eye. Someone had to know what happened yesterday. Someone had to be told what had been going on in his home for the last two months.

"Your commercial has been on the—"

"Rasheed, um, I have something to tell you."

"Um, yeah, what is it, Gary?"

Gary closed his eyes as his lips trembled.

"Gary, are you still there?"

"I...never mind. Forget it."

"Gary, I have a few words for you."

"What's that?" Gary asked, frightened that Rasheed had seen through his smoke screen.

"Ginkgo biloba, memory enhancement pills!"

They laughed. When the laughter died down, Rasheed ended the conversation, by saying, "Well, I am going to the club. I will make sure I toss one alcoholic beverage back for you."

"Have fun," Gary said. "Do it big for me."

"Fa sho, big dog. Give Aisha my regards."

"Huh…who?" Gary asked in a startled voice.

"Aisha, the woman you pledged your life to for better or for worse."

"Yeah. Yeah. My phone was tripping, and I didn't hear what you were saying."

"I was saying to tell your wife I said hello."

"I will. She is out with her girlfriends right now, but I will tell her when she gets back."

"Alright. I will talk to you later."

"One."

Once Gary ended the phone call, he stared at his beaten face in the mirror. He felt empty and shallow. Tears swelled in his eyes as he spoke to his battered reflection, "Y-you should have told him! You should have told Rasheed how Aisha has been beating you!"

Gary wept as he opened up his medicine cabinet and took two pain relievers that would surely put him to sleep. He walked into the living room, sat down on the sofa chair, and put the cordless phone in his lap. Hopefully, Aisha would call. Hopefully, she would come back home.

3

Rasheed felt strange after the call. He knew something was wrong with Gary because he had never seemed so distant. Suddenly, his cell phone vibrated. The sensation ended his thoughts of Gary.

"Who could this be?" Rasheed asked as he glanced down at the touch screen. The touch screen indicated that there was a new text message from Sunshine.

"My homie," Rasheed said as he lightly touched the screen with the tip of his index finger. The text message appeared on his screen and caused his heart to drop to his stomach. It read:

Found strong lead to Gwen. Meet me at club near DJ booth.

"Yes!" Rasheed cried out as he jumped up in the air. As he jumped a second time, the phone slipped from his hands and crashed against the corner of the table.

"Dang! Please don't be broke! Please don't be broke!"

Rasheed picked up the phone and saw a large crack on the screen.

"It's broke! It's broke!"

He tapped the screen with his fingertip, but nothing happened. When Rasheed pressed the 'call' icon, nothing happened.

"I broke my phone! No! I can't access text messages or call out! I've got to get to the club quick!"

Rasheed put the phone in his pocket. Then, he hurried to the elevator. Once he arrived, he rapidly pressed the down button.

"C'mon! C'mon! C'mon!"

In seconds, there was a soft beeping tone. The doors of the elevator slid apart, and a curly haired bellboy, dressed in dark slacks and a red vest, greeted Rasheed.

"Good evening, Mr. Locke," he said in a very cultured voice.

"Good evening, William," Rasheed replied as he stepped into the elevator.

"What is your destination?"

"The lobby, please."

"Very well. The lobby it is, sir."

The doors closed, and William pressed the 'L' button on the golden control panel. As the elevator slowly descended, Rasheed pulled out a picture of his cousin.

"William, have you ever seen this woman before? Please, look hard. I am asking because you see a lot of people out on the strip every day. This is my cousin, and she has been missing for more than two months. I am searching for her. If you have any information, please share it."

William placed his hand on his chin as he thought for a second. Then, he shook his head and said, "Mr. Locke, I have never seen this person before."

At that moment, Rasheed handed William his room key. William asked, "Are you leaving, Mr. Locke?"

"Yes, I am going back to Georgia tonight. Can you send my suit back to the rental and close my account here?"

"Not a problem, Mr. Locke. Will there be anything else, sir?"

"No. Not unless you can tell me where my cousin is. Someone has to have seen her."

"She was taken," William whispered.

"Huh? What did you say?" Rasheed asked as he leaned forward.

William glanced toward the upper left corner of the elevator. Rasheed followed William's eyes and saw a miniature black circle.

"Two's company, but three's a crowd."

"The birds are chirping, and the bees are buzzing in the garden," William said.

"Is someone watching us?"

"Yes!" William coughed.

Just then, the elevator reached the lobby level. The doors of the elevator slid apart, and William beckoned for Rasheed to exit.

"Mr. Locke, you are on the right path. Good luck!"

"Thanks," Rasheed said.

Rasheed briskly walked across the gold trimmed marble floor of the beautifully furnished lobby to the revolving doors that led to Ocean Drive with hope in his heart. Little did he know that his adventure was just beginning.

Rasheed exited the hotel and found himself amidst South Beach partygoers of all ages and races. As he neared the party scene, the crowd thickened.

"This reminds me of New York City during lunch hour. I am about to take to the streets!"

As Rasheed made his way to the curb, Sunshine's taxi sped by.

"Sunshine! It's me! Stop!"

Rasheed leaped into the street, trying to flag down his friend, but Sunshine sped by without even looking in Rasheed's direction. Suddenly, Rasheed heard the deep sound of a car engine revving.

"What in the—," Rasheed gasped. He whirled around and saw a black Impala speeding around the corner, headed right toward him! Rasheed froze with fear. He closed his eyes. He heard a woman in the crowd scream as he was tackled to the ground and, as a result, moved out of harm's way. His dark shades flew from his head and landed on the ground. The black Impala crushed them as it sped in the same direction as the taxi. Rasheed laid on his back and glanced up at two palm trees.

"Are those the pearly gates? Who...who saved me?" Rasheed asked as he rose to his feet, a little dazed.

"That would be me, sir," a calm steady voice answered. Rasheed looked to where the voice had come from. Standing there was a man dressed in torn gray pants, cloth gloves, and a dingy white shirt. He stood beside a shopping cart full of cans. The man looked like a middle-aged version of the great actor Will Smith.

"Mr. Wendal, is that you?" Rasheed asked.

The homeless man shook his head at Rasheed's rude remark and started to walk away.

"Wait!" Rasheed shouted. "Where are you going?"

"Away from you and your rude comments. That's where!"

Rasheed rushed forward and took the man's hand before he could walk away.

"My name is Rasheed Locke. Please tell me your name."

"The name is Adam Smith, but my friends call me Wolf."

"Thank you. Thank you for saving me!"

"It was nothing."

"Dude," Rasheed exclaimed as he continued to shake Wolf's hand, "you were like a superhero, coming out of nowhere!"

"Thanks. Can you stop shaking my hand?"

"Huh?"

"You're hurting my arm."

"I'm sorry about shaking your arm off! I'm just happy to be alive!"

"That's okay. To be honest, it felt good to do something that I used to do every day."

"People go to work every day. People play basketball every day, but people don't dive into the streets to save strangers everyday!" Rasheed rationalized.

"Now that you put it that way, I see your point."

"So, what's your story?"

"I fought in Desert Storm and the Iraq War," Wolf replied. "I led a special operations platoon that played a major role in capturing Baghdad."

"Get out of here!" Rasheed shouted.

"I am serious. My team knocked out their communications and disabled their weaponry. That is how we took the city so fast."

"First News Network missed that one by a long shot."

"Most of what you see on television has been filtered, so you have to get the facts from more than one side."

"I agree with that. So, did you retire from the army?"

"You could say that. I was discharged due to medical reasons."

"Then, how did you become homeless?"

"It's not that easy to explain."

Overlooking the dirty clothes that the man wore, Rasheed put his hand on the Wolf's shoulder and said, "Try. That is all I am asking. I promise that I will listen."

The sincerity in Rasheed's voice caused Wolf to get emotional. Wolf rubbed his nose with his thumb as tears swelled in his brown eyes. This was the first person to speak to him with dignity and respect.

"Are you okay?" Rasheed asked.

"Y-yeah. It's just that you are the first person who has talked to me like a human being. Most just look past me or pretend I am invisible, and the others act like I am no better than the scum on the bottom of their shoes."

"People are naturally afraid of things they do not understand. I just want to understand your situation."

"Okay. Well, I went into the army to better myself and to take care of my family. Then, the war jumped off, and I had to stay longer than expected."

"We all thought the troops would return home quickly."

"Exactly, but when we did not find any weapons of mass destruction, the troops' morale became compromised. We all began to feel like failures."

"You served your country. That is one of the most honorable deeds."

"You're wrong. That is not the most honorable deed."

"Then, what is?" Rasheed asked.

"The most honorable deed a person can do is 'to have and to hold for richer and for poorer and to love and cherish 'til death do us part.'"

"You are married?"

"Yes. Well, I was. When I returned to Miami, my bills were behind, and the house had been foreclosed on."

"What happened to your wife?"

"She had left with another man."

"Stop playing!"

"I wish it was a joke. I wish it was just a bad dream, but my wife left me a certified letter to make sure I got the message."

"You fought for our freedom, then that is what happens?"

"Yep."

"Did you go to any local agencies to help you get back on your feet?"

"Yes, but agencies are running out of money left and right. I have applied for several jobs, but no one is hiring because of this economic slump."

"Damn! That's colder than February!"

"Of all the things I have survived,—suicide bombers, snipers, and roadside bombs— it was my own wife who brought me down."

Rasheed shook his head and replied, "You can't help what your wife did, but those other things should not happen to our troops when they return from duty."

"I am not complaining. Luckily, I am still in my right mind with an excellent bill of health. That's more than I can ask for."

Wolf's positive attitude moved Rasheed even more than Wolf risking his life to save his.

"Well, Wolf, help is on the way."

"What are you talking about?" Wolf asked as he looked at Rasheed sideways.

"I am talking about your very own personal stimulus package," Rasheed said as he reached into his pocket and pulled out six crisp one hundred dollar bills.

"Wh-what's this?" Wolf asked as Rasheed put the money in Wolf's hand.

"Take these benjamins, and get back on your feet."

"I-I don't understand? Why?" Wolf asked as his brown eyes swelled up with tears.

"I know how it feels to be discarded and to feel that no one wants you. All I ask is that when it is time for you to bless someone in need that you do it."

"Yes! Yes! I will do it!" Wolf said joyously as he shook Rasheed's hand. "This is enough for me to catch a flight to my aunt's house in Georgia!"

"Are you from Atlanta?"

"No, I am from Jonesboro, home of Gone With the Wind."

"Wolf, it is a small world!" Rasheed exclaimed. "I grew up not too far from there in a neighborhood named Bonanza!"

"I used to play basketball there. Is there still a fire station on Panhandle Road?"

"Yep! That's my hood!" Rasheed answered proudly.

"Before I went into the army, I used to hang out over there all of the time," Wolf smiled.

"You know, we probably played against each other," Rasheed said as he reached into his pocket. Then, he gave Wolf his business card that had his contact information and said, "Here. Take this."

"CEO of Locke Records," Wolf said aloud as he slowly read the card.

"Wolf, I hate to rush, but I have to meet a friend, and I am running late. Call me when you get on your feet. I could use your security expertise."

"I-I will! Stay out the streets!"

"I will. Have a great day."

Rasheed turned around and faced the congested crowd. People were walking shoulder-to-shoulder. Rasheed swallowed hard before he waded through the crowd. He knew that the only way to get past the crowd was to go through it. Little did he know that the crowd would be the least of his problems.

As Rasheed made his way through the congested crowd, a woman with a light complexion also made her way through the crowd. She sported a short blonde and brown hairstyle. The woman wore a red tank top with spaghetti straps and a black skirt that hugged her hips. She was nothing short of gorgeous. As she plowed past Rasheed, he noticed the woman's flare and could not help but eavesdrop on her conversation as she talked on her Bluetooth device.

"Last night, the club was off the chain!" the woman said.

I know that voice! Rasheed thought to himself. It sounds so familiar, but it can't be her! Her hair is too short!

"I'm going to check out this new spot called Club Fuego," the woman continued. "It is supposed to be hot!"

It can't be her! It can't be! Gary would have mentioned it!

"Tomorrow, I will make you breakfast in bed," the woman said to the person on the other end of her phone. "I will bring the whipped cream and the cough drops."

The remark caused Rasheed to stumble forward and bump the lady, knocking her Bluetooth device from her ear. The device fell in slow motion. Rasheed attempted to catch it but missed. It struck the ground. Before it could roll an inch, someone stepped on it. The woman whipped around with a furious look on her face and went off on Rasheed in a voice that was as sharp as a barber's razor. As she whirled around to face Rasheed, she shouted, "Look at what you did, you stupid idiot!"

"I-I'm sorry," Rasheed replied as he realized that the woman was his childhood friend and Gary's wife.

"Yes! I bet you are sorry. You are just a sorry excuse for a man," the woman said as she picked up the broken device.

"Aisha Campbell, is that how you talk to a friend of the family?"

"How do you…Rasheed, is that you?" Aisha asked as she calmed down.

"Yep! The one and only!"

The two hugged as the people continued to walk around them. Rasheed looked at Aisha in astonishment.

"Aisha, your hair is amazing! You should be in a magazine!"

"Thanks," Aisha replied as she lightly touched the trimmed sides. "My hair had grown down to the middle of my back and was becoming a hassle to manage it, so I had it chopped it off."

"Aisha, I am so sorry about breaking your Bluetooth! I will

buy you another one."

"No need because that was karma," Aisha replied as she put her hands on her hips.

"Why do you say that?"

"When we were in the eighth grade, I broke your walkman and said the same thing. Now eight years later, you break my Bluetooth on South Beach!"

"That is messed up."

"Don't worry about it. I just have to be careful. The touch screen on my phone is extra sensitive. The slightest touch can cause it to redial the last number I called."

"We share the same pains. Just last week, my phone dialed one of my teammates while he was visiting his family in Europe. The phone bill was high to the twenty-fifth power!"

"Ha! Ha! That is why I just carry it in my hands."

"I didn't mean to eavesdrop on your conversation, but are you headed to Club Fuego?"

"Yeah. Why do you ask?"

"I am going there, too. Let's walk and talk."

The two moved forward with the crowd as they engaged in small talk.

"So, Rasheed, are you in Miami to celebrate Valentine's Day with a vixen?"

"No, I am here to close a business deal that Gary set up for me."

"Oh, yeah?"

"Yep. I just got off the phone with him not long ago."

"You talked to Gary?" Aisha asked uneasily.

"Yeah, he said that you were out with your girlfriends, but he didn't mention that you were in Miami."

"Um, I had to close a deal, too. One of my girlfriends had to relocate, so I found her a house here," Aisha said coolly.

"On Valentine's Day? You are truly dedicated to your job!"

"Gary and I...we celebrated on Thursday before I flew down. With the market drying up, a girl has to do what a girl has to do."

"I heard that. Real estate agents took that hit on the chin."

"And in the wallet."

"You know we have been known each other for a long time."

"We are from the same hood, the same block," Aisha replied.

"We both ate ketchup sandwiches and washed it down with sugar water!"

"Ha! Ha! Those were the days."

"Do you remember how we used to play freeze tag in the front yard of your grandmother's house?"

"Yeah, we played from sun up to sun down, but kids don't play outside like that anymore."

"That's because they have video games and MP3 players, now."

"Rasheed, we had video games, but Mama was not having us staying in the house all day. We had to go outside or wash baseboards!"

"When the streetlight came on, you had to be in the house because the switch was on ready!"

"That ain't nothing!" Aisha laughed as they walked past a

palm tree. "My mom used to make me kneel down on rice and face the corner of the wall for thirty minutes!"

"Ouch!" Rasheed said as he rubbed his knees. "That is old school biblical punishment!"

"That's exactly what these kids need today— more pain than pleasure!"

"I blame the parents, not the kids," Rasheed said. "There are so many people advising parents how to raise kids who don't even have kids!"

"Then, the parents wonder why, when they tell Markita or Sean to go to time out, they tell them to go to hell!"

The two laughed. As they laughed, Aisha noticed how well Rasheed's designer t-shirt fit his broad shoulders. When he smiled, she saw his deep, beautiful dimples. The ugly duckling had grown into a handsome young man.

If only I could've seen the future, Aisha thought, I would have chosen more wisely between Gary and Rasheed.

Suddenly, they heard a faint thudding sound in their ears. Club Fuego was near.

"Is that the club making all of that noise?" Aisha asked.

"Yeah, that is my club."

"Your club?" Aisha asked in astonishment.

"That is the deal Gary set me up with."

"So, why a club in Miami and not in Atlanta?"

"I wanted to get my base right. Don't worry. This is the first of many."

"Last night, I paid one hundred dollars to get inside a club called the Dolphin and did not see one celebrity!"

"At Club Fuego, things will be different. We will provide high quality entertainment at an affordable cost."

"So, are you going to corner the market?" Aisha asked.

"Exactly!"

"Boy, you are going to make so much money! Who does your club cater to?"

"Grown and very sexy with a dress code. Slacks, blazers, or button-ups. No tall tees, please."

"Wow! Sounds like you are the man with the plan!" Aisha cried out.

"It wasn't just me. If I tried to take all of the credit, Gary would slap me with a skillet!"

"A skillet?" Aisha asked as a cold feeling went down her spine.

"I'm just saying that I can't take any of the credit. It was all Gary's idea."

Aisha quickly changed the subject, stating, "CEO of Locke Records, star athlete, and now entrepreneur. Is marriage next on your list of things to do?"

"That is a negative!"

"Someone is going to lock you down. You're too much of a catch to be alone."

"I am not looking for love. If it finds me, then it finds me."

"Usually, that is how it happens."

"Yeah, that's what the people in the old school songs keep telling me," Rasheed said.

"At least, someone is. New school songs are all about sex and drugs."

"That is why I keep a Mary J. Blige CD close by. Her songs counsel and give me hope about relationships, unlike some of the other singers I've heard."

"Cheating is the next best thing when you're unhappy at home," Aisha said wistfully.

"Cheating always leads to someone getting hurt or, in some cases, worse."

"Umm hmm," Aisha agreed as they passed an ice cream and hotdog stand that was by a palm tree. At that moment, the thudding of the music became even louder. They turned a corner and beheld a large parking lot and an L-shaped building. Above the building was a large billboard with neon orange flames that read CLUB FUEGO.

"Rasheed, your club is huge!"

"It is over six thousand square feet with an ocean view on the backside. It used to be an independent film studio."

"Well, the VIP line is empty. What's up with that?"

"Don't know, but let's check it out!"

They hurried into the parking lot and passed the men's line.

"What's up? How are you? Good evening," Rasheed coolly said to the women as he slowly walked past. There were numerous women dressed in short shorts, tight jeans, clingy blouses, and short summer dresses.

"Tonight, somebody is gonna put a ring on it!" Rasheed bellowed. "I might just put a ring on it! Oh, no! No, oh!"

"Rasheed, you are crazy!" Aisha laughed.

As Rasheed led the way to the VIP line, Aisha glanced over her shoulder at the women in line. These women are looking good. Yes, they are looking real good, Aisha thought to herself. Tonight, it's going down! Then, she turned and followed Rasheed. As they neared the VIP line, Rasheed's broken cell phone buzzed again. He pulled the phone from his pocket and looked at the screen. It informed him that he had two new text messages from Sunshine.

"Hold on, Sunshine. Here I come," Rasheed muttered. Rasheed entered the empty VIP line. Standing at attention was a tall light complexioned bodyguard with his hair braided in cornrows. He was dressed in black boots, black cargo pants, and a black t-shirt with the word SECURITY written in white across the chest.

"That is a big security guard," Aisha whispered.

"I think I remember his résumé. He used to play football at Miami State until he damaged a tendon in his arm."

As Rasheed approached him, the security guard held out his large hand and spoke in a deep voice, "Let me see your ID."

"How much for this line?" Rasheed asked.

"Eighty dollars."

"Eighty dollars! Good Lawd! Do you get something to eat, too?"

"Eighty dollars," the security guard repeated.

"Eighty dollars? What about the other line?"

"Forty, but, you ain't in dress code, so the price is one-fifty!"

"Whoowee!" Aisha shouted. "So much for affordable entertainment!"

"What's your name?" Rasheed asked the security guard.

"A-Grip."

"Your name is A-Grip? Are you serious?"

"As a heart attack. A grip is what you are going to have to pay to get in tonight. Ha! Ha! Ha!"

Rasheed did not laugh. Instead, he said, "I am going to be honest with you, A-Grip. I am not paying any money to get into this club tonight, and these people aren't, either."

"Then, what you got for collateral, homie?"

"What do you mean?"

"You got dat weed? You got dem pills? You got that fry? I got deals and can get you whatever for the right price."

"Nah, I don't do drugs."

A-Grip smiled at Aisha and said, "I can settle for a little bang-bang skeet-skeet!"

"You are disgusting!" Aisha remarked.

"It's time to end this foolishness. Here is my driver's license," Rasheed said, handing his identification to the security guard. A-Grip read the card line by line. The security guard's hand quivered as he handed the driver's license back to Rasheed. A-Grip realized his mistake and attempted to speak, "I-I-I—"

"A-Grip," Rasheed said in a calm tone, "my mother always said, 'Be careful of what you say to a person because he could be your next boss.'"

"I-I-I'm sorry, sir. I need this job! I have kids, and one has asthma!"

"Should I give him another chance?" Rasheed asked, turning to Aisha.

"Rasheed, I don't know. It's on you."

Rasheed nodded his head and said, "A-Grip, if you do me a favor, I will go easy on you."

"W-what is it? Just name it!"

"I want you to let all of these people in the club for free. Can you do that?"

"Y-yes. I can do that!"

"Good. And, after tonight, find yourself another job!"

"I thought you were going to give me another chance?"

"I did. You're out here dealing drugs on my property! You are lucky that I don't have you arrested!"

He walked past A-Grip. Then, he turned around to face the people with his hands in the air and said, "Locke Records is in the building! Everyone gets in free all night long!"

The people in the line shouted at the same time, "Yeah!"

"Let the people in!" Rasheed shouted. He walked into the building, feeling like a champ as the people cheered him on. So far, so good. Everything seemed to be going his way.

Meanwhile, A-Grip stomped away from the partygoers and toward the parking lot.

"I ain't no do-boy," A-Grip complained. "Like I'm just gonna let everyone in the club and then go home with a coke and a smile. Boy, stop!"

A-Grip turned around and shouted at the club, "I ain't no do-boy! I'm a boss! I'm a boss!"

Suddenly, four black Impalas skidded into the parking lot.

"What in the world? Is this a jack move?"

Four men, each dressed in gray business suits and dark shades, quickly leaped out of each car and surrounded A-Grip before he could flee.

"Yep, I'm being jacked," he said as he held his hands up in surrender. Their leader strolled forward. The man lit a skinny cigarette, inhaled, and then blew out a white circle of smoke. The man was Cien Muertes, the right hand man of El Hombre Guapo.

"Little brother, you look like you are a little vexed," Cien Muertes said.

"I just got fired by the jackass who owns this club! Now, y'all are 'bout to jack me!"

"Depressing, mi amigo. Most depressing."

"You telling me," A-Grip said as he looked at the men a little closer. "You guys look like you are in the business."

"And what business might that be?"

"Dope running."

"And what would you know about that, señor?"

"I know how not to get caught. I have street sense. I know how to stuff my gas tank and tires with those white dragons."

The man took another puff of his cigarette and blew a smoke circle. As he exhaled, he noticed the golden ring at the end of a necklace around A-Grip's neck and asked, "Do you mind if I take a look at your ring, mi amigo?"

Before A-Grip could reply, he saw the men slightly pull back their suit jackets, revealing their holstered pistols. A-Grip hurriedly took off the necklace and handed the man the ring.

"Here! Take it! Just don't kill me, please!"

"This is a nice ring," Cien Muertes said as he studied the ring.

"It's okay."

"The ring is heavy, and the orange stone is precious. How did you come across such a ring?"

"That was my father's ring. He died when I was little. I never knew the loser."

The man inhaled his cigarette deeply, but this time he blew a stream of smoke from his nostrils like a dragon.

"Little brother, do you know who we are?"

"Um, not really."

"We are Cien Fuegos, the Legendary One Hundred Fires!"

"Then, you must be—"

"Cien Muertes."

"I've heard about you! The streets talk about you!"

"And what do they say?"

"They say that you are the butchers of La Committee, and you bleed whoever crosses you!"

Cien Muertes took another drag of his cigarette.

"Little brother, chance has orchestrated this meeting. Your father was La Committee."

"My father was La Committee?"

"Sí, he was a dealer, a slanger, and a runner. It is in you to be these things as well. You shall be all of these things and so shall your children."

"How do I get started?" A-Grip asked as dreams of fame, fortune, and women quickly filled his mind.

"Go to this address," Cien Muertes said as he reached into his suit jacket and gave A-Grip a business card.

"Alright."

"Make sure you are wearing your ring or else you will be murdered on site."

"Thanks."

Cien Muertes did not reply to A-Grip.

"¡Vamos! We have a lesson to teach," Cien Muertes said. "Tonight, blood will run in the streets!"

"Now, that is gangsta," A-Grip said, watching the Cien Fuegos walk to the club entrance. He had heard terrible stories of them cruelly killing anyone who crossed La Committee. A-Grip crossed his chest with the sign of the cross and hurried away. Tonight, the local news would be quite interesting.

Chapter 4
Damages

As Cien Muertes and A-Grip held their conversation in the parking lot, Rasheed and Aisha walked down a corridor that was decorated with several mirrors and flashing red lights.

"Rasheed, this hallway looks like the inside of a kaleidoscope," Aisha said.

"Not only that, Aisha. Look at the walls carefully."

Aisha turned her undivided attention to the wall closest to her. After a full minute of concentrating, she said, "I don't see anything."

"Keep staring. You will see something," Rasheed assured.

Suddenly, Aisha took a step back, pointed, and exclaimed, "Oh, my God! The walls are moving!"

"They move so slow that you can tell only if you stare at the walls. Come on. There are more sights to see."

As they walked down the mirrored corridor, they could hear Kanye West's synthesized voice coming through the archway as the DJ spun his smash hit, "Heartless".

Aisha nodded her head to the song as she shouted and rhythmically snapped her fingers, exclaiming, "Ahh, junk! That is my jam!"

"Kanye is the best rapper of all-time. He gives a performance whether it is on CD or in concert," Rasheed said as they reached the doorway, "After you."

"Thank you."

Aisha stepped through the archway and into the main section of Club Fuego.

"Look at the crystal chandeliers," Aisha said in amazement. "Look at the…look at the beef cakes dancing on the raised platforms! Rasheed, how many people can your club hold?"

"On a good day, three thousand. Tonight, I want to push the limits."

"Rasheed, you hired strippers," Aisha said in astonishment as she watched a bare-chested man dance with a woman in a bikini.

"I have two customers: men and women. It is a scientific fact that partially naked men and women attract fully dressed men and women!"

"Well, I am not attracted to just anyone or anything!"

"Then, what's your vice?"

"That is my weakness," Aisha said as a male dancer with long black dreads walked toward her. He was dressed in black tights, a pair of white wrist cuffs, and a white neck collar.

"Aisha, are you okay?" Rasheed asked as he noticed how she was holding her chest.

"Rasheed, I can count all the muscles in his stomach, and I mean all of them!"

"Ha! Ha! Ha!" Rasheed laughed. "I thought you were not attracted to just anything!"

Ignoring Rasheed, she called out, "Excuse me! Muscle man, come here!"

The male dancer turned and pointed at himself.

"Yes, you! Come here right now!" Aisha commanded.

The man walked over and stood in front of her. She knocked on his hard chest as if it was a front door.

"So hard! Oh! Hard as an oak tree!"

The male dancer made his chest muscles twitch. Aisha leaped for joy and exclaimed, "Boy, I will take you home and do you wrong! Can you turn to the side?"

The male dancer turned to the side and crossed his arms as he allowed Aisha to examine him.

"This is quality ribs, chuck wagon, and rump roast! Rasheed, can you say Sunday dinner!"

"Um, no. I'm sorry I can't!" Rasheed replied. "Girl, you are tripping! Leave that man alone and let him do his job!"

Aisha leaned on Rasheed and sighed, "Rasheed, you have brought sexy back!"

"Sexy was last year! This year, we are bringing love back!"

"I feel you! I am going to text my girlfriends and tell them to come out tonight!"

Aisha pulled out her cell phone and quickly texted her friend. Then, she lightly punched Rasheed in the shoulder and said, "I am proud of you, Mr. Entrepreneur. You've created such an amazing party atmosphere!"

"This is just one part of the club. When you go to the back, you are going to see pool tables, skee ball machines, and flat screen TVs along the walls."

"So a person can dance, play games, or catch a sports game?"

"Exactly. There is even a working kitchen for you to order wings and seven bars positioned along the walls where you can get your drink on."

"That is all I needed to hear," Aisha said as she put her lip gloss on. "Let's get a drink."

"No, you go. When you get to any bar, tell the bartender you are with me. They are going to ask for the code. The code is 725— my birthday."

"Okay, but where are you going?"

"Do you see that platform in the middle of the dance floor that looks like a small tower?"

"Yeah," Aisha said.

"That is the DJ booth. I have some important business to attend to there that can't wait any longer."

"Well, Mr. Entrepreneur, thanks for showing a sister a good time. I will see you around! Peace!"

Rasheed watched as she disappeared into the crowd. There was something different about Aisha, something that he had never noticed before. Whatever it was, Rasheed didn't like one bit of it.

2

Rasheed carefully waded through the crowd toward the DJ
"You cool, partnah," one of the guys replied.
"That's fine, baby. Come back later, so we can talk," a woman said.
"Riiiiight!" Rasheed said to her as he continued to make his way through the crowd. Just before he made it to the steps of the DJ booth, a man dressed in a gray suit with dark shades bumped into him hard and almost made him fall.
"Excuse the hell out of you!" Rasheed yelled.
The man did not reply.
"Are you deaf or something?" Rasheed asked.
Again, the man did not respond. He kept walking through the crowd, just turning his head from right to left like a robot. Rasheed dismissed the encounter and quickly ascended the steps to the DJ booth where the legendary DJ Hurricane controlled the crowd by operating three laptops and a turntable. DJ Hurricane spoke first as they gave each other dap, "What up, my dog?"
"Ain't nothing changed, but the day on the calendar."
"It is what it is, my dog!"
"You're doing your thing!" Rasheed said as he pointed at the crowd. "I like what I see!"
"Yo, dog! I was getting worried!"
"Bout what?"
"The club was empty. I mean like ghost when I first got here.

Then, boom! It was full!"

"Like that?" Rasheed asked, surprised.

"Like that, my dog. I've been doing this for ten summers, and I never saw a new club get packed so fast!"

"If you keep the crowd dancing, then I will do my part to get people in here!"

"No doubt! Watch what I can do with the help of a little technology!"

After quickly tapping on the keyboard of one of his laptops, T-Pain's classic "Chopped and Screwed" came in over the fast tempo of Luke's "Don't Stop! (Get It! Get It!)". In seconds, DJ Hurricane had blended a perfect melody with the old and the new.

Rasheed waved his hands in the air and sang, "Don't stop! Get it! Get it! Old school with a new school twist!"

DJ Hurricane pointed to his right and shouted aloud, "Rasheed, look down on the dance floor over there!"

"Ooooh Wee!" Rasheed cried out as he looked in that direction and saw a group of women booty-shaking outrageously! A woman, dressed in a white shirt and daisy dukes, bent over, put her hands on her knees, and started working her butt cheeks one at a time.

"Dude, she is making her cheeks go up and down one at a time!" Rasheed shouted.

"Yeah, that is what you call talent!" DJ Hurricane shouted.

"I can't believe what I am seeing," Rasheed said as he leaned back.

After taking in the spectacle, DJ Hurricane handed Rasheed a microphone. Confused, Rasheed asked, "What's this for?"

"After this song, I am going to cut the music and introduce you to Miami. No host has ever come to Miami and not welcomed the crowd. I can't let you break tradition!"

"Let's do it."

As the song approached its end, DJ Hurricane cut the music and yelled a special announcement over the microphone, "Club Fuego, when I ask, 'Who's the best?', you say, 'We the best!' Club Fuego, Who's the best?"

"We the best!" cheered the crowd.

"Club Fuego," DJ Hurricane shouted, "who's the best?"

"We the best!"

"Club Fuego, I am pleased to bring to you the man not the myth, the club owner, and CEO of Locke Records Rasheed Locke!"

A spotlight fell on Rasheed as he let the cheers die down. Then, he spoke into the microphone with an energetic voice, "What up, South Miami? What up, Opa-locka, Carol City, Liberty City, Hialeah, Coconut Grove? Who's the best?"

"We the best!"

"If you have more than twenty dollars in your pocket, say I'm the best!"

"I'm the best!" the crowd bellowed.

"To my fellas, if you're putting food on your table and keeping the lights on at your crib, say I'm the best!"

"I'm the best!" the men yelled.

"Ladies, if you are single, sexy, and I.N.D.E.P.E.N.D.E.N.T, say I'm the best!"

"I'm the best!" the women shouted.

Rasheed pointed into the crowd as he continued, "Tonight is for you and you and you! Thank you for coming out to celebrate the grand opening of Club Fuego! Tonight, all drinks are free! Who's the best?"

"We the best!" the crowd cheered.

Rasheed waited until the cheering had subsided. Then, he continued, "I know you all do it crazy in South Miami but, DJ Hurricane, take us to Atlanta!"

"Yikki yik! Zzzzurp!" scratched the record as DJ Hurricane started up the rap song titled "Dey Know" by Shawty Lo. The party raged on. The people danced to the exciting song as DJ Hurricane congratulated Rasheed on a job well done. He said, "That's how you crank up the crowd, my dog!"

"Thanks! I have always—"

Rasheed cut his sentence short when he saw two men in gray suits walking through the crowd. He watched as they met up with four more men, chatted briefly, then separated again.

"What are they looking for?" Rasheed asked aloud as he watched the men in the gray suits rove through the crowd.

"Huh? Are you alright, my dog?"

"Yeah, I-I'm fine," Rasheed responded.

"Are you sure? You look like you just saw a ghost."

"I just saw something odd. It is at least eighty degrees outside, and there are guys wearing two piece suits in here."

"Are they in gray suits?"

"Yeah, they look like they are going to a funeral."

"Are you sure you saw men in gray suits?"

"Yeah, there go three of them right there."

"Damn!" DJ Hurricane said as he also spotted the men in the gray suits, prowling through the crowd.

"What's wrong?"

"My dog, have you heard of these guys?"

"No. Who are they?"

"They are a gang of killers called Cien Fuegos," DJ Hurricane said.

"I am about to go tell security about our situation. I think I saw one by the restroom," Rasheed said.

The word 'restroom' jogged DJ Hurricane's memory. He said, "Yo, my dog! I knew there was something I had to tell you! It completely slipped my mind!"

"What up?" Rasheed asked.

"A white boy came by the booth looking for you! He said it was urgent!"

"Did he have brown hair, blue eyes, look like he went to Harvard?"

"Yeah, yeah! That's him! Ivy League-type dude! Look like he played water polo."

"How long ago was that?"

"About thirty minutes before you came to the booth."

"Did he leave a message for me?"

"Yeah. He said to tell you to meet him in the restroom near

the pool tables."

"Are you sure that's what he said? That is the ladies' restroom."

"My dog, that's what the man said."

"Thanks, man."

"No problem."

As DJ Hurricane mixed in another song, Rasheed began to wonder, Why would Sunshine ask for me to meet him in the ladies' bathroom? Is Sunshine the person the gray suits are looking for? Rasheed hurried to the stairs and quickly descended them. Just as he was halfway down the steps, Sunshine came dashing up the steps.

"Whoa! Sun—"

Sunshine did not see or hear him. Instead, he ran right smack into Rasheed. The force of the impact knocked both of them to the ground. Rasheed rose to his knees as he dusted his black jeans off.

"Sunshine, you need to play football. That hit would have taken any running back down!"

Sunshine did not respond. He laid motionless on his side.

"Sunshine, did you hear me?"

Rasheed looked closely at Sunshine. Chill bumps formed on his arms as he heard Sunshine's gut-wrenching moans. His face was ghastly pale, and he was clutching his stomach.

"Sunshine, what's wrong?"

"Ohhh…it hurts!"

"What hurts?"

"Ohh...Ohhh...My stomach...Ohhh, it hurts!"

"Sunshine, let me see."

Rasheed removed Sunshine's right hand. Rasheed's eyes grew as wide as billiards. Stretching from one side of his stomach to the other side was a deep gash. Blood squirted from it like a leaky faucet. Portions of Sunshine's large intestine bulged through the wound. Immediately, Rasheed put pressure on the wound. He could feel the warm blood on his palms.

"Sunshine, you're bleeding bad! Your body cavity has been breached! We've got to get you some help!"

"Ohhh...it hurts!" Sunshine repeated.

"Help! Somebody help! Oh, my God! Please help!"

Rasheed's cry was drowned out by the loud music that blared within the club. Rasheed knew he had to do something quick, or Sunshine would die.

"Stay here, buddy. I am going to get you help!"

"No!" Sunshine shouted as he grasped Rasheed by the arm with his bloody hand.

"Sunshine, I have to get you some help! You're losing too much blood!"

"It doesn't matter."

"Yes, it does! If I don't do something quick, your lungs are going to fill up with blood and choke you to death!"

"No. Stay. I am getting cold. Rasheed, it's too late for me! D-don't let me die alone!"

"Alright. I'll stay."

"T-thank you, Rasheed."

Rasheed sat Indian-style and placed Sunshine's head in his lap. His skin was cold and clammy.

"Sunshine, you've been like a brother to me. You took up this burden of helping me find Gwen without questioning the outcome. Thank you!"

Sunshine spat up some blood and said, "Y-you are a good man with a good heart, Rasheed. A good heart is better than riches."

"Thank you," Rasheed said as he looked into Sunshine's blue eyes. "God, why is this happening?"

"Rasheed, th...," Sunshine struggled as his lip trembled.

"Take your time. Take your time."

"T...th...the-they are h-here."

"Who is here?" Rasheed asked frantically. "Who are you talking about?"

"T-the... gray suits. They took Gwen!"

Rasheed's heart thudded in his chest at the mention of his cousin's abductors.

"Sunshine, did the men in the gray suits do this to you?"

"Y-yes. One attacked me."

"Those bastards," Rasheed muttered.

At that moment, Sunshine's eyes rolled into the back of his head and his body began to shake violently as he went into a state of shock. Tears streamed down Rasheed's eyes as he continued to honor his friend's dying wish.

"Sunshine, hang in there!"

In seconds, Sunshine's trembling ceased. Sunshine looked up at Rasheed with his blue eyes. He licked his dry lips and struggled to say, "Rasheed, save the girl. Last stall of the women's restroom. Beware of La Committee."

Sunshine's body shook one last time. Then, his head slowly rolled to the side. A stream of blood escaped from the corner of his mouth.

"Sunshine! Sunshine! Sunshine!"

Rasheed sat in a daze for a moment as he held Sunshine. Behind him, DJ Hurricane's voice bellowed over the microphone, "All my single ladies! Tell whoever you are standing beside that you can have whatever you like!"

D.J Hurricane mixed in T.I.'s "You Can Have Whatever You Like". T.I.'s lyrics that complimented the beauty of a woman snapped Rasheed from his daze. He reached into Sunshine's pocket and found his cell phone. Quickly, he tapped on the keys and sent a text message to the pilot of his leer jet. It read: NORMAN, THIS IS RASHEED. GET THE PLANE READY! WE ARE LEAVING PRONTO!

Rasheed exited the text message feature and clicked on the dial pad where he dialed 911. A female operator answered the phone in a perky voice, "Nine-one-one. What is your emergency?"

"A man in a gray suit stabbed my friend at Club Fuego on Ocean Drive! My friend is a police officer!"

"What is the condition of the police officer?"

"Dead! Hurry! The maniac is attacking other people!"

Rasheed hung up the phone. Then, he closed Sunshine's eyes.

"Rest in peace, my friend. Your death will not be in vain."

Rasheed looked up at the flashing lights of the club as vengeance filled his heart and murder came into his mind. He did not know which of the men in the gray suits had done this to Sunshine, but each one of them would pay dearly for his actions.

3

Rasheed hurried down the stairs and dashed through the crowd, not caring who he bumped into. As drinks spilled, tempers flared. As he approached the restrooms near the pool tables, he bumped into a guy dressed in a brown blazer.

"Yo! You just spilled my drink, partnah!"

"Get a life!" Rasheed shouted. He kept moving through the crowd. Next, he stepped on a woman's sandaled feet.

"Hey!" the woman shouted. "Those are my toes, you asshole!"

"You have bunions anyway!" Rasheed replied.

From across the club, Cien Muertes saw Rasheed plowing through the crowd like a madman and said, "Hmm. This could be interesting. Let's see where the fire is."

He popped his knuckles and followed Rasheed.

Rasheed could see the pink neon lights of the women's restroom. Save the girl. Who is the girl? Rasheed wondered.

Suddenly, a waitress, carrying a tray of hot wings, stepped in his path.

"Quick decision!"

Rasheed spun to his left to avoid colliding with the waitress but chest bumped another. He quickly reached down to help the woman up.

"My bad. I didn't...Aisha?"

"Yes, it's little ol' me! You almost put out my fire!"

"I'm sorry. Let me help you to your feet."

Rasheed reached down and helped Aisha to her feet. Her red spaghetti strap was hanging off her shoulder, and she was smoking a cigarette.

"What's the hurry, Mr. Entrepreneur?" Aisha asked as she took a puff.

"Aisha, when did you start smoking? Don't you have asthma?"

"Yes, you can have asthma and smoke a pack a day," Aisha said as she took another drag from her cigarette and blew the smoke out her mouth. "They do have breathing treatments, you know?"

"You smoke a pack a day and do breathing treatments?" Rasheed asked, amazed.

Aisha coolly flicked the ashes of her cigarette onto the club floor as she replied, "Don't act like you are Mr. Goody Two-Shoes! I know you got dirt. Besides, there are plenty of things about me that you don't know about!"

"I am not trying to find them out either. Anyways, this is a non-smoking environment. Put the cigarette out."

"Such attitude. I find it so beastie! Grrr!" Aisha growled.

"Put the cigarette out," Rasheed sternly repeated. "I am not going to say it again."

"Anything for you, Mr. Entrepreneur."

Aisha took one last, long drag of the cigarette. Then, she dropped it onto the ground where she smashed it with the toe of her right shoe. She blew smoke through her nose as she rapidly fanned herself with her purse.

"Aisha, are you hot or something?" Rasheed asked.

"Yeah, those shots of tequila, Nuevo, and bourbon got me a little heated."

"Aisha, are you crazy!" Rasheed shouted. "You can't mix liquors like that!"

She cocked her head and gave Rasheed a sidelong look as she rolled her eyes, saying, "That's the only way I can get a buzz, ya dig?"

"Aisha, you are going to be crawling on the floor! You are poisoning your body!"

"Not me. I am a pro. Certified, stamped, and sealed! Rasheed, you know I am from the ghetto!"

"Aisha, we both know you are from the hood, but if you need to mix liquor like that, then you have an alcohol problem."

"Heh! Heh! An alcoholic needs to attend classes," Aisha laughed. "I already graduated!"

"Then, you need some continuing education."

Aisha rolled her eyes, grabbed Rasheed by the arm, and said, "Come with me, Mr. Entrepreneur. I want you to meet a couple of my friends."

"I don't—"

"Man-up!" Aisha shouted, forcefully jerking him forward.

They walked around a pool table to a nearby wall where a blonde and a brunette stood, drinking apple martinis. They were both dressed in short jean skirts and white tank tops. The only jewelry they wore were rainbow colored candy necklaces and bracelets.

"Mr. Entrepreneur, I want you to meet my girlfriends. The sexy 'blonde-shell' is Sarah, and the brunette chinchilla is Hillary!"

"Hi!" Hillary and Sarah said in unison

"Oh, my God, the Bobbsey Twins!" Rasheed muttered.

"What was that?" Aisha asked.

"I said, 'They look like good friends,'" Rasheed replied. "Um, it was nice to meet you two ladies. Aisha, if you will excuse me?"

"Stay!" Aisha commanded as she grabbed Rasheed by the arm before he could walk away.

"Aisha, your nails are digging into my skin."

"Don't you walk away from me when I am talking to you!" Aisha yelled. "What in the hell is wrong with you?"

"Aisha, I don't know what has gotten into you, but you better let me go."

Aisha released Rasheed's arm but continued to degrade him, screaming, "Man-up, Mr. Entrepreneur, and quit acting weak! You're supposed to be a man not a wimp!"

"Where is all of this man-up stuff coming from, Aisha?"

"Never mind, Rasheed. You're always in a rush! Relax and take a load off!"

"I—"

Before Rasheed could finish his sentence, Aisha grabbed his butt cheeks and squeezed as hard as she could.

"Aisha!" Rasheed shouted in a startled voice.

"Whoa! That thing is tight! With buns like that, the hotdog must be good! Heh! Heh!"

Rasheed could hear Sarah and Hillary giggling. He held his butt cheeks as he confronted Aisha.

"Aisha, you are drunk! Get yourself together!"

"Drunk people tell the truth! Isn't that right, Sarah?"

"By golly. You betcha!" Sarah replied in perky voice. "Let me get some of them buns!"

Rasheed frantically waved his hands and yelled, "Penalty flag on the field! No more grab and squeeze!"

"Sarah, I think he's scurred," Hillary said in her southern voice.

"Let the record reflect that I am never scared or scurred," Rasheed replied. "You just can't take turns grabbing a man's butt in the club!"

Aisha crossed her arms and demanded, "Rasheed, give me one good reason why I cannot."

"The most important reason, Aisha, is you are married to a good man who happens to be one of my best friends!"

"That reason isn't good enough."

"I might as well be trying to make bricks with no straw," Rasheed replied in a frustrated tone. "Now, if you will excuse me, I have something more important to attend to."

"No, you don't," Aisha said as she stepped forward, barring

Rasheed's way.

"Aisha, please move."

"Didn't I tell you to stay!"

"Aisha, I am not playing with you."

"Girls," Aisha said. She snapped her fingers and Hillary and Sarah walked over and stood beside her.

"I don't hit women, but I will push one," Rasheed said. "Now, get out of my way. I have something important to do!"

"Rasheed, are you sure you want to leave now?" Aisha asked softly. "Me and the girls are about to go swimming!"

"Swimming?"

"Darling, he doesn't know what swimming means," Hillary whispered.

"Mr. Entrepreneur, of all of the beauties you've dated, you've never had one take you swimming?" Aisha asked.

"Yeah, my last girlfriend and I went to Jamaica," Rasheed said.

"Not swimming in the ocean or a pool but, you know, swimming?" Sarah said as she added her two cents.

"Well, that's the only swimming I know of."

"Not like that. Swimming means jigging, popping, rolling, or getting powered up," Sarah said.

"Come again?" Rasheed asked.

Hillary said, "Aisha, your friend is as square as a chicken coup."

"Now, now, girls, show some patience. Mr. Entrepreneur is just shy. Let's show him how we power up!"

Hillary and Sarah reached into their pockets and pulled out two fluorescent green glow sticks. They waved the glow sticks as they chanted aloud, "Power up! Power up! Power up!"

Aisha reached into her purse and pulled out a small bag of blue pills. Before she could open the bag of pills, Rasheed snatched them from her.

"Give me those!" Rasheed shouted.

"Those are mine!" Aisha yelled angrily. "Give me my pills back, Rasheed! You have no right!"

"You smoke cigarettes, drink liquor like a wino, and also pop pills! What else are you doing behind Gary's back?"

"Give me back my ex! Those things are ten dollars a pill!"

"For what? So, you can overdose! Not on my watch. Aisha, you need serious help. I need to call Gary—"

"Don't ridicule me, Rasheed!" Aisha interrupted.

"Aisha, what else is going on with you? This is not you!"

"The pills are me! The liquor and smokes are me, and this is me as well!"

Aisha turned around and French kissed Hillary then Sarah. Rasheed watched in disbelief as the three women groped each others' bodies.

"Rasheed, did you enjoy the show?" Aisha asked.

"If you are referring to your soft porn clip, then no; I did not enjoy it one bit."

"Rasheed, I saw how you looked at me when you recognized me outside on the strip," Aisha said.

"Girl, you're high! I looked at you the same way I looked at you when I came by to see Gary last week."

"Shhh," Aisha said. "Don't talk. Just listen. Rasheed, I want you to join our swingers' club."

"Swingers' club?" Rasheed asked.

"Yes. Last month, we did New Orleans. Next month, we will do DC. We want to do it in every major city."

"Let me get this correct. You and the Bobbsey Twins plan to have sex with at least fifty people?"

"Fifty is the minimum."

"Did you meet Sarah and Hillary on one of your travels?" Rasheed asked.

"No," Aisha explained, "I used to work with Hillary and Sarah at the law firm."

"So, I guess all of those late nights of filing paperwork was sex-related, not job-related," Rasheed said.

"This is a once-in-a-lifetime offer, right, girls?"

Sarah leaned on Aisha's shoulder and winked at Rasheed. She said, "We would love to have Mr. Entrepreneur for dinner."

"That's right, and," Hillary added, "we are not vegetarians. We like—"

"Aisha, what about your husband?" Rasheed interrupted furiously. "What about Gary?"

"What about Gary?" Aisha asked rudely.

"You are over one thousand miles away from him, kissing other women and recruiting people for your swingers' club! I am sure that was not included in your marriage vows!"

"He didn't tell you, did he?" Aisha asked as she crossed her arms.

"Tell me what?"

"Gary and I are exploring the option of seeing other people!"

"This isn't real. This isn't real."

"And that's what I kept saying when Gary couldn't get it up anymore. I got tired of dressing up in police uniforms and plaid skirts to try and get a rise out of him, so I left him."

"Just as simple as that?"

"As simple as a, b, c and easy as 1, 2, 3," Aisha assured.

"Men go through that every day, but there are other options like counseling or getting a prescription! You just can't walk out on Gary with two bimbos and forget about your marriage!"

"Whatever!" Aisha cried out as she waved her hands. "Rasheed, you're acting like the sky is falling or something!"

"The sky is falling for Gary!" Rasheed exclaimed. "He loves you! He is probably at home tearing himself to pieces!"

"Rasheed, don't make this about Gary! You don't know what it feels like to wonder why your man is not attracted to you anymore!"

"You're right. I don't know that feeling, but this is not about feelings. This is about choices."

"I'm not even studying you, Rasheed."

"Aisha, you chose to base your relationship on sex not unconditional love. Now, you're lost, and you don't even know yourself!"

"Go to hell, Rasheed, with gasoline soaked boxers! C'mon, girls! There are other men here who wouldn't mind coming to our slumber party!"

Aisha and her friends walked away, disappearing into the crowd and leaving Rasheed at a loss. Rasheed placed his right hand over his face as he absorbed everything that had recently transpired.

"First, Sunshine dies in my arms. Now, I discover that Aisha is a full-fledged drug addicted swinger! What's next?"

Save the girl…

"The girl! I almost forgot!" Rasheed shouted.

Quickly, Rasheed headed toward the women's restroom. Standing not too far behind him was Cien Muertes. He had witnessed everything that happened and was eager to see where Rasheed was going.

Chapter 5
When the Smoke Clears

Rasheed stopped outside the women's restroom. His heart pounded inside his chest. He licked his lips. This was it. This was the moment of truth.

"I stopped playing professional basketball for this, bought a night club for this. Now, I am one step closer to finding you, Gwen."

Rasheed took a deep breath and entered the restroom. He turned the corner and stood in the main part of it. Four stainless steel stalls were positioned in a straight line. Standing in front of a full length mirror was a busty woman adjusting her undersized bra. At a nearby sink was another woman touching up her makeup.

"These thangs just keep popping out," said the woman adjusting her bra. "When I get my taxes back, I am going to get a reduction!"

The woman at the sink replied, "You should try taping them down. That is what runway models do."

"I ain't got time for that! I am gonna claim my sister's girl to get a couple extra thousand back on my taxes."

"Oh, yeah?" the other woman said as she put on her lip liner.

"Yeah, my niece is over at my house just about every day anyway. She drinks up all my milk and eats up all my cereal!"

Rasheed stepped from around the corner, scratched his head, and said, "You know if you do cardio for at least thirty minutes a day, it will reduce your overall body fat percentage which will ultimately reduce your cup size."

"You're not supposed to be in here!" the woman screamed as she adjusted her bra. The two women fled the bathroom, leaving Rasheed alone. He looked down the row of stalls. Each door was opened except the last one.

"Eeny meeny miny mo. Catch a tiger by his toe," Rasheed whispered. As he passed the first stall, he emptied Aisha's bag of blue pills into the toilet and flushed it. Then, he cautiously walked to the last stall. There was no sound. All was quiet, too quiet. Rasheed reached out and touched the cold stainless steel of the handle of the last stall. He pushed against the door, but it didn't budge. It was locked. Rasheed leaned forward and placed his right ear against the door. Behind the door, he could hear someone sniffling.

"I know you are in here," Rasheed said softly. "I can hear you. I know you don't know me, but you have got to trust me. My best friend risked his life to save you. Now, he is dead. I need you to open the door please. You are the only person who may know where my cousin is! The last time we heard from her she had a photo shoot for some magazine called Sea Through. God, please. You are my only hope!"

She slowly unlocked the door.

"Thank God," Rasheed said as the door slowly opened.

Standing a step away from the doorway was a terrified woman dressed in a pink v-neck t-shirt and jeans. She wiped the tears from her face and introduced herself in a trembling voice, "M-my name is Keysha Belle."

"Hi, I'm Rasheed Locke. Nice to meet you."

Rasheed reached out to shake Keysha's hand, but she scuttled back to the rear of the stall and shouted, "Stay away! Stay away! I'm not going back! I'm not going!"

"It's okay. I'm here to help you. I'm Sunshine's friend."

"I-I am so sorry about Sunshine. H-he was a great guy."

"It's okay. He is in a better place now. Sunshine sent me to take care of you. Do you understand?"

"Y-yeah, I-I understand."

Rasheed looked past the stress and uneasiness that shadowed Keysha's face. He noticed her oval eyes, her curly hair, and even skin tone. The woman's natural beauty washed away the thoughts of the dangers at hand and made him want to know more about her.

"Keysha, how did you get caught up in all of this?"

"A-about a month ago, I went to a photo shoot for Sea Through magazine and was kidnapped."

"I see," Rasheed said as he pulled out a picture of his cousin. "Do you recognize the girl in this picture?"

"I didn't see her with the other women in the cages, but these clothes that I am wearing are the same ones that your cousin is wearing in the photo!"

"What! Where did you get them?"

"They were in a closet where I was held captive."

"Did you see any other women there?"

"I am sorry, but I was the only prisoner there!"

"Damn! She is gone! Gone! I am too late!" Rasheed cried.

"Here. Take this and wipe your face," Keysha said as she handed Rasheed some toilet tissue.

"Thank you. Who kidnapped you?"

"The group is called La Committee, and their leader is El Hombre Guapo."

"You mentioned a boat with cages earlier," Rasheed said as he wiped his eyes. "Can you explain?"

"They kidnap women and send them to Costa Rica to become female slaves, but El Hombre Guapo keeps one or two for himself."

"Is that why you were not sent away?"

"Yes, he wanted me to be one of his wives, but I refused, so he locked me in a roach infested room, fed me moldy bread, and gave me a syringe of heroin to commit suicide with."

"So, how did you escape?"

"Just when I was about give up, I heard the commercial for your club. I burst out of a window, and Sunshine picked me up in his cab."

"Just like that?"

"Just like that."

"If I wasn't part of this, I would think that your story had been created in Hollywood during the screenwriter's strike."

"Tell me about it. There is still hope for your cousin, Rasheed."

"Yeah, right."

"Seriously," Keysha said as she placed her hand on Rasheed's. "If your cousin's clothes were in the closet, then El Hombre Guapo tried to make her one of his wives."

"Then, that leaves two options. Either he murdered her, or he shipped her to Costa Rica. It's too much to take in all at one time!"

"Rasheed, please don't give up hope. It is never too late to hope!"

"You're right," Rasheed said as he took a deep breath. "I have to keep hope alive. Any news is good news."

"I know that's right. I wish we had some news about that man in the gray suit that was chasing me and Sunshine."

"I've seen these men. They are out there now, relentlessly searching the club for someone!"

"They are looking for me! How many are there?"

"Too many."

"Rasheed, what am I to do?" Keysha asked, rubbing her bare arms as chill bumps formed.

"Keysha, we are going to get through this together. I don't

think that God brought us together just to die."

"Are you a preacher or something?"

"No, I just don't believe in coincidences. Everyone has a purpose, and everything happens for a reason."

Keysha squinted at Rasheed and said, "There is something different about you, something special."

"I hope you don't mean special as in I wear plaid shorts with striped shirts."

"Ha! Ha! No, special as in you have a knack for making the best out of the worst situations."

"My mother taught me to look at the glass as half full," Rasheed smiled.

"My glass is so, so empty," Keysha said sorrowfully.

"Then, come with me, and I will help you fill up your glass."

"I need a moment to understand what you are saying," Keysha said as she smiled from ear to ear.

"Read my lips, Keysha. I am going to take care of you. From this day forward, I am going to protect you."

"How do you plan to do that? There are men in gray suits stalking me like the Terminator!"

"With all my heart and soul."

"What if I am not ready to be protected?"

"Then, I will patiently wait for you to be ready."

Keysha gazed at Rasheed as she felt both joy and fear pumping through her veins. The feeling was like freezing ice and sizzling fire colliding. Keysha's ears had heard something unique in Rasheed's voice. What she heard was not jealous or envious.

It was patient. It was kind. It was love.

"Rasheed, this is too good to be true. You're my knight in shining armor."

"Then, take my hand, my princess, and let's leave this place."

Keysha took Rasheed's hand in hers as he helped her out of the stall. She looked into Rasheed's dark brown eyes as she spoke to him in a soft voice, "Rasheed, my hand fits perfectly in your hand."

"Like a key in a lock."

"I'm glad we met," she said as she hugged him.

"Me, too."

"Rasheed, what is happening?"

"Whatever it is, I don't want it to end."

"Is this what love at first sight looks like?"

"No, this is what it feels like."

"So good, so right?"

"So right, it can't be wr—"

"Señor Romeo and Bonita Chica, I have bad news," an accented voice interrupted. "The honeymoon is over!"

Rasheed whirled around to see Cien Muertes standing in front of him.

"Get out of here, Keysha!"

"No, Rasheed! I won't leave you!"

"You don't have a—"

WHAM!

Cien Muertes punched Rasheed in the face and sent him flying against the wall.

"Rasheed!" Keysha cried out.

"Bonita Chica, looks like your boyfriend is knocked out cold!"

"Rasheed! Wake up!"

"Señor Romeo can't hear you."

"You gray suit wearing bastard!" Keysha shouted angrily.

"Such words, Bonita Chica, should not be spoken before dying."

"You are just like El Hombre Guapo—heartless and insane!"

"I am sorry for your ill opinion, Bonita Chica, because El Hombre Guapo sends only the best regards."

Keysha cringed as Cien Muertes reached beneath his gray suit coat and withdrew a black pistol. Keysha dropped to her knees as she begged for her life, "Please don't kill me! Please! I beg of you!"

"Bonita Chica, may the angles welcome you whether into heaven or hell!"

Keysha's eyes grew wide as she watched Cien Muertes's index finger wrap around the trigger. In that moment, Rasheed kicked the gun out of his hand. The gun flew across the floor and banged against Keysha's knee.

Cien Muertes grunted, "Señor Romeo, you broke my hand!"

"Surprising what a couple classes in martial arts can do for you," Rasheed said as he pounced from his back and onto his tiptoes.

"Señor Romeo," Cien Muertes shouted as he pulled a large knife from out of his suit jacket, "I am going to carve out your heart and let you watch it stop beating!"

"Bring it!" Rasheed replied.

Cien Muertes groaned as he lunged forward and swung the knife at Rasheed's stomach. Rasheed darted backwards just as the tip of the blade ripped his black shirt and nicked his abdomen.

"Señor Romeo, you are fast, but I am faster! Soon, your blood will drip from this blade!"

"Let me clear up your sinuses!"

Rasheed swung his right fist, hitting Cien Muertes in the nose and making him stumble. Rasheed darted forward. Cien Muertes tripped Rasheed, causing him to fall. Cien Muertes, then, placed the knife against Rasheed's throat. Rasheed could feel the cold blade against his skin.

"Señor Romeo, how does it feel? Is it cold?"

"Go sit on a bike with no seat!" Rasheed shouted.

"You are funny, Señor Romeo, but you will not get an Oscar."

"Shut up, you nut brains!"

"I am going to cut you from ear to ear, Señor Romeo! ¡Buenas noches!"

Just as he was about to slit Rasheed's throat, something cold pressed against his temple. Then, Keysha spoke in an angry, compelling voice, "Señor Bastard, put the knife down!"

"Bonita Chica, welcome to the party," Cien Muertes coolly responded.

"Drop the knife, you bastard! Drop it, or I will shoot!"

"You…you don't have the nerve, Bonita Chica!"

"Try me! At point blank range, I can blow your sick thoughts onto that wall over there!"

"La perra," Cien Muertes muttered as he dropped the knife.

"La perra this!" Keysha shouted as she slapped Cien Muertes across the face with the barrel of the pistol. Then, she kicked him in his ribs. There was a cracking sound.

"My ribs! You broke my ribs!" Cien Muertes shouted.

"Get up against the wall before I break something else!"

"As you wish, Bonita Chica," Cien Muertes said as he leaned up against the wall.

"Are you okay, Rasheed?" Keysha asked as she held Cien Muertes at gun point.

"Thanks, Keysha," Rasheed said in a calm voice. "Now, please hand me the gun."

"I don't think so! He just tried to kill us, and Keysha don't play that!" Keysha sharply replied as she cocked the gun back.

"I know you are angry, but I won't let you become what he is. Please give me the gun!"

"Rasheed, you don't understand La Committee. They have no boundaries, no rules! They will keep coming after me, after us!"

"Keysha, listen to me. I called the police before coming here. They should be here by now."

"The police? That's great!" Keysha sarcastically replied. "They will solve the case! Oops! I almost forgot. La Committee practically owns the Miami Police Department!"

"That is right, la perra!" Cien Muertes smirked. "We will hunt you down and slaughter your family and your family's families!"

"Not in this lifetime, you bastard!"

Before Rasheed could react, Keysha fired the gun.

BLAM!

"My leg! My leg!" Cien Muertes screamed as he fell to the ground, hugging his thigh. Seeing Cien Muertes in pain pleased her and made her feel better than good. Keysha bit her bottom lip as she aimed at Cien Muertes's chest and said, "A leg for a leg. Now, a heart for a heart!"

"Stop it, Keysha!" Rasheed commanded. "Keysha, the police are almost here. I told them an officer was down!"

"Buenas noches, Cien Muertes," Keysha said, sounding as if she were in a trance.

"No, Keysha!" Rasheed exclaimed as he saw the seriousness in Keysha's eyes. He quickly wrestled the gun from her hands. She angrily shouted at him, "Rasheed, you have to kill him! They are everywhere!"

"I will not kill him and neither will you! I will not let you become what he is!"

"I am going to enjoy cutting you like a fish, la pendeja!" Cien Muertes cursed as he pointed at Keysha.

"Shut up, you piece of trash!" Rasheed shouted as he shoved him into the stall of the bathroom. "I wish I could flush you down the toilet with the rest of the crap!"

"Señor Romeo, La Committee is everywhere! We will find you!"

Suddenly, there were several booming sounds that shook the bathroom.

KABOOM! KABOOM! KABOOM!

There was a brief moment of silence. Then, the screams began.

"Help! Help!"

"Somebody! Anybody help!"

"I'm bleeding! I'm bleeding!"

"I can't find my arm! I can't find my arm!"

Keysha looked at Rasheed with wide eyes and asked, "What in the world was that? Why are people screaming?"

"Don't know," Rasheed replied.

"Señor Romeo, you are so naïve," Cien Muertes said. "You don't know the sound of an explosion when you hear one?"

"What exactly exploded?" Rasheed asked as he pointed the gun at him.

"My men, of course."

"Your men?" Rasheed asked in a confused tone.

"They are called Cien Fuegos! When one is facing capture, everyone faces capture. Death before dishonor!"

Cien Muertes snapped open his shirt and revealed several wires connected to bombs that were interlaced around his waist. Rasheed's eyes widened when he saw the letters C-4.

"Oh, my God! They're suicide bombers!" Keysha shouted.

"Sí, Bonita Chica, and so am I," Cien Muertes smiled. "¡Buenas noches!"

He pressed a button on his belt buckle. Immediately, Rasheed grabbed Keysha by the arm and yelled, "Run, Keysha! He's going to blow!"

Keysha screamed. They sprinted to the exit of the bathroom as Cien Muertes spoke his final words, "May the angles welcome you whether in heaven or—"

KABOOM!

The force of the explosion hurled Keysha and Rasheed through the air and into the main room of the club. Debris pelted Rasheed as he lay on the ground. Rasheed moaned as he rolled onto his back. Smoke filled the air. He opened his eyes and stared at the blasted ceiling.

"Part of the ceiling is gone," Rasheed moaned. "What have I done? I should have never called the police!"

Suddenly, he felt someone trying to pick him up. He turned around. That person was Keysha. She said, "Come on, Rasheed! Get up!"

"Keysha, this is my fault! I killed these people! I shouldn't have called the police!"

"Get up, Rasheed! You didn't know those goons were wearing explosives!"

"Keysha, I can't."

"You picked me up when I was down, and now it's my turn! Now, get up!"

Keysha's voice gave Rasheed the strength to rise to his feet. He leaned on Keysha as he stared at the devastation. The ceiling now had a huge hole, and small fires blazed throughout the club.

"Keysha, thank you for not giving up on me," Rasheed said.

"Where I am from, friends never give up on friends."

"I would buy you a drink, but, under the circumstances, I hope you will take a rain check," Rasheed said. "This place is a mess."

"I am going to hold you to that drink. Can we leave now?"

"Sure, take my hand and stay low. Try not to breathe in the smoke."

"Okay."

Keysha held Rasheed's hand as he led her to the exit. They saw pool tables overturned, and some of the metal platforms were twisted.

"How many of those suicide bombers were there?" Keysha asked.

"I counted at least five, but I am sure there were more."

"It looks like a war zone in here," Keysha said. "The force of the explosions had to be tremendous!"

Suddenly, they heard cries for help nearby.

"Help! Please help!" a woman cried out. "I can't see! God, something is in my eyes!"

"Help me! I can't find it! I have to find it!" a man cried out.

"We have to help them," Keysha said.

"Let's hurry," Rasheed replied. "Who knows how long this place is going to be standing!"

Rasheed and Keysha walked through the smoke and stopped when they came across a woman crawling on the ground. The woman had pieces of metal lodged in her eyes. Then, they saw a man hopping around in one place. His leg had been blown off. Suddenly, there was a loud creaking sound. A part of the roof dangled menacingly above them. Next, that swinging piece of the blasted ceiling crashed down to the ground.

"We have to get out of here quick!" Rasheed shouted. "The ceiling is damaged, and it could collapse at any moment!"

"But what about the people?" Keysha asked.

"We can't save everyone! You grab that woman over there. I am going to grab the guy with one leg."

Keysha grabbed the woman and helped her to her feet while Rasheed assisted the man with one leg as the smoke overwhelmed them.

"Rasheed, the smoke is stinging my eyes. Where is the exit?" Keysha asked.

"We are going to take them over there!" Rasheed said as he pointed. "There is a hole in the wall, and it looks like people are helping other people through."

As they hurried to the hole, more debris began to fall from the ceiling.

"Hurry!" Rasheed shouted. "The roof is falling!"

Rasheed and the injured man made it to the hole as the flaming debris fell. Before the man stepped through the hole, he thanked Rasheed for saving his life.

"You're welcome," Rasheed smiled. As Rasheed helped the man through the hole, he heard Keysha scream from behind him.

"Rasheed, help! She's fainted, and I can't carry her!"

Suddenly, there was another loud creaking sound as the ceiling indicated that it was about to give way. A small piece of the ceiling fell down not too far behind Keysha.

"Keysha, run! The ceiling is coming down!" Rasheed shouted.

"What about the woman?" Keysha panicked.

"I will save her!"

Keysha sprinted toward the hole as Rasheed sprinted toward the woman. The two looked like they were participating in a relay race of some sort. In seconds, Rasheed had scooped up the unconscious woman in his strong arms.

"Hurry, Rasheed! The roof is falling!" Keysha yelled.

Rasheed bit his bottom lip, took a giant step, and leaped toward the hole.

"Make way!" Rasheed screamed.

Streams of dirt, fire, and debris fell around him as he soared through the air with the unconscious woman in his arms. Everyone watched as he floated through the hole just as the ceiling crashed to the ground. He cradled the woman in his arms like a wide receiver making a spectacular catch.

"Rasheed!" Keysha shouted.

"Yeah! He made it!" cheered the bystanders.

A nearby man quickly assisted Rasheed with the unconscious woman and helped him to his feet.

"Hi. My name is Dr. Smith."

"Hi. I am Rasheed Locke."

"That was quite a long jump," Dr. Smith said. "You should go to the Olympics. I bet you would win the gold medal in the long jump!"

"Thanks. Do you know if the police have arrived yet?"

"Yes, they have. The police showed up and apprehended a man dressed in a gray suit. Then, the explosions went off!"

"The ambulance and more police should be here any minute. Go over to the sidewalk and get some fresh air. I will check out the woman you saved. You're a hero."

Rasheed nodded his head in appreciation. Then, he said, "Thanks. I will."

Rasheed stood there, watching his club collapse to the ground. At least, it had served its purpose in his life, and he had met a wonderful person. He pulled out Sunshine's phone and called Gary. He had to tell him about Aisha.

2

Gary laid sprawled out on the couch. The pain relievers had kicked in, and he was knocked out, dead to the world, so as his house phone rang, Gary did not answer it. The answering machine picked up, and Rasheed left a message.

"What's up, Gary? It is Rasheed. I bumped into Aisha in Miami, and she was acting weird. Call me, so I can fill you in. What I saw, you don't deserve. Just know that I am here for you. Peace."

The message ended. Gary continued to sleep, not feeling the pain from his wounds or from his broken heart.

3

As Rasheed ended his phone call, Keysha energetically leaped onto his back and hugged him. He felt her curly hair tickling the nape of his neck as he gave her a piggyback ride to the curb.

"You are my hero!" Keysha said.

"Thanks. If you don't mind, I am going to put you down."

"My bad!"

Rasheed lowered Keysha to the ground and glanced to his left. He saw Aisha, Hillary, and Sarah walking away from the scene with two guys.

"When I get home," Rasheed said. "I am going to make sure Gary takes the trash out!"

"Huh?" Keysha asked.

"Do you see that girl over there walking with those two guys?"

"Yeah. Do you know her?"

"I thought I did. It's a long story, but here's the short version. She is married to one of my best friends, but the way she is gripping that guy's butt cheeks doesn't make her look very married. When I break the news to Gary, she is going to be gone like the wind."

Keysha kissed Rasheed on the cheek and smiled, "Gone like the wind? Rasheed, that was corny."

"I know, but you liked it."

"So, what? You know you look like that basketball player that plays for Cleveland. What's his name?"

"LeBron James."

"Yeah, you looked like LeBron James going up for a dunk when you leaped through the hole with the lady in your arms!"

"When we play them next season, perhaps you can come to

one of my games and watch me dunk on him."

"Games? You mean you're a basketball player?"

"Yeah, I play for the Atlanta FireHawks, but I took the season off to look for my cousin."

"This is too unreal," Keysha said.

"What's wrong?"

"Nothing," Keysha said as she leaned forward and kissed Rasheed on the lips.

"What was that for?"

"That is for all of the sacrifices you've made."

"Ah, it was nothing."

"It is something. This is a bittersweet moment for me."

"Oh, yeah? Why is that?" Rasheed asked.

"I am glad you came looking for your cousin and found me, but I am very sad you have not found her. I owe you my life."

"We both owe our lives to God. Come on. Let's get out of here before more La Committee goons show up."

Keysha and Rasheed walked away as paramedics, firemen, and the news media rushed up to the burning building to assist those in need. As they walked down the boardwalk, Rasheed pulled out Sunshine's telephone and called his pilot.

"Good evening," Norman greeted.

"Good evening, Norman. Is the jet ready?"

"Yes, sir. Locke-One is gassed up and ready to fly the friendly skies!"

"Okay. ETA is about twenty minutes."

"Roger-that. See you when I see you."

Just as Rasheed hung up the phone, a black Impala swerved in the middle of the street. Leaning out of the passenger's side of the car with an AK-47 machine gun was El Hombre Guapo, yelling at the top of his voice, "Bonita Chica! Nobody leaves me! Nobody leaves La Committee without being in a body bag!"

"Quick! Jump behind that hotdog stand!" Rasheed shouted. Rasheed and Keysha leaped behind it just as El Hombre Guapo fired the machine gun. Bullets riddled the metal frame of the hotdog stand. Quickly, Rasheed pulled out the handgun he had taken from Cien Muertes.

"I've got something for that," Rasheed said as he ejected the clip. "Full clip with one in the chamber!"

He reloaded the pistol and took a deep breath as bullets whistled past him and Keysha.

"What are you about to do?" Keysha asked.

"I am about to win the game with a three pointer off the glass!"

"What?" Keysha shouted. "Are you crazy? Do you hear those bullets?"

"Yep, but all that is about to be silenced!"

The driver of the Impala reversed the car just as Rasheed rolled forward and rose to a bent knee position. He fired his pistol four times. The shots hit all three of their intended targets: front tire, rear tire, and front glass. The car came to a screeching halt.

"Forward! Drive! I want to crush the cucarachas!" El Hombre Guapo shouted, but the car did not move.

"Didn't you hear me? Drive! ¡Ándale!"

Again, the driver did not respond, and the car did not move. El Hombre Guapo glanced over to his left and saw his driver slumped over the steering wheel with a bullet in the side of his head. The sight enraged El Hombre Guapo. He leaped out of the car and fired into the sky.

"Vengeance will be mine! The angel of death is here!"

"We have got to go," Rasheed said as he leaped to his feet and grabbed Keysha by the arm. They dashed down the boardwalk. Behind them, El Hombre Guapo let loose another barrage of automatic gunfire in their direction.

"Jump!" Rasheed cried. They leaped behind a palm tree as windows and doors of nearby restaurants were blasted by the bullets.

"We can't keep this up!" Rasheed said. "A pistol can't beat a chopper!"

"We need a fast getaway!"

Rasheed glanced up ahead at a group of high performance sport motorcycles that were parked on the nearby sidewalk.

"If only I knew how to drive a motorcycle."

"I know how to drive a motorcycle, Rasheed!" Keysha replied.

"Good! This is our only chance! The keys are in the ignition of that red one."

"I need a destination," Keysha said. "That is a Ducati racing motorcycle with some large pipes on it. I am not going to be able to hear you once we take off."

"Take us to Miami Airport, Runway C. Go jump on the bike, and get it ready. I will cover you!"

Keysha nodded her head, leaped to her feet, and dashed to the motorcycle. Not too far behind them, El Hombre Guapo shouted as he aimed the AK-47, "Die, los cucarachas! Die!"

"You wanna play? Come play with me!" Rasheed shouted.

He fired the pistol, but El Hombre Guapo leaped behind the riddled hot dog stand. Suddenly, there was the sound of a motorcycle revving its engine.

"Got to go! Got to go!" Rasheed shouted.

El Hombre Guapo whirled from around the hotdog stand with Rasheed in his sights. He aimed the AK-47 with a sinister grin on his face and threatened, "I am going to chop you down like grass! May the angles—"

"Freeze!" a police officer shouted from behind him.

El Hombre Guapo froze.

"Drop the weapon and turn around!" commanded the police officer.

"I can't do that, my friend."

"Drop the weapon!" commanded the police officer again.

El Hombre Guapo slowly turned around and stared at the police officer. The officer stared back as he aimed his gun from behind the door of his black Chevy Charger squad car.

"Do you know who I am, Señor Officer of the Law?"

"I don't give a damn who you are! Drop the gun, or I will shoot to kill!"

"I respect your answer, Señor Officer of the Law. Too bad

you are not on my side, but it seems that you have made your choice. May the angels welcome you to heaven or hell!"

"Drop the gun! Drop it or—"

The police officer fell to the ground from multiple wounds to the chest and head. Suddenly, there was the sound of a powerful motorcycle engine speeding away.

"Los cucarachas, you can run, but you can't hide!" El Hombre Guapo shouted as he saw Rasheed and Keysha making their getaway. He rushed over to the black Chevy Charger, pushed the wounded officer to the side, and leaped behind the driver's seat. The wheels of the car squealed as the black Chevy Charger sped off in the direction of the red motorcycle. Keysha and Rasheed sped south on Ocean Drive, then they veered right, onto US Highway 41, cutting off a taxi cab.

"Use your freaking signal light before you become dog food!" the taxi driver shouted.

Keysha glanced in her side mirror. We've lost him, thought Keysha. She brought the motorcycle to a skidding halt at the red light at Collins Avenue and US Highway 41. The quick motion caused the pistol to slip out of Rasheed's hand and slide into the gutter.

"I just saw something fall. Was it the gun?" Keysha asked.

"Yeah, you see what-had-happened-was the 'nersha' got me."

"You mean Newton's First Law of Motion called inertia," Keysha corrected.

"Yeah, something like that."

"Newton's first law of motion says an object at rest tends to stay at rest and an object in motion tends to stay in motion with the same speed and in the same direction unless acted on by an unbalanced force."

"Huh? You lost me," Rasheed said.

"When I braked, the gun went forward at the same speed and in the same direction because of inertia," Keysha explained.

"Are you a scientist?" Rasheed asked.

"Chemistry was my major. I graduated Summa cum laude from LSU."

"Well, I graduated but nothing close to summa," Rasheed said softly.

"At least, you did graduate," Keysha replied. "Too many of us don't finish or ever get started."

"True that," Rasheed said.

"We need to produce more graduates," Keysha said. "Not everyone is going to be the next Diddy, you know?"

Then, Rasheed changed the subject when he said, "What is going on? This light is longer than Interstate 95!"

"This is the most dangerous intersection in Miami," Keysha replied. "When I first moved here, I saw a wreck every day."

"Then, carry on," Rasheed said. "We will wait our turn!"

Finally, the light turned green, and Keysha sped off. The intersections became a blur as they sped forward, weaving in and out of traffic. Rasheed glanced to his right at the names of the streets as they flashed by: Euclid Avenue, Meridian Avenue, Jefferson Avenue, Michigan Avenue, Lenox Avenue, Alton Road, West Avenue. Finally, the motorcycle crested upon the MacArthur Causeway, a thirteen-mile bridge lit with small purple lights that connected Miami to Miami Beach. Keysha maneuvered the motorcycle into the slow lane and reduced her speed as she gave Rasheed a brief tour.

"What islands are those?" Rasheed asked.

"Star Island and Dodge Island are over there. I am going to pull over in a second, so you can get a good view of the city."

"Alright."

Moments later, a beautiful glowing city loomed to his right. Keysha pulled over onto the shoulder of the road, where she put on her hazard lights. They sat there, staring at the bright lights from the numerous towering buildings glaring against a fleet of purple storm clouds.

"Voilà! Rasheed, I present to you Miami the Magic City!" Keysha announced.

"Wow! I wish I had a camera! This view would make a wonderful poster!"

"Too bad we don't have time to drive through the city. It is an amazing sight with the buildings and canals."

"I can only imagine, but those look like rain clouds," Rasheed forecasted as he pointed at the gray area in the sky.

"That is the usual. We get a shower about once every two days."

"I can't remember the last time we had a good downpour in Georgia. The drought is drying everything up."

"Everything stays green here. It is timeless."

Suddenly, a police siren screeched across the bay as blue and red police lights flashed in the distance.

"Do you think we were clocked?" Rasheed asked.

"No, we were going too fast. Miami PD has a strict policy about pursing speeding motorcycles."

"What? They just let them go?" Rasheed asked.

"Yes. They never pursue."

The police siren drew closer, and the lights brighter. Cars pulled over to the right and left, making way for the police car. Keysha squinted her eyes and saw a black Chevy Charger relentlessly racing up the bridge.

"Rasheed, there is something funny about that police car."

"What's funny about it?" Rasheed asked.

"It is a South Beach squad car, and it's way out of its jurisdiction! Wait! Oh, my God. It's El Hombre Guapo!"

"Shoot! Let's go!"

"Hold on!" Keysha yelled as she slowly pulled into the right lane. She increased her speed from 35 miles per hour to 65 mile per hour in seconds, weaving in and out of traffic. At that moment, automatic gunfire erupted.

"Yep, that's El Hombre Guapo!" Rasheed shouted. "Shoot first, and ask later!"

"Hang on! I am going to try to lose him in traffic!"

Rasheed glanced back as the black Chevy Charger sped forward and the road slightly curved. A midnight blue Ferrari beeped its horn as the police car drifted over into its lane. The Ferrari swerved to the right as the Charger slammed into its bumper. The tires of the Ferrari squealed. It lost control and slammed into the cement wall where it exploded into a fireball of flames.

"This isn't real!" Rasheed shouted. "A hundred thousand dollar car just went up in smoke!"

The black Charger burst through the fire like a bat out of hell. It sped forward with magnificent speed as the other cars behind them slammed into each other, causing a multiple car pileup on the bridge. Soon, Rasheed could hear the Chevy Charger's engine revving. Quickly, Rasheed shouted in Keysha's ear, "How fast are we going?"

"One hundred twenty-five miles per hour!"

"Impossible!" Rasheed cried out. "We are going 125 miles per hour, weaving through traffic, and he is still catching up with us!"

"That is a South Beach police car! They supercharge the engines with liquid nitrogen to chase drug dealers!"

Keysha quickly passed a minivan and a sedan. Then, she sped between two sport utility vehicles. For a moment, Rasheed lost sight of the black Chevy Charger.

"My God! I don't know which is going to kill me first—your driving or that maniac!"

"Hang on!" Keysha shouted as she swerved back to the left. Rasheed glanced over his shoulder and saw the black Chevy Charger two cars behind them. He could see El Hombre Guapo smiling as he gripped the steering wheel with both hands. Rasheed knew exactly what his intentions were.

"Keysha, he is going to run us down!" Rasheed shouted.

"Then, let's give him what he wants!"

"What are you doing?" Rasheed asked.

"Trust me, Rasheed! I know this road!"

"I trust you, but I don't want to be a grease spot on the road!"

"Just follow my lead!"

Keysha decreased her speed by downshifting the gears of the motorcycle. Rasheed gulped as the speedometer decelerated from 125 mph to 90 mph. El Hombre Guapo pressed his gas to the floor as he yelled through the black Chevy Charger's loudspeaker.

"I will now crush you, los cucarachas! Die!"

"Keysha, whatever you are going to do, you had better do it now!" Rasheed screamed.

"Trust me! It is already done!" Keysha replied.

The cars veered out the way of the black Chevy Charger. Keysha swerved right. The black Charger swerved right also and closed the distance.

They were caught. There was no escape. Rasheed closed his eyes just as the front bumper of the black Chevy Charger sped towards the motorcycle's black tire. At that moment, the road took a wide unexpected turn.

"Lean left, Rasheed!" Keysha shouted as she shifted the gears. "Lean now! Do it now!"

Keysha leaned, and Rasheed followed her lead as they sped into the curve.

"¡Ay, carumba!" El Hombre Guapo shouted. He gripped the steering wheel as he tried to brake. The steering wheel jerked out of his hand, and he lost control of the car.

"Los cucarachas!" El Hombre Guapo screamed.

The police car smashed into a concrete wall and burst into flames.

Rasheed screamed, "That is how you drive a motorcycle! Evil Knievel Keysha stunt driver! Whoa!"

Keysha smiled as they sped over and onto the mainland of Miami. She glanced up at the cloudy sky and quietly thanked God. She was finally free to start her new life. Perhaps, she could start that new life with Rasheed in Georgia. Perhaps.

Chapter 6
Turbulence in the Skies Over Georgia

Keysha drove the red motorcycle to a nearby alley that sat between a group of abandoned warehouses and parked it.

"That was some wicked driving. Where did you learn to ride like that?" Rasheed asked.

"My father was a bike rider. God knows Mama that would have killed him if she had known he was taking us riding on Interstate 10!"

"It paid off. I am sure someone has reported a red motorcycle speeding on the bridge. The authorities will be looking for us."

"Well, by the time they find this bike, we will be long gone. There is a taxi over there."

Rasheed hurried to the corner and flagged down the taxi. In seconds, a taxi cab driver stopped to pick them up. As they sat in the back seat, the cab driver asked them where they were going in a most unique way, "Where to, my comrades against the evil empire?"

"What is he talking about?" Keysha whispered.

"Easy. He is a Star Wars junkie," Rasheed softly replied. "You have to speak his language. Watch this."

Rasheed cleared his throat and spoke in an authoritative voice, "Greetings, rebel starfleet commander, this is x-wing leader Locke. Please take us to Miami Airport, Runway C. We are headed to the Atlanta, Georgia System."

"The coordinates are set, x-wing leader!" the taxi driver replied. "We will be there in ten parcs."

Rasheed nodded his head as the taxi pulled off. First, Keysha giggled. Then, she asked, "Are there any other languages you speak?"

"Qui! Qui!" Rasheed said.

"So, you speak French?" Keysha asked.

"No, no!"

Rasheed and Keysha laughed. The pleasant sound caused the taxi cab driver to glance in his rearview mirror. He thought that they made a good couple.

"So, Keysha, where are you from?" Rasheed asked.

"I am from Lafayette, Louisiana."

"Is that near New Orleans?" Rasheed asked.

Keysha rolled her eyes as she replied, "New Orleans isn't the only city in Louisiana."

"My bad. My bad. Whenever I meet someone from Louisiana, they are always from New Orleans."

"Okay, I guess I will go easy on you. Lafayette is forty-five minutes west of Baton Rouge."

"Cool. Gwen always goes to the Alcorn State verses Southern University football games there."

"That is always an exciting game. Rasheed, are you from Atlanta or did you just move there?" Keysha asked.

"Neither. I am the only child and was born twenty-five miles south of Atlanta in Jonesboro, the home of Gone with the Wind."

"Gosh. I had to do a book report on that back in the seventh grade!"

"Really?" Rasheed replied in astonishment. "They made us watch the movie as part of my eight grade history class."

"Rhett Butler and Scarlett O'Hara. Now that was a relationship that was doomed from the beginning."

"So, what do you think makes a successful relationship?" Rasheed asked.

"It is all about communication, sharing your feelings with one another, and understanding why love is essential."

"I feel like a guest on the Keysha Belle Show," Rasheed laughed. "Tell me why you think love essential?"

"Once the aches and pains start, your eyes don't see that far anymore, or if you have a tragic accident, all you are going to have is love. Without love, you have nothing."

"You are correct. Love is everything. Too bad other people don't see it as that."

"I have a question for you, Rasheed."

"Go head. Give me your best shot."

"Where is your wifey?"

Rasheed laughed as he held up his index finger first and asked, "What does this stand for?"

"Um, a number one."

"That's right," Rasheed said as he raised his middle finger, forming a peace sign. "So, one plus one equals two, right?"

"Yes, but where are you going with this?"

"There is a level of progression to these things. First, one has to have a girlfriend, then you can have a wife!"

"Hmm! That is a rule that is too frequently broken. You would probably break it if you could."

"Nah, that isn't my style. I had a girlfriend. We were serious, but now we are over."

"If you say so. You may think it is over, but she may not. She is thinking that y'all are just taking a break."

"If that is what she is thinking, then she is quite mistaken because I made it clear in a court of law that we were over."

"What happened?"

"She tried to take over my record label by using fake documents!"

"Fake documents? Sounds juicy!"

"She had fake W-2's, inventory records, and even contracts! The whole nine!"

"Wow! What was this maniac's name?" Keysha asked.

"Kandis Wright. I still remember what my mother told me when she met her."

"What did your mother say?" Keysha asked.

"She said in her tiny little voice, 'Rasheed, everything that glitters is not gold.'"

"Your mother told you the truth. Some people have good looks but bad intentions!"

"I know. We had a good relationship. We went places and did things together."

"Wow, and she acted like that?" Keysha said.

"Yep, the lies and arguments just became overwhelming."

"That is enough to break the strongest relationship."

"She is the type of person who is in a league of her own, so you have to show her that you mean business."

"How long did you all date?"

"Umm, about a year and a half."

"I'm sure things were good in the beginning."

"Everything is always good in the beginning. Haven't you read the Bible?'

Keysha giggled, "Yes, silly, but are you sure the groupies waiting for you at the end of the games didn't transform her?"

"That wasn't it," Rasheed responded as he shook his head. "I took her everywhere I went, and when she wasn't there, she was still there, know what I mean?"

"Yeah," Keysha said.

"A person just doesn't change the way she changed overnight. She was already like that."

"Maya Angelou says that when people show you who they are, you should believe them."

"Come to find out. When Kandy wasn't with me, she was

making fake documents that said she was the CEO of Locke Records and was responsible for distributing all compensations!"

"That chick is straight out of the soap operas!" Keysha exclaimed. "I am surprised she didn't make you drove!"

"Drove? What's that?"

"I'm sorry. That is my Louisiana lingo coming back to haunt me. It is short for driving someone crazy."

"That is okay. Just to let you know, we speak slang in Atlanta, too."

"Like what? 'Shawty' and 'crunk'?"

"That is old school. Now, people say 'ham on 'em'! For example, if I am going to go off on someone, I would say I am about to go ham on 'em!"

"Ham on 'em?" Keysha giggled. "That is definitely an Atlanta thing 'cause I've never heard it before!"

"We are the originators of uniquely crafted euphemisms."

"Well, hopefully, your bad days are over when it comes to relationships."

"You think?"

Keysha put her hand on Rasheed's hand and asked, "Do you feel that?"

"What? Your pulse?"

"Yes. And that other thing that has you smiling from ear to ear?"

"Get out of here," Rasheed laughed. "You think you are running game."

"When we get to Atlanta, what do you plan on doing with

me?" Keysha asked.

"I am going to give you some money to go back to Lafayette to your family. I know they miss you."

"Thanks, but what if I just want to visit them and stay in Atlanta with you?"

"That-that can be arranged," Rasheed stuttered.

The two kissed as the taxicab driver made a right hand turn and entered Miami Airport. When they separated, Rasheed looked at Keysha.

"What is that look for?" Keysha asked.

"I just recognized something that I have only ever seen glimpses of."

Keysha looked around wildly and asked, "What was it? Was it a spider? Was it a roach?"

"None of the above. What I saw and what I am still seeing is love."

Keysha cooed, "Awww! You are so sweet!"

"Keysha, the only thing that you don't know about me is my social security number, but I don't feel like I know anything about you. Do you have brothers or sisters?"

"I have two sisters and no brothers," Keysha said, "and I am part of a book club called Book Jazz."

"So, you like to read books and discuss them with your friends?"

"Along with making special dishes for baby showers and birthday parties. Oh yeah, we also go to basketball games."

"I am definitely going to have my next birthday party down

there, so Book Jazz can hook me up!"

Keysha looked Rasheed up and down in sexy way and said, "Make sure you do that. I will make sure you are well taken care of."

The taxi cab coasted onto Runway C and toward a white leer jet with the navy blue words LOCKE-ONE printed on the side.

"This is your jet?" Keysha asked in awe.

"Yes. It has a galley with a kitchen for meal preparation, two single full-sized beds, and an office area just in case I have a business meeting to conduct while in the air."

"What do you know? A house in the sky," Keysha said. "You could practically live on there."

"I could, but the yard space is very limited."

The taxi slowly approached a raised platform that led to leer jet. At the bottom of the platform stood a tall bald headed white man dressed in a dark suit.

"That's my pilot, Norman," Rasheed said. "Rebel Starfleet Commander, pull up near that guy."

"Roger that, x-wing leader," he said as he parked the taxi near the airplane. Rasheed handed the cab driver a fifty dollar bill and opened the door.

"Keep the change, and may the force be with you," Rasheed said as he exited the vehicle.

"Good bye," Keysha said.

"The force is strong in that one. Strong, I say." the driver said.

Rasheed and Keysha walked to Norman, who reached out and shook Rasheed's hand as he greeted him, saying, "Glad to see you made it, Rasheed."

"Me, too. Norman, this is Keysha. She will accompany us back to Atlanta."

"Pleased to meet you, Keysha," Norman greeted.

"Same here."

"I was watching the news. There seems to be some trouble on the bridge," Norman said.

"You could say there were some fireworks. C'mon, Norman. Let's get out of here."

"As you wish."

Keysha looked uneasily at Norman. There is something strange about him, Keysha thought to herself, but I can't put my finger on it. Keysha dismissed the thought as they boarded the airplane and entered the luxurious cabin that was decorated with tan leather recliner seats. Keysha sat down on one of the nearby sofa recliners, and Rasheed sat down beside her.

"Finally, we've made it!" Keysha sighed.

"This recliner has never felt so comfortable," Rasheed said. "Let's roll, Norman!"

Norman pressed an orange button on the side of the wall that caused the steps to retract, and the door to close automatically. There was an audible hissing sound as the cabin was pressurized. Norman entered the cockpit and closed the door. Rasheed heard the twin turbine engines starting up as they began to move slightly. Below them, on the runway, employees of Miami Airport directed the plane to the designated area for takeoff.

"Everyone, please fasten your seat belts," Norman said over

the intercom. "We have clearance for takeoff."

Rasheed and Keysha buckled their seat belts. The engines whirred to a crescendo. Norman released the lever, and the leer jet sped down the runway. The jet took off into the night sky then leveled off. Norman picked up the intercom and addressed the two passengers, "Locke-One is cruising at an altitude of fifty thousand feet above sealevel at a cool 600 miles per hour. We will be arriving in Atlanta in one hour."

"This beats driving nine hours," Rasheed said.

"You should try driving fourteen hours from Lafayette to Miami!" Keysha joyfully spoke. "I was practically the poster child for energy drinks!"

"Now, it's time to relax. Just like my granddad would say, 'We got it made nah!'"

Keysha leaned over and rubbed Rasheed's cheek. Then, she said, "Earlier, you mentioned your mother. Is she still living?"

"Nah, she is in heaven," Rasheed replied.

"Oh, I'm so sorry," Keysha apologized.

"It's okay. The breast cancer was aggressive, and God answered our prayers by not letting her suffer."

"That's a good way to look at it," Keysha said. "I once read in a magazine that there is a belief among older blacks that if they have surgery the cancer spreads quicker."

"I can believe that. Before the surgery, Mom was fine, taking chemotherapy on schedule, and going fishing! After the surgery, the cancer started eating away at her with a vengeance!"

"I was unaware of the toll cancer could take on a person until my aunt was diagnosed. It affected my family mentally and physically."

"In less than four weeks, Mom went from 135 pounds to 99 pounds! Just to see that type of transformation tore us up!"

"I know it had to be hard to watch her go through that," Keysha said softly.

"It was hard, but she was a strong woman whose faith never wavered."

"I can see some of that in you."

"Thanks for the compliment. She definitely rubbed off on me."

"What was your mother's name?"

"Her name was Ellen."

"That's a pretty name. Whenever you have a daughter, you should name her that."

"First," Rasheed replied, "I have to find someone. Then, I have to get to know her."

"Finding someone…check," Keysha replied as she smiled at Rasheed. "Getting to know someone…pending."

"You better not have a glitch or let someone hack the system."

"My operation is secure. I am talking Fort Knox, baby."

"I like a woman who can talk junk!" Rasheed shouted.

"I can back it up, too! Watch yourself! Don't get beside yourself!"

"Can you just hold me? It's been a long time since I was close to someone."

"Sure," Keysha replied in her pleasant voice. Rasheed raised the armrest that was positioned between them. Then, he laid his head on Keysha's lap where she caressed his head.

"That feels so good," Rasheed moaned. "Keysha, your hands could melt butter."

"Shhh!" Keysha said in her soft voice. "We've had a long day. Let's take a nap."

In minutes, the two love birds had fallen asleep as they flew the friendly skies at fifty thousand feet. The two slept believing that they were now safe.

2

Behind the cockpit door, Norman's cell phone beeped. He answered the phone without checking the caller ID.

"Hello. This is Norman. How may I help you?"

A raspy, accented voice replied to him, "Señor Norman, this is the El Ojo."

"E-El Ojo?" Norman stammered. "The El Ojo who took me in as a kid when I was living on the streets of Costa Rica and sent me to flight school?"

"Sí. It is I."

"El Ojo, it has been a long time," Norman said.

"For twenty summers, I have watched you from afar. You have always carried yourself in an esteemed manner."

"Gracias, El Ojo. How may I serve La Committee?"

"I call you with a notification. I am assuming control of La Committee. El Hombre Guapo is dead."

"Dead?"

"We are all mortals and subject to remarkable fates, Señor Norman. The angels have welcomed El Hombre Guapo into their gates, and it is now time for vengeance!"

"Tell me who killed El Hombre Guapo, and I will rip them apart," Norman angrily responded.

"This person is with you now, Señor Norman. The person is on your airplane as we speak."

"The woman?" Norman asked.

"Sí, she was a wife of El Hombre Guapo."

"I see," Norman said.

"Just like you and other possessions of La Committee, a tiny GPS microchip was inserted into her arm, showing her location and vital signs. She and the boy are a threat to La Committee."

"They shall be dealt with," Norman said harshly.

"Death before dishonor is the code of La Committee. It has been for hundreds of years! Señor Norman, I ask you to put the code to the test!"

"El Ojo, I will not forsake the code or La Committee."

"Then, make me proud, Señor Norman. Extinguish yourself, and crash the plane!"

"Why not let me do them myself?"

"When a leader of La Committee is killed, a sacrifice is required. Señor Norman, the angels await you."

"Whether in heaven or hell."

He ended the phone call and reached for the landing gear unit. Norman grunted as he kicked the side panel. His shoes busted an opening into it. Then, he pulled out a short knife and cut the wires that lowered the landing gear.

"Let's see how you land with no wheels."

Norman violently and repeatedly kicked the lever until the bolt broke.

"Now for the final touch, the death touch."

Norman pressed a button on the control dashboard labeled FUEL. A message appeared on his monitor as a computerized voice spoke to him.

"Are you sure you would like to purge the fuel tanks?"

"Yes."

"Fuel tanks purging."

He watched the fuel level decrease. Then, he reached into his suit pocket and pulled out a syringe of morphine.

"China White, take me to the angels!"

Norman plunged the needle filled with powerful drug into his heart. Norman began to sweat profusely. He became dizzy. Norman's hand flopped to the left and struck the butterfly control stick of the airplane, causing the leer jet to rock from side to side.

3

The turbulence snapped Rasheed from his nap.

"Keysha, did you feel that?" Rasheed asked in a concerned voice.

"Nah, but your big head made my leg go to sleep," Keysha said as she stretched her legs out.

The airplane rocked again, but this time more than the first time and flung Keysha to the floor.

"Are you okay?" Rasheed asked.

"Yeah. Are we flying through a storm or something?"

"We are not in a storm," Rasheed said as he looked out of the window. "The night sky is clear! Something is wrong!"

Suddenly, the airplane rocked again.

"Rasheed, check on the pilot!"

Rasheed hurried to the cockpit door and knocked on the door. "Norman? Norman, is everything okay?"

There was no response. Rasheed knocked harder and raised his voice, "Norman! Norman, answer me!"

"Rasheed, why isn't he answering?" Keysha asked.

"I don't know, but step back. I am about to kick the door in!"

Keysha backed up to the far end of the cabin as Rasheed slammed his foot into the door two times. On the third kick, the door to the cockpit flung open. Slumped forward with his hand slightly bumping against the control mechanism was Norman.

"Norman!" Rasheed shouted.

Rasheed hurried to Norman's side and leaned him back. Rasheed saw the syringe protruding from his chest. Suddenly, Norman opened his eyes and with his last breath, he whispered, "La Committee…"

Keysha held her hands against her chest as she stared at the dying pilot.

"What does he mean by La Committee?" Rasheed asked.

"They can't be here."

"Rasheed, is there a golden ring on his finger?"

"Yes," Rasheed said as he studied Norman's ring. "There is a golden ring with a single yellow stone."

"They all wear golden rings!" Keysha said frantically. "El Hombre Guapo said I would never be able to leave them! He was right! He was right!"

"I need you to calm down, Keysha."

"How am I supposed to calm down? Rasheed, we are fifty freaking thousand feet in the air traveling at six hundred miles an hour with no pilot! Don't tell me to calm down! We are going to die!"

"Keysha," Rasheed said in a calm steady voice, "I am not telling you, but I am asking you to calm down. I need you."

"You need me for what? What can I do?"

"I need you to co-pilot," Rasheed said.

"Huh?"

"We are going to land the plane in Atlanta. If we are to survive, we need to act now!"

Keysha stared at Rasheed. Their eyes locked. In those dangerous seconds, they fell deeper in love with one another.

"You have the longest eyelashes and the brownest eyes," Keysha said.

"Keysha, I need you to focus."

"Okay. Okay. Just tell me what to do."

"First, we need to get Norman out of the cockpit. Then, I want you to sit in the co-pilot seat and work the speaker-radio."

"I can't touch a dead person," Keysha said as she stepped aside.

"I got him," Rasheed replied as he grabbed Norman by the shoulders and hoisted him from the pilot's seat. He dragged him to a nearby sofa recliner that was located near the window.

"There you go, buddy. Look out the window and watch this miracle!"

Rasheed walked into the cockpit and sat in the pilot's seat. Keysha sat next to him. He stared at the computer monitor that was surrounded by numerous gauges and dials. Rasheed gripped the butterfly control stick of the airplane and pulled back. The airplane began to rise in elevation.

"That was easy. Back for up, forward for down."

"Cut that out, Rasheed, before I throw up in your lap!" Keysha yelled as she held her stomach.

"My bad. Can you start the transmission to Air Traffic Control? Just say, 'Mayday! Mayday! Mayday! Locke-One 029er is in distress."

"Okay," Keysha replied as she nodded her head. "Mayday! Mayday! Mayday! Locke-One 029er is in distress! I repeat! Mayday! Mayday! Mayday! Locke-One 029er is in distress."

In a few seconds, Air Traffic Control responded to their distress signal via the intercom within the cabin, saying, "Locke-One 029er, we hear you loud and clear. This is Jake with Air Traffic Control, requesting your distress. Over."

"Locke-One 029er, the pilot is dead. Mr. Locke is attempting to land the airplane. We are in need of assistance. Over," Keysha explained.

There was a moment of silence. Keysha looked at Rasheed

with fearful eyes.

"Do you think La Committee is there?"

"Who knows? I've known Norman for years, and he turned out to be a maniac! I don't know who to trust. Transmit the message again!"

"Air Traffic Control, Locke-One 029er is in distress. Please respond."

"This is a bad sign!" Keysha said in a somber tone. "They are not answering!"

"Retransmit," Rasheed said. "Don't give up!"

"Air Traffic Control, please excuse my language, but we are in major shit! Respond! Please respond!"

Suddenly, Jake with Air Traffic Control came back online and said, "I apologize for the delay. I had to look up your leer jet's model and get a diagram of the layout of your cockpit."

"I am sorry for cussing at you!" Keysha replied. "Please help us, Jake."

"I understand your level of frustration. Locke-One 029er, you have clearance on runway X-1A. Please input the following coordinates into you dashboard to activate your smart-guidance system. The coordinates are 0-7-5 degrees west and 8-3-5 degrees north. I repeat. The coordinates are 0-7-5 degrees west and 8-3-5 degrees north. Over?"

"Roger. Rasheed, I am typing in the coordinates. Zero-seven-five degrees west and 8-3-5 degrees north," Keysha informed. She typed the coordinates in, and the monitor came on as the smart-guidance system became engaged.

"Jake, the Smart-Guidance System has been activated," Keysha said.

"Locke-One 29er, do you see the lines that form lanes with the triangle in the middle?" Jake asked.

"Yes," Keysha replied.

"That is a virtual mapping of the best projection to your desired destination. Keep the triangle in the middle and wait for further instructions."

"Aye! Aye! Captain!" Keysha said. "Looks like we are out of the woods after all."

"Don't pop the champagne, yet." Rasheed said. "We still have to land this giant bird!"

The leer jet soared through the night sky. Ten minutes later, Jake hailed Rasheed and Keysha, saying, "Locke-One 029er, you are going to have to start your descent and drop some speed!"

"Um, Jake, how do we do that?" Rasheed asked.

"Lock-One 029er, you have to increase the size of your wings!"

"Jake, speak English. How do I do that?" Rasheed asked.

"Press the orange button located on your upper right," Jake instructed.

"Upper right?" Rasheed muttered as he glanced up. "Where is my upper right?"

"Calm down. Look up then right," Jake instructed.

"Got it," he said as he pressed the button. Extra wing surfaces slid out on the wings and extended downward at a steep angle. There was a noticeable change in their speed.

"That did something! That did something!" Rasheed chanted excitedly.

"The extended extra wing surfaces make your drag larger," Jake explained. "Now, lower your speed by about 150 mph by lowering the throttle."

Rasheed followed the directions and watched the speedometer decrease from 600 mph to 450 mph.

"Speed is decreasing, Air Traffic Control."

"Good. Now, look on your dashboard. There should be a graphic of the runway."

"I see it," Rasheed said.

"Keep the triangle in the middle. Now, lower your landing gear and try to keep your nose up."

"How?"

"Pull back the lever with the chrome handle."

Rasheed pulled the handle back, but the mechanism came loose with severed wires attached.

"What in the hell?"

Jake noticed that the landing wheels had not been lowered.

"Locke-One, what is the situation? Why are the landing wheels not lowering?"

"Air Traffic Control, we have a problem," Rasheed transmitted. "The freaking landing gear is damaged and cannot be lowered."

"Pull up and stop your decent!" Jake shouted.

Rasheed pulled back on his control stick and retracted the smaller wings that had increased his drag. Just then, a warning message appeared on the monitor: FIVE PERCENT FUEL.

"Oh, my God," Keysha gasped. "Our fuel is almost depleted!"

"Jake, we have another problem," Rasheed said. "Our fuel has been purged! We have to land!"

"Your craft is not made to handle such an impact without landing gear!" Jake exclaimed. "If you land on your belly, you are going to burst into flames!"

"What are our options?" Rasheed asked.

"It depends on how much fuel is remaining," Jake said.

"The monitor says we have five percent fuel remaining!" Rasheed responded.

"Five percent fuel remaining," Jake sadly responded. "You are running on fumes and can crash at any moment!"

"What about sending an airplane to refuel us like they do on television?" Keysha asked.

"It takes time to load up a fuel tanker, and time isn't a luxury we have," Jake replied. "I am sorry, Locke-One 029er, but we have to prepare a crash site."

"No! God, no!" Keysha sobbed as she dropped her head.

"Jake, listen up! I am requesting fire and rescue teams along the Chattahoochee River near the junction of Interstate 75 and 285! Give me the coordinates!"

"What for?"

"I am going to land this white duck in the water near Cumberland Boulevard!"

"Okay, that will work! The coordinates are 0-4-8 degrees east and 7-1-2 degrees north."

"You got that, Keysha?" Rasheed asked.

"Got 'em," Keysha replied as she typed in the coordinates.

The Smart-Guidance System steered the aircraft in the best possible direction to its desired destination.

"Jake, I am going directly through the city!" Rasheed said.

"I have diverted all flights away from the airport and the city. Good luck!"

"I don't believe in luck. I believe in God!"

"Then, He will see you through," Jake replied.

Rasheed concentrated as he navigated the leer jet. He glanced over at Keysha. They both had not come this far to end like this. Rasheed licked his lips and concentrated even more.

Seconds later, Jake saw the white leer jet speed by the airport. He had already notified the emergency agencies. The Atlanta skyline towered before Rasheed.

"There is the city!" Rasheed said. "Keysha, give me an update on the fuel!"

"Rasheed, we are at two percent fuel!" Keysha said. "How far is the river?"

"Just north of the city."

"At this speed, we are not going to make it," Keysha realized. "You have to increase the speed!"

"Then, I will burn fuel faster!"

"If you don't, we will crash faster and kill thousands!" Keysha said.

Rasheed knew Keysha was correct. He pulled the emergency lever. Oxygen masks and flotation devices dropped from the ceiling.

"Keysha, go take a seat in the cabin and assume the crash position. Don't forget to put on your swimming vest."

"But—"

"I will be fine. Go!"

Keysha hurried to the cabin of the airplane where she slipped on her flotation device, tucked her head near her knees, and began to pray. Rasheed increased the speed of the leer jet as the city drew closer.

"I am going to cut through this city like a hot knife through butter," Rasheed said.

The leer jet boomed over Turner Stadium where a baseball game was being played. The fans cheered because they thought it was part of the attraction.

Rasheed glanced at the monitor. It read: ONE PERCENT FUEL REMAINING.

"Let the good times roll!" Rasheed shouted. He accelerated the speed even more. The airplane boomed past the Westin Hotel and shattered some of its windows. Rasheed glanced up ahead and saw the express way split into two directions: one northwest and the other northeast.

"I am going to follow I-75 north, northwest. The Chattahoochee River should be coming into view."

Rasheed pressed the orange button, causing the smaller wing surfaces to extend to lower his drag. He glanced at the monitor again. It read: ZERO PERCENT FUEL.

"God have mercy," Rasheed muttered.

Along the highway, traffic had been stopped by police cars and fire engines. Some of the rescue vehicles even bordered the river just as he had requested. Rasheed aimed the plane towards the Chattahoochee River.

"Good job, Jake. God, it is in your hands now!"

Suddenly, the twin turbine engines stopped. Rasheed fastened his seatbelt and braced himself as they fell from the sky at a tremendous speed. The airplane vibrated terribly as the rate of decent increased. Rasheed held onto the control stick for dear life as he prayed.

"God, please forgive me for all my sins and welcome me into your kingdom."

The leer jet ripped through strands of misty clouds as Rasheed saw the river drawing closer. He braced himself for impact. It was entirely out of his hands now. Hopefully, Keysha and he would be spared.

On the ground, Sergeant Gaston with Cobb County Fire and Rescue evacuated the area as he saw the lights of the airplane in the sky.

"Everyone get back! He is coming in too fast!"

The rescue and emergency teams took cover as the leer jet

thundered across the interstate and down the river like a runaway train. There was a moment of silence, then the explosion followed.

KABOOM!

Sergeant Gaston shielded his eyes from the glare of the explosion. He picked up his portable radio and broadcasted on all channels, "The bird is down in the river! All teams commence search and rescue!"

He hopped from the river bank and onto a small boat where his team awaited him.

"Sergeant Gaston, do you think anyone survived?" an officer asked.

Officer Gaston shook his head and said, "That craft is more fiberglass than anything. There will probably be a lot of burnt remains floating in the water."

The rescue team silently navigated the Chattahoochee River toward the crash site, bracing themselves for the worst. The smell of smoke and water drifted to their noses. It was disgusting and gut-wrenching.

Hundreds of miles away in San Jose, Costa Rica, an elderly man with stringy white hair sat in a leather executive chair at a mahogany desk. Brown spots covered his bony hands and black dirt was under his yellow fingernails.

The man was El Ojo, the Eye of La Committee. He picked

up a remote and clicked a button. A one hundred-inch television television came on, featuring the most watched broadcast of the First News Network. At the top of the screen was the caption: BREAKING NEWS: DRAMA IN THE SKIES OF ATLANTA!

"This is Monica Drake, with 'First New Network', reporting live from a crash site just north of Atlanta! A leer jet belonging to local star athlete Rasheed Locke has crashed in the Chattahoochee River!"

"Bueno, Norman," El Ojo said in his raspy voice. "I am very proud of you."

Monica Drake held her hand up to her ear as new information came in. Then, she reported, "I have just been informed that Rasheed Locke is alive, but an unknown female passenger is not accounted for! Stay tuned. We will return after this commercial break as the drama unfolds!"

"This is not what I had hoped for," El Ojo said.

He quickly opened up a nearby laptop that displayed a graphic of heart rate and pulse for Keysha. His anger grew each time the device beeped.

El Ojo slammed his feeble hand on the countertop of his mahogany desktop and screamed, "The wench still lives!"

He picked up a nearby phone and made a call to a very pricey assassin that La Committee used only for special missions.

"This is the Eliminator," answered a deep voice.

"This is El Ojo. La Committee requires your talents."

"You know the price is seven figures."

"Money is not a factor," El Ojo coldly replied.

"Wire the money to my Swiss account. Where is the target?"

El Ojo licked his thin lips. Then, he said, "The target is in Atlanta, Georgia. A girl that belongs to La Committee is missing. However, the chip inside her arm is still transmitting favorable vital signs. I want her deader than dead!"

"The Eliminator is en route, El Ojo. Your problems will be solved by tomorow evening!"

"Very well," El Ojo said.

He hung up the phone. Then, he accessed the menu of his television and chose SECURITY CAMERA: PACKAGING AREA. Suddenly, he was viewing a well-lit room of naked women as they packaged bricks of cocaine, packets of pills, and bundles of marijuana. The women were there courtesy of El Hombre Guapo. Using the direction pad on the remote control, El Ojo zoomed in on a young black woman who was bagging drugs near the end of the table. The woman had an English Ivy tattoo that ran up her hand.

"Priceless, priceless as gold," El Ojo muttered. "The product never loses its value."

The pleasures of the flesh did not excite his aged body, only the sight of continuous drug flow. He turned the television off and hobbled out of the room. There would not be a need to spend any time or resources searching for the woman. The Eliminator was the best at turning living people into dead people.

Chapter 7
Degrees of Separation

The morning sun glared through the window and fell on Rasheed's face. He slowly opened his eyes. As they focused, Rasheed became aware of his surroundings.

"Where...where am I?"

A television was positioned in the right corner of the room. On the other side of the room was a sink with a mirror and GET WELL balloons.

Beep! Beep! Beep!

What's that noise? Rasheed wondered. He glanced down and saw a device attached to his first finger with a small cable that was connected to a small machine that registered his heartbeats.

"I'm in a hospital. H-how did I get here? W-where is Keysha? Keysha!" Rasheed moaned as he tried to detach the device from his finger.

"Slow down, cowboy," a familiar voice said, "before the cavalry comes running!"

Rasheed rolled his head to the left. Sitting in a chair, dressed in blue jeans and a black-tee shirt, was a young black man with a low fade.

"DeWayne," Rasheed shouted, "how did I get here?"

"Courtesy of a Life Flight helicopter."

Rasheed rubbed his eyes as he began to piece together the events that had occurred within the past couple of hours.

"What are you doing here? Don't you have some customers to help at Shop-Mart?"

"Yeah, but they can wait. I'm here to see my best friend and favorite pilot Mr. Unbreakable."

"Who?" Rasheed asked in astonishment.

"Mr. Unbreakable is the nickname the tabloids and media have coined for you."

Rasheed sat up in his hospital bed and asked, "And where is Keysha?"

"I don't know about Keysha, but Monica Drake, that black reporter on First News Network, is reporting some juicy stuff about you."

"And what is she saying?" Rasheed asked.

"She reported, and I quote, 'The Atlanta FireHawks' star player is in financial straits and tried to fake his death to avoid creditors!'"

"She is still mad that I shot her down in Vegas in front of her girls."

"You already know. She thought she had you, dressed in that purple mini skirt. From the neck down, she is a model, but from the neck up, she has the face of a dinosaur!"

"That woman has more teeth than a gremlin!" Rasheed laughed.

"I love you! You love me! I am a bitter woman who's lonely. With a mini skirt, a hug, and kiss from me to you. You better say you love me, too!" DeWayne childishly sang.

Rasheed and DeWayne laughed at the joke. When the laughter subsided, Rasheed became serious.

"I wish people like Monica Drake would look for the facts first. It's already open season on young black males, whether we are successful or not."

"Yesterday, one cop pulled over my cousin then called five of his buddies for backup," DeWayne said, leaning forward.

"Wow! Was he drunk driving or something?"

"No, he has an old school car with the big rims, and they said all they wanted was to check his license and registration."

"Let me guess. The cops were white."

"White as refined sugar! You never hear about six black cops stopping one white person just to check his license and insurance!"

"See, that's what I am talking about! Instead of Monica Drake reporting I'm broke, she should be reporting on the injustices that are happening every day. Why is that? I mean why don't we get the support we deserve during a bad situation? I'll tell you why. The bottom line is that black people sell."

"You lost me, Rasheed," DeWayne said as he shook his head. "I was with you until you said that."

"Trust me. Black people sell."

"Everyone sells," DeWayne said. "White people, Black people, Latin people, and people who check 'Other' under the ethnicity category on an application sell."

"You're right, but not only do we sell products, we sell ourselves," Rasheed said. "If you don't believe me, just look at the television."

"Rasheed, I'm sorry, but it sounds like you are hating on black people."

"Everything I am is because of black people," Rasheed clarified. "I love Black people. Black people are me, but we need to clean up the images that are being broadcasted."

"Rasheed, I'm still lost," DeWayne said. "Give me a flashlight."

"Let me put it this way," Rasheed explained. "If I was from another country and I watched television every day, I would think that all black people did was shoot each other and sell drugs. Not to mention reality shows. What we need are more broadcasts that display family values, education, and a sense of responsibility."

"We do need more role models other than athletes and musicians," DeWayne rationalized. "We need a combination of blue collar and white collar workers stepping up as the voices of the community."

"Whenever that day comes, we, the people, will have to show that our value is the same as an athlete or rapper."

"True. True, but there is hope to remake our image!" DeWayne shouted. "There is Obama!"

Rasheed nodded his head and said, "Now that he is the president, the face of our country, black people will view themselves in a better light. No longer will you have to say you have to be a star athlete to make it out of the hood."

"Now, we can say, even if my mother is a single parent, as long as I work hard, I can still go to the best schools and be the president," DeWayne said.

"That's right," Rasheed replied. "As for the crash, the airplane's controls were damaged, the pilot was dead, and we were out of fuel. I just did what I had to do."

"If the plane would have hit one of those skyscrapers downtown, hundreds of lives would have been lost. You are a hero."

"It was all God."

"It had to be or else Monica Drake would be leading a mob with torches to your home!"

"Ha! Ha! Ha! You're right," Rasheed laughed. "Let's see what is on the news right now. Maybe there is some news about Keysha."

Rasheed turned the television on and put it on the local news channel where Any Time News chief meteorologist Jeff Marksman pointed to a graphic of the word COLD slowly creeping from the north to the south.

"This rapidly approaching cold front will cause changes throughout Georgia after lunch today and will not let up until Sunday," Jeff Marksman forecasted.

"The weather is about to change," Rasheed said.

"That is Georgia for you," DeWayne replied. "Hot one day, then freezing the next!"

Jeff Marksman continued his forecast, "Be prepared for high winds, dropping temperatures, and ugly rain showers. What you have today won't be there tomorrow. Paul, back to you."

The screen switched to the brown haired clean shaven news anchor, Paul Pritchett, as he reported a developing story, saying, "In the wee hours of the morning, the popular sports bar known as Dee's Kitchen, located on Tara Boulevard in Clayton County, was the scene of another smash and grab robbery."

"Ridiculous," DeWayne said.

Paul Pritchett continued, "This group of thieves, known as the Jump Out Boys, have robbed numerous businesses across Metro Atlanta. Last night, surveillance video captured them in action, snatching flat screen televisions from the walls and pillaging the safe in less than thirty seconds, leaving the owner baffled. Here is what the surveillance cameras caught."

Any Time News switched to the video feed, showing how the men ran to and fro, grabbing the flat screens off of the wall and hurrying out the store. Before they left, a black ski masked figure with a mouthful of gold teeth looked into the camera and waved good bye.

Paul Pritchett resumed the broadcast and said, "Standing by in downtown Atlanta is 'Any Time News' anchor Dana Anderson."

The camera switched to a blonde haired, blue eyed sexy woman dressed in a navy blue business suit standing outside a hospital. With an authoritative voice, she said, "Good Saturday morning, Atlanta. This is Dana Anderson, reporting live from outside Saint Frances Memorial Hospital where star athlete Rasheed Locke is resting after surviving last night's plane crash!"

"Now, that is a reporter!" DeWayne said. "She used to be a supermodel, right?"

"Yeah," Rasheed replied. "I went to high school with her and her late husband."

"What happened to him?"

"They were crossing a street in downtown Atlanta, and a driver wasn't paying attention and ran right into them. Dana's husband pushed her out of the way, but the car hit him. The impact immediately killed him," Rasheed explained.

"Dang! Was the driver drunk or something?"

"No, the driver was sending a text message while driving!" Rasheed exclaimed.

"That accident could have been avoided," DeWayne replied.

"Yes, sir. That is also what made Dana give up modeling and go into journalism."

"She has my undivided and unsubtracted attention!" DeWayne said humorously.

Dana Anderson continued her report as the wind lightly blew through her blonde hair, "Rasheed Locke, also known as Mr. Unbreakable because of how he emerged from the wreckage without a scratch or broken limb, is recovering at this local hospital!"

DeWayne sat Indian style in his chair as he held his fingers together in a gesture of meditation and spoke in a monotone voice,

"Rasheed, I see many new endorsements in your near future, perhaps a Mr. Unbreakable action figure with the kung fu grip!"

Dana Anderson continued her report, "People, this just in! Rescuers have recovered the body of Mr. Locke's female passenger miles down the river! She is being life- flighted to Jackson Memorial!"

Rasheed leaped out of his bed in astonishment and shouted, "Keysha!"

"Are you crazy? What are you doing?" DeWayne asked.

"Keysha needs me!" Rasheed answered as he unhooked the device on his finger.

The device beeped uncontrollably.

"Dang!" Rasheed said as he reattached the device. "I need to get my clothes, but this thing is not going to let me get to the closet!"

"Wait! Wait! Pump your brakes!" DeWayne said. "Where do you think you are going?"

"I have to find Keysha! Please get my clothes out of the closet?"

"Rasheed, you just survived a plane crash. Your clothes are half burnt up, and you look like you opened up a present from Jokey Smurf! The only thing they could salvage was your cell phone."

"Then, give me your clothes and take my place in the bed!"

"Let's rewind," DeWayne said as he did a triple take. "Zurp! Now, please repeat what you just said?"

"You are going to give me your clothes and put on this gown

and get in that bed! I will explain later."

"You know this isn't going to work, right?"

"Why not? They say all black people look alike."

DeWayne pointed to his nose and said, "I have a 1978 Michael Jackson nose, and you have 2009 Samuel Jackson lips! That's why it isn't going to work!"

"It will. Besides, you owe me."

"For what?"

"For the summer of 1996, when I let you play with me in that basketball league with recording artists and record producers, when you met what's her face."

"Simple Sparrow," DeWayne sighed.

"Yeah, that poor simple minded girl, so you owe me."

"But she broke up with me in the fall of 1996."

"Didn't you listen to Ms. Jackson?" Rasheed asked as he patted DeWayne on the shoulder. "That's the way love goes. Now, give me those pants!"

"Okay, but if they put some plastic gloves on and try to take my temperature, I am going to jump out the window. Then, they are going to say you tried to commit suicide!"

Rasheed and DeWayne quickly changed clothes. Rasheed made sure he took Sunshine's cell phone. DeWayne reluctantly pulled the covers up to his neck as he called out in a kiddy voice.

"Rasheed?"

"Yes."

"Can you give me a cup of water?"

"Sure. Anything else?"

"Add six cubes of ice."

Rasheed smiled as he opened the miniature icebox and put half a scoop of ice into the cup.

"There you go! Six plus some!"

"Rasheed?"

"Yes, DeWayne," Rasheed replied in frustrated tone. "What is it now?"

"Can you tell me a story?"

Rasheed handed DeWayne the cup of water as he talked through his clenched teeth, "Once upon a time, a friend aggravated another friend, and he did not invite him to his next Super Bowl party!"

"Nice story. Now, just don't fart in my jeans!"

"If I do, I will make sure I leave a stain to keep the other stains company. Where did you park?"

"In the handicapped parking spot in the emergency room parking lot," DeWayne said.

"Why did I even ask? I should have known. Now, real talk. DeWayne, thanks for coming to see me."

"That's what friends are for. I hope you find, Keysha."

"I will. Thanks."

Rasheed walked out of the hospital room. He picked up a newspaper that someone had left outside another room and, while pretending to read it, crept down the hallway. Rasheed made it to the elevator and pressed the ground level button. As the elevator descended, he formulated a plan.

"First, I am going to go home, change clothes, and get my

other cell phone. Then, I am going to look for Keysha."

The elevator stopped on the ground level. Rasheed stepped out of the elevator and headed for the exit.

2

Just as Rasheed walked across the sitting room of the emergency room, Dana Anderson came around the corner after coming from the restroom. She recognized the man's walk. It was smooth, goofy, refined, and immature at the same time. Only one person had a walk like that.

"Rasheed Locke!" Dana Anderson whispered. She closely followed him as he entered the parking lot and pressed the panic button on the keypad. She observed as the alarm of a silver Trans-Am sounded as Rasheed tried to unlock the doors. Once he was successfully inside, Dana Anderson watched as he hopped into the car and started the engine. As the beastly engine growled, Dana said, "Nice car, but you are supposed to be upstairs recuperating from a plane crash not going for a joy ride!"

Dana pulled out her two-way radio and chirped her camera man, "Brian, where are you?"

"I just finished loading the camera into the van, and I am coming around the corner to pick you up."

"Good, we are about to break an exclusive story!"

"Gravy."

"And biscuits," Dana Anderson said.

The white van pulled up, and Dana Anderson hopped in and

instructed Brian to follow the silver Trans-Am. She knew this story was going to blow the other stories off the network.

3

On the other side of Atlanta, on the tenth floor of a high rise condominium, an exotically beautiful woman laid on her king sized bed watching Any Time News on a flat screen television that suffered some nicks and scrapes along the edges of the black frame. The woman was Rasheed's ex-girl Kandis Wright.

"Tsk! Tsk! Flying bimbos around in your private jet. Well, Rasheed, your worries are far from over."

She thrust the comforter back and rolled out of her bed. She was dressed in only a red bra and matching lace underwear. Then, she walked to an adjacent restroom where she stared in the mirror as she brushed her long black hair and gave herself a pep talk.

"You are so beautiful, so gorgeous! No one is as breathtaking as you!"

Kandis pulled her hair back as she continued, "You are a sexy diva! Everyone else is below you! No one else is above you, not even God!"

Kandis poured herself a cap of mouthwash and gargled then swished the fluid around in her mouth. After rinsing her mouth, she exited her bathroom and went into the kitchen where she picked up her cell phone and accessed her address book. Kandis clicked on a contact named Pressure.

"Let's see what my little ghetto boy is doing," Kandis said as his phone number was dialed.

On the second ring, Pressure answered the phone in his deep southern voice, "Sweet Kandy! What it is, shawty?"

"Good morning to you, too."

"Good morning, good night! I'm all about the goods, ya dig?"

She rolled her eyes at Pressure's overuse of slang words and phrases. It seemed to be a way of life for him.

"Yeah, I know you are about the goods. The television you gave me is working, but next time try not to scrape the sides! It makes it look so ghetto!"

"I'm gonna do what a goon got to do, but I always come through for my bottom chick."

"I am not a bottom chick," Kandis muttered under her breath.

"Did you say something, shawty?" Pressure asked.

"I said that your bottom chick needs a favor."

"I am right round the corner from you, and my phone is about to die. Do you mind if I stop by?"

"No, come on by," Kandis said.

About fifteen minutes later, there was a knock at the door. Kandis opened the door and let Pressure in. Pressure wore a pair of designer jeans that he sagged well below his waist and a lime green collared shirt. The tips of his shoulder length dreads were bleached blonde. He looked at Kandis, who was now dressed in her pink robe, and licked his lips.

"Shawty, uh! Nah, you wrong for answering the door like that! You putting on a brotha's mind!"

"Boy, you are crazy! Have a seat. We need to talk," Kandis

said in a serious tone.

Pressure sat down in a nearby chair, brushed his dreads out of his face, and said, "Go head. What's crackin'?"

"Pressure, do you remember what we spoke about last week?"

"Yeah, I 'member."

"What was it about then?"

"It was 'bout how the president race was so close? My dude Barack is da truth!"

"No, we didn't talk about that."

"Um was it 'bout how much my gold teeth cost? 'Cause my grill is sick like that swine flu!"

"No, we didn't talk about that, either."

Pressure clapped his hands as he realized what they had talked about and said, "I 'member, now. We talked 'bout that new scary movie with da haunted house!"

"None of the above!" Kandis sharply replied. "We talked about that thing I need you to do for me!"

"What thang?"

Kandis shouted in frustration, "Uggh! All of that weed has your memory jacked up!"

"Ain't no proof that weed is bad for the body! It is from the earth, shawty!"

"That is nonsense, but let's go back to the subject at hand. Pressure, we talked about getting back at my old boss!"

"Oh, yeah! Yo' boss! I 'member now."

Kandis sighed as she shook her head and muttered, "You are slower than pond water."

"Take that back, shawty!" Pressure shouted. "That ain't nuthin' to play around with!"

"I always protect my investments, Pressure. Remember, I made you and the Jump Out Boys. I gave you contacts you didn't have."

"Yeah, you gave me dat work, but I mastermind and plan better than a championship coach. You need me mo' than I need you, shawty. 'Member that!"

"But I am the one sticking my neck out, doing the dirty work, even if it means sleeping with someone just to get a security code!"

"Sweet Kandy, that's why I'm sweet on you! You are the perfect set-up broad! You take pride in yo' work. I like that!"

"Once you do this thing for me," Kandis said softly as she walked over to and then straddled Pressure, "I won't have to spend my time seducing these cheap tricks. I can spend my time seducing you!"

"You ready for me to lay da smack down, huh?"

"Like a pro-wrestler!" Kandis said as she unloosened her robe and revealed her red lingerie.

Pressure, mesmerized by Kandis' succulent cleavage and smooth, soft stomach, asked, "What is the prick's address that you want done in?"

"It is 2534 Mallard Court in Jonesboro."

"That is off Tara Boulevard, right?"

"Yes," Kandis replied.

"Can't do it," Pressure quickly responded. "Can't do it! Can't do it! I put that on my unborn son!"

"Why can't you do it? What is the problem?" Kandis asked.

"Kandis, don't you watch the news?"

"Yes, and?"

"We just did a job in Clayton County! The spot is too hot! The police will be combing the area for the usual suspects!"

"You have to! This is your only chance!"

"This is a chance alright! A good chance to get locked up!"

"Pressure, the house is empty, and I have the safe code!"

"How do you know all of this?"

"I dated him for a while and had access to personal files. Inside the safe is four hundred thousand dollars!"

"Four hundred stacks! Is he trying to be a bank?"

"No, he isn't trying to be a bank. It is his spending money and how he pays for cars, houses, and private services."

"Well, what's the catch, Sweet Kandy? What did he do to you? Did ol' boy dump you, and you want revenge?"

Kandis ran her hands through her black hair and replied, "That's not important. The only thing I ask is that you trash the place before you leave. No. Better yet, burn it down!"

"That's all. Rob and burn? Nothing else?"

"No strings attached. So, you're game?" Kandis asked as she kissed Pressure on his lips.

"Hell, yeah! I am going in solo. I don't need the Jump Out Boys for this!"

"Call me when it is done," Kandis said as she got off Pressure and pulled her robe back together.

"I won't have to call you. This is going to make the breaking news, morning news, noon news, and evening news!"

"Call me, and you can have desert later," Kandis said as she walked to the foyer and then opened the door. As soon as Pressure left, she walked over to her refrigerator. She pulled out a small box that was filled with stolen credit cards.

"Rasheed, revenge is a dish best served cold!"

She sat the credit cards on a nearby table. Kandis had purchased these cards from a one of her street vendors that helped her finance some of the Jump Out Boys' adventures.

"I think I will go shopping today, so I can wear something sexy while watching the news. I can see the headlines now. Breaking news! Rasheed Locke: A fool parts with his money!"

Kandis danced around her kitchen because she knew that it was going to be an unforgettable day.

The morning sun gleamed brilliantly in the sky over Atlanta as Kandis tidied up her kitchen. Meanwhile, Gary awoke from his slumber. A thudding pain throbbed around his eyes.

"My face still hurts like hell. The swelling didn't go down a bit."

He slowly got off the couch and walked into his kitchen where he poured himself a glass of apple juice. He took a sip then noticed that his message light was blinking.

"I didn't even hear the phone ring! I've missed Aisha's phone call!"

He hurried over to his answering machine as his heart raced with the anticipation of hearing Aisha's voice.

"Can't wait to hear my baby's voice. I know we can get through this," he said as he pressed play. Instead of hearing Aisha's pleasant voice, he heard Rasheed's concerned voice, saying, "What's up, Gary? It's Rasheed. I bumped into Aisha in Miami, and she was acting weird. Call me, so I can fill you in. You don't deserve what I saw. Just know that I am here for you. Peace."

Tears welled up in Gary's eyes as Rasheed's message ended. "Damn. What has Aisha done now?"

He picked up the phone and called the number Rasheed had called him from. The phone rang two times and just when he was about to hang up the phone, Rasheed answered, "Gary, is this you?"

"Yeah, it's me. What's with all of that noise?"

"I am driving DeWayne's car. You know he has that loud engine."

"Yeah, that's right."

"I assume you got my message?"

"Yeah, you saw Aisha, huh?"

"Yeah, and she was in rare form. Gary, are you standing because, if you are, I need you to take a seat."

"Give me one moment," Gary said as he rubbed his bald head. He sat on the sofa chair and stared into a dark fireplace as he answered in a somber voice, "Go ahead. I am sitting down."

"Gary," Rasheed said as he took a deep breath, "this is hard for me to say, so I know it is going to be hard for you to hear."

"Just go ahead and give it to me straight."

"Last night, I went to the club, and I bumped into Aisha and two of her friends."

"Sarah and Hillary. I know them. They all work together at the firm."

"Brother, they do more than work together!"

"What do you mean?" Gary asked naively.

"Gary, your wife sleeps with them and pops ecstasy with them! They have formed a swingers' club. Their plan is to have sex in all the major cities of the U.S.!"

Gary was speechless.

"Gary! Gary, are you still there?" Rasheed shouted.

Rasheed began to fear the worst. Not everyone could take that kind of news. Some people harmed themselves while some people resorted to hurting others.

"Gary, talk to me! Please!"

"I haven't gone anywhere," Gary said sadly.

"Gary, I am sorry, but I had to tell you what I saw."

"I know. I would have done the same for you."

"It was like she had changed into another person. One minute, she was nice, but after a couple of drinks, she became another person!"

"You're lucky she didn't beat you."

"Excuse me?"

"I said you are lucky she didn't beat you."

"Gary, let me pull over on the side of the road. I don't think I heard you right. This engine is too loud."

"No, you heard correctly. Right now, I have a black eye and a split lip from Aisha!"

"What! When did this happen?"

"On Thursday, the day before Valentine's Day. I confronted her about spending more time with her friends than me. She had been drinking. She picked up a skillet and whacked me upside the head!"

"She hit you with a skillet! The one that you fry eggs in or the one you make cornbread?"

"The black iron skillet you make cornbread in."

"My God," Rasheed said.

"When she ain't talking crazy to me, telling me I am not this or that, she is constantly beating me. She even smashed my fingers with a hammer once."

"This is too much. Why didn't you say anything about this before?"

"I felt ashamed. How many men get beat by their drunk wives?"

"There is nothing to be ashamed of," Rasheed said as he pulled into his neighborhood and passed a sign that said NEIGHBORHOOD WATCH.

"Yes, it is!" Gary sobbed. "I am a man! A man!"

"Abuse is abuse, no matter if it is male or female oriented."

"Well, I appreciate the heads up. At least I now know that the marriage is not going to work. I am going to pack my bags after we get off the phone."

"Do you need anything?"

"No, you've done more than enough already. I will take it from here. It is time for me to face the music. Aisha is never going to change."

"I'm sorry, Gary. Just keep me in the loop. Okay?"

"Okay. I will call you later this afternoon. I will probably go to my mother's house. She never really liked Aisha anyway."

"Alright. Tell your mother I said hello and just call me on my cell phone later."

"I will, and Rasheed?"

"Yeah."

"Thanks for the support. I really appreciate it."

"That is what friends are for. Call me later."

"I will. Take care."

Gary ended the phone call and walked to the kitchen where he put the phone on the phone base. Suddenly, his cell phone rang. The ring tone was the Isley Brother's classic "Who's That Lady?". The ringtone was assigned to Aisha's phone number.

"She finally called," Gary said as his heart leaped for joy. "I knew she would! Whoo hoo!"

Gary picked up the phone and answered in an enthusiastic voice, "Hey, honey buns! I was just thinking of you!"

"What in the hell are you doing?" Aisha asked unpleasantly.

"Um, nothing. What's up?"

"Get off your butt and quit running up the power bill!" Aisha yelled. "Turn off those lights!"

"T-they aren't on," Gary said as he looked around to see if any lights were on. "I-I just checked."

"My flight touches down at noon! I want to be picked up at twelve o'clock not twelve o-one, do you understand?"

"Understood. N-no problem. Aisha, can I ask you a question?"

"What is it, Gary? I don't have all day, you know?"

"Um, you know, how was your trip? Was it fun under the sun?"

"It was great! There was a lot to see and a lot to do!"

"That is good. Um, Aisha, can I ask one more thing?"

"Now, you're getting on my nerves with all these questions! I'm in a rush and don't have time for this small talk!"

"I-I miss you. D-did you think about us?"

There was a moment of silence followed by static.

"Gary, my signal is breaking up, and I can't hear you! Be at the airport in two hours and don't be late or else I am going to slap hair onto your bald head!"

"Okay. I-I won't be late. I love— "

"Whatever," Aisha said as she abruptly hung of the phone.

Gary put the cell phone down on the coffee table, walked into his restroom, and filled a capful of mouthwash. Then, he poured the liquid into his mouth and swished it around. Back in the living room, his cell phone rang again, but he did not hear it. The tune finished playing, and the call was directed to his voice mail. Gary finished brushing his teeth and walked into the living room. At that very moment, his cell phone voicemail alert chimed.

"She called back and left a voicemail!" Gary said as he walked over and picked up his cell phone. He held down the number one key and quickly accessed his voicemail.

"Greetings, Gary," a computerized voice acknowledged. "One new voice message. Press one to hear the voice message."

Gary pressed the designated key. Instead of hearing Aisha's seductive voice leaving a message for him, Gary heard Aisha speaking to another man.

"Last night was awesome!" the man said. "We had perfect chemistry! That is what I call the pow with the wow!"

"I really like what you are working with," Aisha replied softly. "My spine is still tingling!"

"Whoa kemosabe! It's my hobby to please that body!"

Aisha and the man laughed.

Gary's face became a portrait of confusion, hurt, and malice as he listened to the laughter of the two people.

"That whorish bastard," Gary muttered.

Aisha continued the conversation with the man, "Kelvin, I appreciate you taking me to the airport. You are quite the gentleman."

"You are quite the lady yourself. As a matter of fact, you are what all men want because you are a freak in the bed and a lady in the streets!"

"The things that I did to you last night were just the tip of the iceberg. Wait till you go deeper."

"And I can go deeper."

Aisha moaned sensually, "Hmm. We will see. We will see."

Hot tears swelled up in Gary's eyes as he heard Aisha confirming what Rasheed had told him.

"I can't believe that whorish bastard!"

Gary bit his bottom lip in frustration as he continued to listen to the conversation.

"Your friends couldn't handle those lines," Kelvin said.

"I know, right? Sarah and Hillary are still snoozing! We shouldn't have mixed the ecstasy with the cocaine!"

"That powder was pure, uncut. I got it from a friend who is from Venezuela."

Aisha exclaimed in amazement, "Wow! If they didn't have drug dogs at the airport, I would buy some grams from you! I was floating like a kite!"

"The next time we hook up, I will make sure we have some."

"That would be great!"

Gary rubbed his bald head and screamed, "I can't believe this! She has been living another life, and she is using drugs!"

"Kelvin, have you ever been involved with a married woman?" Aisha asked.

"Several times. I am a firm believer in if there is no pleasing, then there is no reason!"

"Do you ever feel guilty?"

"For what?"

"For breaking up marriages."

"You only get one life, so you might as well be happy. I don't know about you, but I choose to be happy and make other people happy."

Aisha cleared her throat, "I have a confession, Kelvin."

"What is it?"

"I want to give you my phone number but—"

"But what?" Kelvin interrupted.

"But—"

"If you are not happy, then let me make you happy. It is a simple choice."

"Hmm. I don't—"

"If you are going to deal with me, you have to follow the rules. Rule number one: no phone calls, only emails."

Aisha quickly wrote down her email address on a piece of paper.

"My email addy is 123applewoman@ocho.com. What is rule number two?"

"You have to leave your husband. That's that."

"Like that?"

"I will share you with women but not with men. The offer stands. Take it or leave it."

"I think I will take it!"

"I'm serious. This car is worth two hundred thousand dollars! My house is five hundred thousand dollars, and this watch on my wrist is worth that SUV that just passed us."

"That is a nice watch."

"Thanks. Now, ask yourself? Can your husband buy that?"

"Not in a million years."

"All of this can be yours, Aisha. All you have to do is choose between poverty and riches."

"Stop playing games!"

"I swear. I am not running game on you. I see something in you that I don't see in other women."

"What else do you see?"

"I see that you want more from life, and I can give it to you, physically and financially. Can you dig that?"

"I can dig it, baby!"

"Then, do you choose riches or poverty?"

"I choose you," Aisha said passionately. "I choose you, Kelvin."

"Then, give me a kiss!"

There was a pause followed by a slurping noise as they wildly kissed each other. The sound pushed Gary's anger into madness.

"You kiss like a madman fresh out of prison!"

"I just like kissing you," Kelvin replied.

"Next month, on March the twentieth, the girls and I are swinging to Los Angeles. If you meet me out there, I will have left my husband by then."

"You have thirty days to get yourself together. Don't be late."

"I won't! I promise! Kelvin, I think I love you already!"

The voicemail ended, leaving Gary feeling like nothing less than a volatile volcano that was ready to blow. His eyes were bloodshot red, and his hands slightly trembled as he fumed into a rage.

"I went into debt, sacrificed my 401K, and my dreams to keep you happy, Aisha! Then, you repay me by forming a swingers' club and running around with a two-dollar hustler!"

Gary stood up and hurled a nearby chair at the television that had been braced above the fireplace. The television exploded.

"I wanted kids! I wanted a boy and a girl to take to the park. I wanted to raise them to be model citizens, but you wanted to be a city-to-city tramp!"

Gary walked into the dining room and kicked the dining room table over.

"I trusted you, Aisha! I loved you! I loved you!"

Gary grabbed the china cabinet and slung it to the ground, scattering pieces of broken glass and china across the hardwood floor. He stormed out of the dinning room and rushed upstairs to his bedroom closet.

"This is it! This is how it's going down!"

Gary opened up a shoe box. Inside was a black revolver.

"Aisha, you promised to be my wife for better or for worse. Life or death! Today, you have chosen death!"

Gary loaded the bullets, carefully placing them into each hole of the cylinder. Then, he stuffed it into his pants as he glanced at his watch.

"It is 10:30. Just enough time to go to the bank and make a withdrawal, but first let me check something."

Gary walked into the adjacent bedroom that served as an office. He sat at the computer and went to the Swift Airlines website. He clicked on the tab labeled DESTINATIONS.

"Mexico? Nah, the feds will get me there. I need some place more distant!"

He navigated the page, searching for a place to escape to. In a few seconds, he had found what he was looking for.

"Ah ha!" Gary shouted. "Peru!"

Gary quickly booked a one-way ticket for a six o'clock departure.

"Three thousand dollars well spent. Now, let me get my passport."

Gary glanced out the window and saw the trees blowing in the wind. A light condensation had formed on the lower corner of the glass pane.

"I had better dress warm. It is getting cold outside."

Gary quickly changed into a pair of stonewashed jeans and a dark, long sleeved shirt. He rushed out of the house without locking the door and without looking back. Gary hopped into his gray Magnum with dark tinted windows and sped off. He would not be returning to this house or life anymore.

As Gary drove toward the airport, Rasheed pulled into the winding driveway of his Jonesboro home. He stepped out of the car and looked at his four thousand square foot brick home with Spanish arches.

"Home, sweet home!" Rasheed exclaimed.

He ran up the marble steps to the front oak door and reached into his pockets for his house keys. There was nothing inside of them.

"No keys! Now, I have to break into my own home!"

Rasheed hurried around to the side of his home and jumped the wooden fence. He ran to the back of his home to a low window at his basement where he kicked out the window and triggered the alarm.

"I have thirty seconds!" Rasheed cried out. He quickly crawled through the window. Just before his black shoes disappeared through the opening, an older white man peeked through his bedroom window and over into Rasheed's backyard. The man was Rasheed's neighbor Nicholas Montague and was considered to be a noisy neighbor by all the residents.

"Honey!" Nicholas cried out.

"Yes," Nicholas's wife replied.

"A burglar is breaking into Mr. Locke's house!"

"The black guy next door?"

"Yes! Call the police!" Nicholas shouted. "That burglar will probably be over here next!"

"Okay! Doing it now!"

Nicholas ran his fingers through his snow white hair as he muttered under his breath, "I knew the neighborhood would go down the drain once he moved in."

In the meanwhile, Rasheed rushed up the stairs of his basement and into the spacious kitchen where he quickly entered the pass code: 12546

Beep!

Rasheed entered the code again: 12456.

Beep!

There were only seconds left. Rasheed licked his lips and concentrated. He entered the pass code one last time: 12466.

"Alarm disabled," announced the security system.

"Barely beat the clock. Ugh, what's that smell?"

Rasheed walked over to a closet and opened it, but there was nothing inside the trashcan.

"Dang! What is that smell, and where is it coming from?"

Rasheed rushed over to his sink, but there was nothing in the sink. He leaned forward and grimaced. It was a musky smell.

"Something is rotten, but what is it?"

He looked around the kitchen. It was clean and spotless except for that musty odor. Rasheed felt perspiration forming on his forehead. He reached up to wipe his forehead with the back of his forearm, and that was when the smell became stronger than ever.

"It can't be? Nah, not the kid!"

He slid his right hand under his shirt and rubbed his armpit. Rasheed withdrew his hand, sniffed, and gagged, "Good lawd! What happened to my deodorant? I smell like dump truck juice!"

He sprinted upstairs to his Mediterranean-style bathroom. The stone walls were earth toned and streaked with gray granite. In the far corner of the restroom was a glass shower with a shower head that extended from the ceiling. Rasheed quickly undressed. Then, he hopped into the shower and turned the water on. As he washed, Rasheed rapped his version of the popular song "I Put On" by Young Jeezy.

Suddenly, his house phone rang. The answering machine picked up.

"Thank you for calling," said Rasheed's recorded voice. "I am not available at this time. Please leave a number, and I promise to return your call. Thanks."

Rasheed finished his shower. Then, he stepped out of the shower where he dried off. He walked to his phone and played the message.

"One new message. Press play to hear message."

Rasheed pressed play, and the message commenced. Someone was breathing heavily on the phone.

"What type of psycho was that?" Rasheed asked as he pressed delete.

Rasheed went to dry off. Suddenly, his house phone rang again. This time, Rasheed quickly answered the phone and screamed, "Listen, pervert! If you think that was funny, then wait until the doctor pulls my foot out your butt!"

"Um, hi. May I speak to Mr. Locke?" an unknown man said in a polite tone.

"Yes, this is he. Who is this?" Rasheed asked.

"This is Wolf."

"Wolf? Wolf who?"

"You know. Wolf. We met in Miami yesterday."

"Please excuse me," Rasheed said. "So much has happened to me since yesterday."

"You called me Mr. Wendal, remember?"

"Yeah, I remember! How is everything?" Rasheed asked enthusiastically.

"I am doing fine," Wolf said. "Everything is great!"

"That is good. Are you in Atlanta?" Rasheed asked.

"Indeed, I am back in Atlanta."

"That is good," Rasheed said. "You had said you would be moving back to be with your aunt, right?"

"I made it back in the nick of time. She is recovering."

"Recovering? Wolf, what is she recovering from?"

"My aunt had a massive heart attack right after I arrived last night. Her condition has improved. Now, she is on the second floor."

"I am sorry to hear that. Is there anything I can do?"

"Thanks for asking, but you have done more than enough. You helped a displaced solider get back home just in time. There is nothing else."

"There is always something else. If anything comes up later, let me know."

"Thanks. I really didn't expect you to be back from Miami so soon. I wanted to leave you a message to thank you for helping me get back home."

"You're welcome. I wish there was more I could have done."

"Rasheed, you have a special calling. Hopefully, other people will follow your example."

"What hospital is your aunt in so I can send some flowers?"

"She is in Jackson Memorial, downtown Atlanta. That is the hospital they send you to when you don't have insurance."

Rasheed raised his eyebrows.

"I am going to be there in about an hour to visit a friend. What floor is your aunt on again?"

"She is on the second floor."

"Okay. I will meet you there in a little while."

"Alright. See you then."

Rasheed ended the phone call. Suddenly, he heard a siren blaring and the noise of a hovering helicopter. A person spoke over a bullhorn, "Come out with your hands in the air!"

"What is going on?" Rasheed asked.

"I repeat. Come out with your hands in the air!"

Rasheed rushed to a nearby window that overlooked his street and saw numerous police cars. Slowly, approaching his house was a white police officer. His hand was on the gun that rested on his hip.

"I repeat. Come out with your hands in the air!"

"They think I am robbing my own house."

Rasheed glanced up and to the left, toward the neighboring house. Peeking out of the upstairs window was the elderly white haired man.

"Nicholas the nosey neighbor! I bet he saw me crawl through the window and called the police!"

Rasheed ran to his closet and put on some underwear, blue jeans, and a white t-shirt. As he laced up his tennis shoes, he heard a loud pounding at his front door followed by the loud voice saying, "Come out! We know you are in there! This is your final warning!"

Rasheed hurried down his winding stairs and lightly walked across the marble floor of his foyer. He opened the door with a smile on his face and said, "I'm sorry, officer. There has been—"

"Get your ass down on the floor! Now! Now!"

"But—"

The police officer grabbed Rasheed by his right arm and threw him to the ground.

"You have the wrong person!" Rasheed shouted angrily.

"Shut up! Shut up! You have the right to remain silent."

The police officer put his knee in Rasheed's back and slammed his head against the ground.

Rasheed yelled, "You're not listening!"

"Anything you say may be used against you in court."

"I-I said you have the wrong person!"

"You have a right to consult an attorney—"

Rasheed quickly whirled around, knocking the officer off balance then staggered to his feet. The officer swung at Rasheed, but he blocked the officer's punch and chopped him in the throat with the side of his hand. The police officer gagged.

Rasheed tried to speak again, "Now, I told you. I li—"

All of a sudden, four other cops tackled Rasheed. Not too far down the street was Dana Anderson and her cameraman. They witnessed the altercation as they sat in their television van.

"Are you getting this, Brian?" Dana asked.

"Every punch and kick. Someone just dropped the people's elbow on Mr. Locke!"

"We have to stop this!"

"How do you propose we do that?" Brian asked as he zoomed the camera in.

"Like this!"

Dana cranked the van up and pressed the gas. She sped down the street, honking the horn as she aimed the speeding van away from the police barricade and towards the curb.

Brian put the camera down as he braced himself and screamed, "Dana, that is a curb!"

"And I intend to jump it!"

Brian crossed his chest with the sign of the cross as Dana continued to honk the van's horn.

"Who is honking their horn?" an officer asked. "Officer Dalton, didn't you block the street?"

Officer Dalton looked up, and his eyes grew wide as he said, "Everyone! Make way! It's coming right for us!"

The police officers moved out of the way just as the van jumped the curb. The jolt caused Dana to lose control of the vehicle, causing the vehicle to swerve right to left.

"Hang on, Brian!" Dana shouted as she cut the wheel.

"I'm hanging! I'm hanging!" Brian replied.

The van skidded to a halt on the lawn. The officers drew their guns. Brian ducked down, crunched on the floor board, and screamed, "Dana, they are going to shoot us!"

Dana Anderson, however, had already leaped out of the van with her hands in the air and was yelling at the top of her lungs, "You have the wrong person! This man lives here!"

"Who are you?" Officer Dalton asked.

"I am Dana Anderson with Any Time News! I am scheduled to interview this man today!"

Officer Dalton said,"Officers, stand down!"

The officers holstered their guns and helped Rasheed to his feet.

"That's what I've been trying to tell you!" Rasheed said. "Get off me!"

The police backed up, and one apologized to Rasheed but he declined the apology.

"Apologize for what? That knee in my back. It's 2009, and y'all are still jacking up people! Where's the justice?"

"I am deeply sorry," Officer Dalton responded. "We got a phone call of a burglary, and you fit the description. It was an honest mistake."

"Whatever. Go protect and serve."

Rasheed glanced toward his neighbor's house as the officers walked away and saw that Nicholas was peeking through his window.

"Thanks, nosey neighbor!" Rasheed said as he waved.

Nicholas quickly closed the curtain. The officers walked back to their police cruisers and drove away. Dana shook her head and extended her hand to Rasheed. She said, "Rasheed Locke, it's been a long time."

"Since high school," Rasheed said as he shook Dana's hand. "I remember when your crazed ex-boyfriend came to the school after the Mount Zion basketball game."

"Who knows what would have happened if you and Corey had not been there?"

"He was dragging you by your arm, and you were yelling for help. Luckily, Corey had forgotten something in the locker room or else we would have been on the other side of town."

"You were in the right place at the right time," Dana said.

"When he saw a tall black guy and a tall white guy running towards him, the bum quickly let me go and ran for the hills!"

"After that, a real love story sparked between you and Corey."

Dana dropped her head and wiped her eyes as she remembered the love of her life that had been taken away from her too soon.

"I'm sorry. I shouldn't have said that."

"Rasheed, it's okay. It's okay."

"I'm sorry," Rasheed apologized as he hugged Dana.

"It's just I miss him every second of the day! That person should not have been texting while driving!"

"I know. I know. He is in a better place now and is proud of the things you have done with yourself."

"T-thanks. I just needed to vent. I just needed someone to listen to me."

"No, I should thank you for calling off those vicious pigs."

Dana wiped her face as she lightly giggled, "My camera man recorded the entire incident if you want to take it to the authorities."

"I don't plan on pursuing it. So how did you know I was home?"

"I have my sources, but we can discuss that over an exclusive interview," Dana said as she pulled her blonde hair into a ponytail.

"I can do that," Rasheed said as he reached out to shake her hand. "Just let me know when and where. I hope you have a nice day."

Rasheed started to walk away when Dana called out his name.

"Yeah, what's up?"

"I am a little curious. If you are here, then who is that in the hospital?"

"My stunt-double," Rasheed replied as he held his hands in the air.

"You are something else," Dana said as she walked back to her van.

Rasheed watched them disappear then hurried back into his house. Outside, the wind started to pick up as rain clouds rolled in. The warm temperature had dropped. The weather was changing for the worst.

Meanwhile, DeWayne sat in the hospital bed with his arms crossed behind his head singing the gospel song "On the Rough Side of the Mountain" in an cracking voice. Before he could finish singing the song, a young nurse walked into the room. She was dressed in a white nurse's uniform that stopped well above her knees. The woman's dark hair flowed down her shoulders, and her glittering green eye shadow was spectacular.

"I hope I am not intruding," the nurse said in her sexy voice.

"Girl, you can't be busting up in here like the CIA!" DeWayne shouted as he jerked his blanket up to his nose. "I have a black belt in issuing BW's!"

"What are BW's?"

"BW is a top secret ghetto acronym for Butt Whipping!

Heyyyyah! Waahh!'" DeWayne replied.

"Oooh. Sounds dangerous," the nurse giggled.

"Danger is my middle name," DeWayne replied. "What is your name?"

"I am sorry for startling you, Mr. Locke. My name is Betty."

"Nice to meet you, Nurse Betty."

"The pleasure is all mine," Nurse Betty said as she fanned her neck. "Ooh, it's warm in here. Don't you think?"

"Yeah, it's warm. It feels like Cancun during Spring Break!"

"I know. Do you mind if I get comfortable?"

"No. M-make yourself at home. I pay taxes, so this is just like my home."

"Thanks," Nurse Betty said as she took off her dress. "I am glad you are so understanding."

"I am very, very understanding," DeWayne said as he saw a portion of a red lace bra.

"Mr. Locke, I have a confession," Nurse Betty said softly.

"I-I'm listening. I am all ears and eyes."

"I am you're biggest fan, and I just wanted to wish you a Happy, Happy Valentine's Day!"

"Wish it! Wish it!" DeWayne urged. "Nurse Betty, you just wish your little heart away!"

Nurse Betty walked to the edge of the bed and pulled the sheet back. At that moment, she paused then scratched her head.

"What's wrong?" DeWayne asked.

"On television, your legs looked longer and more muscular."

"It's all about the lens of the camera. Some make you taller, and some make you wider."

"Oh, I see."

"Come, lay next to me," DeWayne said as he patted the space next to him. "In bed, people are always the same height."

"I thought you would never ask," Nurse Betty said as she laid down beside DeWayne.

"Nurse Betty, we can't do this."

"Why? Are you not attracted to me?"

"Yes! Very attracted, but I don't have any protection."

"Mr. Locke, this a hospital, and I am a nurse. I am an expert at protection."

She reached into a side pocket and pulled out a condom.

"Whoop, there it is!" DeWayne smiled. "Let the games begin!"

DeWayne pulled the covers over their heads and began to play beneath the sheets.

7

At a small airport about three hours north of Atlanta, a small private plane skidded across the runway and maneuvered towards a hangar where it parked. In seconds, a white man with a square forehead stepped out of the airplane dressed in a black suit.

The Eliminator had arrived. He carried a small briefcase as he walked to a navy blue Crown Victoria. The doors were unlocked, and the keys were in the ignition. He popped the trunk and put his briefcase inside. He sat in the driver's seat and pulled down the front visor. There was an envelope. He opened it and quickly read the single sentence on the paper.

"May the angels welcome you whether in heaven or hell."

He crumbled up the letter and tossed it out of the window.

"The Eliminator does not believe in angels! The Eliminator believes in annihilation!"

He pulled out his high-tech cell phone that doubled as a GPS device. He entered a code that activated a diagram of surrounding streets on the screen. A pink pulsating dot appeared in the city of Atlanta.

The Eliminator quickly reversed the car out of the hangar and sped toward the city. He would enjoy inflicting his cruelty upon the woman and whoever else stood in his way.

Chapter 8
Judgment Day In Atlanta

Gary parked in the designated curb side parking area at the Atlanta Airport and put his hazard lights on. Wearing a baseball hat and a pair of dark shades, he stepped out of the car.

"The temperature is dropping," Gary said as he felt the cold air. "Good time to take a vacation."

At that moment, Aisha came strutting around the corner, pulling her carry-on luggage. She spotted Gary and quickly approached him. As she walked toward him, Gary experienced both pleasure and discontent as he stared at his wife's hips. She was not wearing the jeans; the jeans were wearing her!

Those hips, Gary thought as he licked his lips, Those thighs—

"Hello! Earth to Gary!" Aisha shouted. "What in the hell are you doing?"

"Um, nothing," Gary said, startled. "I was just daydreaming."

"Daydreaming? And why are you dressed in a hat with shades? You look like a broke down P. Diddy! Boy, you have lost it!"

"The—"

"The hell!" Aisha harshly interrupted. "Take my luggage! I am ready to go!"

Gary took the luggage by the handle as he popped the trunk. While loading the luggage into the trunk, he said, "Aisha, I did the dishes that were in the sink. The house is spotless."

"It had better be clean! Geesh! Can you hurry up so we can leave?"

"One moment," Gary responded as he put the luggage into the trunk. People looked strangely at Gary and Aisha as they passed. Aisha noticed the ugly stares they were receiving but did not care as Gary casually walked around to the front of the car and sat in the driver's seat where he adjusted his mirrors.

"Do you have to do all of that?" Aisha asked. "You're acting like you are about to fly an airplane or something!"

"Safety first," Gary calmly replied. "I am just thinking about us being safe."

"Just drive the freaking car!" Aisha exploded angrily. "Do you need instructions on how to do that?"

"No, I have it," Gary replied.

"News flash! You don't have it. You never had it! Not in life, not in bed, and definitely not ever with me!"

Aisha leaned back and put on a pair of dark shades as she

mumbled a series of curses under her breath. Gary endured the complaints as he slowly drove away from the curb side parking and headed for the interstate. Moments later, the road split into two directions, Gary took the Interstate 285 North exit instead of the Interstate 285 South exit which led back to their home.

"Gary, where in the hell are we going?" Aisha questioned abruptly as she became aware of the change in direction.

"I have a quick errand to run."

"I just got off an airplane! I am ready to go home, take a hot bath, and lay in my bed!"

"Haven't you been on your back enough?"

"What was that? Are you getting smart with me? Because you are not smarter than a fifth grader. Trust that!"

"I didn't say anything."

"Like I thought. I think when I get home, I am going to get the extension cord and teach you how to man-up!"

"Aisha, I didn't say anything."

"So, I just imagined it like when I let you imagine that you make me reach my peaks when we make love."

"Whatever."

WHAM!

Aisha's open palm knocked the shades off of Gary's face.

"Ouch! You busted my lip again," Gary shouted as blood leaked down his chin.

"That's what you get for running off at the mouth! What's that look for, Gary? Are you going to do something? Huh?"

"No. No, I'm not going to do anything," Gary said as he

wiped his busted lip.

"I thought so! Now take me home, or I promise to beat you like a mangy mutt!"

"You want to go home," Gary muttered. "I'll take you home."

Gary pressed the accelerator and zoomed past a car in the slow lane. Aisha glanced over at speedometer. They were traveling at 70 miles per hour. The speed limit was 55 miles per hour.

"Gary, slow down now!" Aisha commanded. "Are you insane?"

"Hold that thought for one moment."

"One moment? We could be dead in one moment! Slow down!"

"Aisha, I need to ask you a question about your trip," Gary said as he took his hands off the steering wheel.

"Gary, what are you talking about?" Aisha bellowed. "Put your hands back on the steering wheel!"

"Who in the hell is Kelvin?" Gary asked sharply.

"Who?" Aisha asked as her facial expression went blank.

"Kelvin! You heard me!"

"Gary, put your hands back on the steering wheel!" Aisha yelled as she felt the car drifting towards the cement wall.

"You have about five seconds before this car hits the wall! Now, who is Kelvin?"

"I met him in Miami! I met Kelvin in Miami, okay? Now, put your hands back on the steering wheel."

"A guy you just met in Miami, huh?" Gary repeated as he grabbed the steering wheel and guided the car back into the proper lane.

"Yes! Yes!"

"I gave you a chance to come clean, but you couldn't even tell me the truth!"

"Gary, it's not what you think."

"How do you know what I think?"

"Because I know how guys think, Gary. I know how you think. Now, shut up and take me home!"

"You are such a pathological liar! You can't help but lie! It is in your blood!"

"Gary, I am tired of you pretending to be Matlock! All you know is that I met a guy named Kelvin, and there is nothing else to it!"

"You're wrong. There is something else."

"Give me your best shot, Gary. I am tired of your whining!"

"Aisha," Gary said as he looked Aisha in the eye, "I heard it all! Your phone called me back! I know all about you, Sarah, Hillary, and Kelvin!"

Aisha glanced down at her cell phone as it laid on her purse. The sensitive touch screen had betrayed her for the worst.

"Gary, I can explain."

"I understand quite clearly. You are a lowlife whore! I know that you plan on leaving me next month!"

"But—"

"Now, it's time for you to shut up," Gary said as he accelerated the vehicle from 70 miles per hour to 95 miles per hour.

"Rasheed was in Miami and introduced him to me!" Aisha

blurted out.

"For some reason, I don't believe you!"

"You have to! I am your wife!"

"Aisha, save the drama for yo' momma. Rasheed had already called me and told me what happened before your phone even called me back!"

"You have to believe me!" Aisha pleaded. "He told me to leave you and get with Kelvin! Did he tell you that?"

"Aisha, I wish I had never met you, you skank!"

"Gary, I am your wife, we exchanged vows, for better or for worse!" Aisha said as tears streamed down her face.

"You were my wife!" Gary replied coldly. "Now, you are just some two dollar whore who turns tricks for fun!"

"Gary! Watch out for that eighteen wheeler!"

"I got this," Gary shouted as he swerved the speeding Magnum to the left, barely missing the tail end of the truck. The driver of the eighteen wheeler honked its horn.

"Gary, I never meant to hurt you!"

"What did you intend to do then?" Gary angrily shouted. "Destroy me?"

"If it means anything to you, I never stopped loving you!"

"Aisha, save your lies! You couldn't have been loving me when Kelvin was making your spine tingle and you were doing lines of coke!"

"Gary, I am lost," Aisha said as she rubbed her forehead. "Please help me find me! You know what type of background I came from. I don't want to go back there!"

"How can you expect me to trust you after all of the lies?"

"I experimented with drugs, and now I can't kick them. I need you, baby. Oh, I need you so much right now!"

For a moment, Gary saw the woman he had pledged his life to instead of an over-sexed drug addict.

"I am here for you, Aisha. I am sorry for the things I said. I really didn't mean them. I am just angry."

"After you couldn't get it up in bed, I figured you didn't love me anymore! I figured that I was unattractive to you!"

"Baby, I have always been attracted to you!" Gary said passionately. "It was just the stress of bidding on those new jobs that was affecting me! I was getting worried that I couldn't take care of you!"

"Oh, baby!"

"It is my number one job— taking care of you," Gary said as he maneuvered the car into the right lane where there was no traffic. "I was afraid that I couldn't."

"You've done such a wonderful job," Aisha said as she unbuckled her seat belt and kissed Gary deeply.

"Wow!" Gary smiled. "That one sent a shudder down my spine!"

"Gary, are you still in love with me?"

"Y-yes, with all my heart, Aisha."

"I love you, too," Aisha said as she unbuckled Gary's pants. "I love you, too. Do you know what I want?"

"Um…what is it that you want?"

"Do you remember what we used to do at the drive-in on

movie night?" Aisha asked as she unzipped his pants.

"Y-yes," Gary said as he felt her warm hand on his genitals. "How could I forget?"

"I want to feel you."

"You want to feel me?" Gary asked as his eyes rolled towards the back of his head.

"I want to taste you."

"Go-go ahead. Get your taste on," Gary moaned.

"Then, I want to make love to you, Kelvin!"

Gary snapped out of his trance and shoved Aisha back into the passenger seat of the car as he shouted out in anger.

"Hell to the nawh! You just called me that other dude's name! Are you stupid!?"

"G-gary, please!" Aisha begged. "It was an accident! An accident!"

"You really think that I am a dumb ass, don't you? How could you accidentally say his name? Gary does not sound like Kelvin!"

"I promise. It was an accident!"

"Just to think that I almost gave you my sympathy! I almost gave you my trust!"

"Gary, please believe me!"

Gary put the pedal to the metal and accelerated the hemi engine.

"Gary, we're doing 135 miles per hour!"

"Oh, we are going to go faster."

"Gary, I beg you! Please slow down!"

"Shut up and enjoy your last moments. I was going to kill you and take a trip to Peru, but now, now I am going to do us both in!"

"Don't say that, Gary," Aisha pleaded. "Don't say that. We can get through this!"

"Shut up! I have nothing. You hear me? Without you, I have nothing! It is over!"

Aisha noticed how everything was a blur: the cars, the small trees that bordered the highway. She closed her eyes as thoughts of how to escape her enraged husband raced through her mind. She knew that she did not have that much time. She had to do something.

2

Sipping a cup of joe with no cream or sugar was State Patrol Johnson. He had volunteered to work for one of his fellow officers who needed to go see an ailing family member. He finished off his cup of coffee and looked at the traffic as he sat in his squad car that was positioned on the side of the road.

"So far, everyone is respecting the road, their cars, and the law," State Patrol Johnson said. "Let's hope it continues."

As he put on a pair of dark shades, a gray car sped past him, rocking the police car as it passed.

"Dispatch, this is State Patrol Johnson in pursuit of a gray Magnum with dark tint on Interstate 285 North, accelerating at 140 mph!"

"Proceed with caution," dispatch replied.

The state patrol's car pulled onto the road without turning on his lights and siren. State Patrol Johnson picked up speed, but the gray Magnum was already out of sight.

"Dispatch, the suspect is out of sight. Put out an All Points Bulletin."

"Roger that. An A.P.B is being issued right now."

State Patrol Johnson followed the suspect with caution. Hopefully, he would be able to catch the culprit and teach him a lesson in respecting the road, the vehicle, and the law of the land.

3

As State Patrol Johnson cautiously pursued the car, Gary and Aisha's argument escalated even further.

"Aisha, how could you forget about our love?" Gary asked furiously.

"Gary, it doesn't matter," Aisha replied.

"You traded a life of happiness for drugs and sex! How could you trade that for love?"

"Don't try to chastise me!" Aisha sharply replied.

"You're right. You don't even know how to love! You might as well be a rock at the bottom of the sea!"

"News flash!" Aisha shouted as she waived her hands. "I don't love you because I never loved you!"

"You never loved me?"

"I loved that marketing degree and the money it was bringing us, but I never loved you! You're not even my type!"

"Then, it's over. It's over," Gary said quietly.

"It has been over! Now, quit acting like a little bitch and take me home!"

"I'll show you a bitch," Gary said as he pressed the accelerator further, increasing their speed past 150 miles per hour.

"Gary, you're going to kill us!"

"Now, that's a bitch."

The road ascended and curved along a four foot reinforced cement wall. Aisha's eyes widened as Gary aimed for the wall.

"Gary, what are you doing? Are you crazy?"

"I told your father I would take care of you through sickness and health! I am not going to look like a failure!"

"You're not a failure! Please stop!" Aisha pleaded.

"It always takes two to fall out of love! I loved you, Aisha, with all my heart! Too bad you didn't love me the same!"

"Gary! The wall!"

"Goodbye, Aisha!"

"The wa—"

Just before they smashed into the wall, Aisha opened the door and rolled out of the car. She hit the pavement hard, snapping her right collarbone and breaking her right leg in three places. As she rolled on the pavement, an intense burning sensation ran along her back, arms, and legs.

"Aggh!" Aisha screamed "It hurts! Aggh!"

She opened her eyes just in time to see the Magnum smash into the cement wall and fly sideways through the air. There was a tremendous noise as cars came to screeching halts on the freeway, followed by the terrible crashing sound of cars smashing into each other. Suddenly, a loud fireball exploded.

"Gary!" Aisha cried out. "My God! Gary!"

The only response to her cry was the horn of a car. Aisha lifted her head and saw a car headed right for her.

"God have—"

The car slammed into Aisha, sending her body flying onto the shoulder of the road. Shortly after, State Patrol Officer Johnson arrived on the scene and radioed dispatch.

"Dispatch, we need ambulances, and we will possibly need a helicopter on the 285 northbound lane, half mile south of Washington Road exit and I-85 southbound lanes! Multiple DOA's!"

"Roger that. I am dispatching nearby EMS. The estimated time of arrival is thirty seconds."

State Patrol Officer Johnson turned on his lights and sirens as he pulled over onto the shoulder of the road. Then, he set down some flares and began to work the accident scene.

Miles away, at his home in Jonesboro, Rasheed turned on his house alarm as he closed the kitchen door, and walked into his garage which contained a fleet of luxury vehicles.

"Which one am I going to take today?" Rasheed asked himself. "Will it be the navy Porsche, the wine berry Benz, the champagne Mazarati, the soot black Hummer, or the 1968 candy red Cutlass Supreme?"

He walked past each one. Then, he finalized his decision when he said, "I think I am going with the candy red Cutlass today."

He hopped inside the old school classic with plush white seats and pressed the button that operated his garage door. It slowly rose up and the red Cutlass pulled out. The sunlight reflected off of its twenty-two inch rims. Peeking out of his window was Nicholas.

"Hmm! What a waste of money! They spend all of their money on cars and never make any long term investments!"

Nicholas, however, was not the only person watching Rasheed. Parked at the corner of a nearby street was a black van. Inside the black van was Pressure with his mouthful of gold teeth. He zoomed in through a pair of binoculars and caught a glimpse of the cars before the garage door closed.

"This dude is living it up, MTV Cribs style," Pressure said. "I am gonna kidnap this fool then hold him for ransom! Today is gonna be a bad day for him but a good day for me!"

Pressure put down the binoculars and slipped on a black-ski mask that only exposed his eyes and gold teeth. After Rasheed's candy red car passed by, Pressure's black van pulled out and followed closely behind him.

The sun became a pale orb in the sky as gray storm clouds moved into the area. Shoppers moved from boutique to boutique in a busy marketplace near Downtown Atlanta as they searched for deals and steals. On this day, only a few shoppers entered the expensive boutique called Taste. Among those shoppers was Kandis Wright. She entered the high-priced boutique dressed in a green sweater, pink tights, and green heels. As she entered the building, the flamboyant front clerk Jeremy rushed to greet her. He gushed, "Honey, you are startling! I just love the pink and the green! It is so Valentine's Day!"

"Indeed it is, Jeremy," Kandis replied. "I adore your pink sweater and your charcoal skinny jeans. The flat-ironed hair-do is so you!"

"My better half Myka knows my fashion degrees," Jeremy replied.

"So he knows the rules?" Kandis asked.

"Yes. He knows what is hot and cold!" Jeremy shouted as he snapped his fingers.

"Is that right?"

"We are too hot to touch! Szzz!"

Jeremy brushed back his trimmed eyebrows, collected himself, and said, "So how may I help you, today? Since the last time you were here, a new shipment of Prada and Dolce has arrived."

"Then, show me the new Prada!"

"Certainly! Follow me!"

Jeremy led Kandis to a nearby wall and took a yellow shirt off the wall. It had tiny, shiny stones and an image of a fiery orange phoenix. He put the shirt up against Kandis body as he gave the product information.

"These new shirts have a designer flare. Note the three-quarter sleeves."

"Spectacular," Kandis replied.

"The material is a silk blend that makes it sheer, and it will beautifully hug those tight dangerous curves of yours!"

"I like," Kandis said.

"You can dress it up with a pair of jeans, short shorts, or even some skimpy impy panties for when that gentleman comes a-calling!"

"Jeremy, you are so naughty!" Kandis giggled.

"Grrrr!" Jeremy growled. "I am a naughty pussy cat!"

"I'll take it."

"Great!" Jeremy exclaimed in a high-pitched voice. "Will there be anything else?"

"No, I am going to take your advice and dress it up with something skimpy."

"Then, follow me to the register, Ms. Skimpy Impy. Will that be cash or charge?"

"Charge as usual," Kandis said as she extracted a credit card.

"Thank you!" Jeremy replied as he swiped the card.

Jeremy handed it back to Kandis, where she tucked it into her purse and leaned on the counter as she spoke in a sinister tone, "Jeremy, tonight is a special night."

"Okay! Like my horoscope said that an unexpected visitor would be coming, and I was like no way!"

"For me, tonight symbolizes a new beginning."

"I like new beginnings!" Jeremy joyfully replied.

"What goes around is finally going to come around," Kandis

said.

"Sounds freaky to me. That will be three hundred and fifty dollars charged to your account!"

"Pennies on the dollar. Charge it."

"'Charge it,' she says!" Jeremy replied.

Jeremy folded the shirt and bagged it. Then, he handed the bag to Kandis.

"I will see you when I see you. I hope you and Myka enjoy each other tonight!"

"We will! Tootles!" Jeremy replied as he wiggled his fingers at Kandis.

Kandis walked out the store and down the street. As she disappeared around the corner, Jeremy picked up his phone and made a phone call. When it connected, Jeremy spoke in a deep masculine voice, "The cat has the bag and is on the move. Execute Operation Hawkeye."

Jeremy hung up the phone and fell back into character, waiting for new customers to serve. Tonight would not be as special as Kandis hoped it would be.

On the busy road known as Tara Boulevard, Rasheed pulled up to the red light, nodding his head to a popular song by the legendary rap group Outkast. He glanced to his left. There was an older black couple sitting in their car, looking straight ahead. Their necks were stiff. Rasheed reached down and turned the bass level down on his radio. As the music decreased, the older black woman turned to face him and smiled. Rasheed nodded his head. At that moment, his gas light came on.

"I haven't driven this car in a while. I've got to get some petro quick!"

The light turned green, and Rasheed pulled off. He drove to a nearby gas station where Rasheed pulled up to pump three and swiped his credit card. He started pumping his gas. When he was done, he put the receipt in his pocket.

"Can't forget the tax write-off."

Rasheed opened the door of the candy red Cutlass Supreme and hopped back into the car. Just as he cranked the car, a masked man leaped into the passenger side of the vehicle and pointed a pistol in his face. The masked man yelled, "Break yo' self, partnah! This is a jack move. Ya heard me?"

"Here! T-take the car!" Rasheed fearfully spoke.

"Fool, I don't want the car," Pressure shouted as he smacked Rasheed across the face with the back of the pistol, splitting Rasheed's lip.

"What-what do you want?" Rasheed asked in a muffled voice as he held his bloody mouth.

"Fool! If this don't go right, I am going to take your life! Now, drive before I leave your thoughts splattered all across that dashboard!"

"Aight-Aight!" Rasheed said as he licked his battered lip. Slowly, he pulled off from pump three as intense thoughts raced through his mind. He knew that his survival rate would greatly diminish if he did not follow the mad man's instructions.

"I said to drive not creep!" Pressure shouted. "Step on it!"

"Aight! Be easy!"

Rasheed lightly pressed the gas and the 442 engine growled loudly. The sound reminded Rasheed of the raw power held captive within the transmission. He punched the pedal to the floor and turned the steering wheel wide, causing the old school classic to spin out of control.

"You think you're slick," Pressure shouted as he cocked the gun back and aimed at Rasheed's head. "Die, you bastard!"

"Not today!"

Quickly, Rasheed spun the wheel in the opposite direction and pressed the accelerator as he leaned back. The pistol fired. The bullet burst out the driver's side windshield as Pressure fell to the floorboard of the car. Rasheed quickly tried to turn the wheel but nothing happened.

"I must have broken the struts!" Rasheed said as the car sped toward the power pole. "Got to put on my seat belt!"

The car rammed into the power pole. For a few seconds, Rasheed sat in his car, in shock. Then, he snapped to, unhooked his seat belt, and stumbled from the wreckage. He glanced over at the broken power pole. Broken lines sparked and smoke rose from the damaged transformer. Suddenly, he heard moaning coming from the passenger's side of the vehicle.

"P...please don't leave me! Please! I don't want to die!"

"Don't move. Here I come."

Rasheed could faintly hear sirens as he stumbled over to the passenger's side of the vehicle and jerked the door opened. On the floorboard, grasping his shoulder was Pressure.

"P-please help me! My shoulder, my s-shoulder is broken!"

"Okay. Just bear with me."

Just as Rasheed bent down, Pressure raised the pistol up and snarled, "Tommy Tucker, you neighborhood sucker! I will see you in hell!"

Suddenly, something knocked Rasheed down as the pistol fired. Rasheed rolled a couple of feet. Then, he glanced at his savior and gasped, "It's you, again! You!"

The good Samaritan was Wolf.

"Looks like you are a man of adventure," Wolf said.

"That's what the people tell me," Rasheed replied. "Wolf, thanks for saving me, again!"

From inside the wrecked car, Pressure shouted, "When I get out of this car, I am going to peel your cap, fool!"

Wolf walked over and kicked the door closed.

"Speak when spoken to, maggot!"

"Wolf, how did you get here?" Rasheed asked.

"I was actually pumping gas on the other row when you were carjacked," Wolf replied. "I saw the whole thing and followed you after I called the police."

"Thank God you were in the right place at the right time," Rasheed said.

"If you don't mind," Wolf said, "I'll hang around until the police come."

"Sure," Rasheed said as he brushed off his clothes. "Wolf,

have you ever thought about being the head of a security firm?"

"Are you offering me a job?"

"That is the least I can do," Rasheed responded. "You've saved my life twice!"

"Then, I gladly accept your offer. Thank you!"

Rasheed and Wolf shook hands as two police cruisers pulled up. Officer Dalton leaped out of the squad car with his shotgun extended.

"Mr. Locke, it is you again! Are you okay? We had a report of an attempted carjacking."

"The guy who tried to carjack me is in the car, and he has a gun!" Rasheed said.

Officer Dalton cocked his shotgun as he warned Rasheed and Wolf, "Get out of here! It is about to get ugly!"

Wolf and Rasheed stepped away as Officer Dalton and his fellow officer circled the wrecked car. Officer Dalton nodded as the other crouched and grasped the door handle. The officer swung open the door as Officer Dalton leaped forward and said, "You have the right to remain—"

Broken pieces of glass were in the seat and floorboard, but the car was empty.

"Where is he at?" Officer Dalton asked.

"There!" the other officer shouted. "Near the train tracks!"

Officer Dalton rose to his full height and saw a man dressed in black limping from the scene while holding his shoulder.

"Got him!" Officer Dalton shouted. "Freeze!"

Pressure aimed over his shoulder and wildly fired his pistol.

The bullets struck the hood of the wrecked car. Officer Dalton aimed and fired the shotgun. Immediately, Pressure fell to the ground, screaming in agony, "My legs! My legs! You shot my legs!"

Officer Dalton and the other officer cautiously walked over to where Pressure was screaming. Rasheed shook his head as he said, "That cop is trigger happy. He is just itching to shoot something!"

"Yeah, but he won't be reprimanded because the thief gave him a reason to shoot," Wolf replied.

"I hope he gets his life together," Rasheed said.

Wolf looked at Rasheed in amazement and said, "You sure have a lot of compassion for someone who has been pistol-whipped and has a busted lip."

"It's just how I was raised," Rasheed said. "You know. Forgive but don't forget."

"That's from the old school," Wolf said. "People don't play by those rules anymore."

"I know, but it's just that too many of us are in jail and not in school or with our families."

"We all have to make choices," Wolf said. "Just like my mother says, 'You make the bed that you lie in.'"

"You're right. The choices we make in life are the actions that define us."

"Come on," Wolf said. "Let's go give the police our statements. You can ride to the hospital with me."

"Thanks," Rasheed said. "The temperature is getting colder,

and it looks like it is about to rain."

Wolf nodded his head, and they walked over to the police cars that had pulled up. Rasheed glanced at his watch. It was almost four o'clock, and the sun would be going down soon.

#

As Rasheed felt the deepening chill, Kandis returned home and saw that she had three new messages on her phone.

"Let's see who has called the baddest chick in Atlanta," Kandis said as she pressed the play button.

"First message: 11:00 am. Please call Loyalty Bank. This is an attempt to collect a debt."

"Good luck with that," Candy replied.

"Message deleted. Second Message: 11:30 am. Please call Knowledge Credit Card. Your account is delinquent."

"Gibberish!"

"Message deleted. Third Message: Ma Ma, yetterday I went to the zoo and saw a lion! It said raaagh!"

The innocent voice of the little girl moved Kandis and caused a tear to drop from her almond shaped eyes. The voice of the little girl belonged to her daughter Chanise.

After being convicted of shoplifting, Kandis' mother had won custody. Rather than moving back to Colorado, Kandis' mother had moved thirty minutes away from Kandis to Hampton, Georgia, so Kandis could have some type of relationship with her daughter.

"Chanise...my grace! You sound like a big girl! Oh! I need

a drink!"

Kandis walked over to the cabinet where she kept her liquor. She reached inside and picked up a bottle of bourbon. She untwisted the cap and poured herself a shot. She tilted her head back and allowed the liquid to hit the back of her throat. Kandis gasped, "Whoa!"

Then, she picked up her house phone and dialed her mother's phone number. In a couple of seconds, her mother Donna answered the phone in a pleasant tone, "Look at what the cold weather blew in! Good afternoon!"

"Donna, I don't have time for your snide, sarcastic remarks."

"We haven't heard from you in at least a month, Kandy! Where have you been?"

"Where is Chanise?" Kandis asked, ignoring Donna's remarks.

"Where she belongs," Donna said. "Where she is wanted."

"I want to speak to her," Kandis demanded.

"I have a better suggestion. Why don't you leave your high rise condo and lavish lifestyle and visit your daughter for a change?" Donna replied.

Before responding, Kandis poured herself another shot and tossed it back. Then, she said, "And give you a chance to talk about where I went wrong in life? Please!"

"Kandy, what have you accomplished by staying away from your family, from your daughter?"

"More than you could ever know, Donna!"

Kandis remark cut Donna deep. She had had enough of this

stubborn, snobbish rhetoric.

"When you get some manners, I will let you speak to my granddaughter."

"Whatever! I am tired of playing with you, Donna. Put Chanise on the phone!"

"Child, I gave you a pot to piss in and a window to throw it out! Don't make me come up there and snatch the life out of you!"

"There you go again, Donna. Blah! Blah! Blah!" Kandis mocked.

"When you were locked up for putting shirts in Chanise's stroller, I came to your rescue! I am still here for you, but you are just so stubborn!"

"Look, Donna!" Kandis snapped. "I did not call to fuss with you! May I please talk to Chanise?"

"You may. Chanise, telephone!"

Kandis drank another shot as she heard her daughter's footsteps racing to the phone. Her heart skipped as she heard Chanise's voice in her ear, "Hi! Ma Ma!"

"Hey, Chanise! How is my big girl?"

"I am fine! Grandma took me to the zoo. That's where the animals live."

"I know. I got your message. Tell me what the lion says."

"Ma Ma, the lion said, 'Rarrgh!'"

"Ha! Ha! Ha!" Kandis laughed. "You are so silly!"

"Ma Ma?"

"Yes, Chanise."

"When are you coming to live with me and Grandma? We miss you."

Kandis looked down at her kitchen floor because more than the alcohol was affecting her. She rubbed her nose with her thumb as she responded, "Ma Ma can't come live with you and Donna. It is complicated."

"What is complicated?" Chanise asked.

"It is when something is hard to do. Like when you try to put all of your toys in your red wagon."

"Okay. I get it. You can't put all your toys in your wagon."

"Let me talk back to your mother," Donna said in the background.

"Bye, Ma Ma! I love you!"

"Love you, too."

"Here, Grandma!"

There was a ruffling sound as Chanise handed the phone to Donna.

"Hello?" Donna asked.

"How dare you pit my daughter against me!" Kandis shouted.

"Kandy, you need to calm down before you find yourself talking to the dial tone!"

"Calm down for what, Donna? Huh? Please tell me!"

"For your daughter," Donna replied. "She is two and a half years old and quickly beginning to understand that you should be with her!"

"How in the world would she know that?" Kandis asked.

"She watches all of those educational DVDs over and over!

She can almost read and write! Your daughter is exceptionally intelligent!"

"That's nice," Kandis responded in a nonchalant voice. "I hope that she goes to college and betters herself."

"That's all you can say?" Donna asked.

"What else is there to say?"

"She is the spitting image of you, Kandy!" Donna shouted furiously. "You've become more distant since you lost your job!"

"That rat bastard is about to go bankrupt for firing me! Locke Records is going to pay with more than money!"

"Kandy, you were caught with fake documents in your own hand writing. It is a wonder the man didn't press charges and send you away for a long time!"

"You're full of it, Donna! You always take other people's sides and never want to hear my side! Just like when Simon reenlisted in the army and got killed in Iraq!"

Donna finally realized that the depth of Kandis' pain included the loss of her husband Simon. A road side bomb had killed him during his second tour.

"You can't let that hurt keep you away from your child, Kandy! We all loved Simon and miss him, too!"

"No one told him to leave us! All he had to do was come home, and everything would have been different!"

"He died for our freedom and for those who were being persecuted in Iraq! He is a hero, not a person who abandoned his family!"

Kandis poured another shot and tossed it back. She was good

and drunk by now as she said, "He abandoned us! That's the bottom line! That creep! That sucka!"

"Kandy, you have to keep the family legacy going. You have to be with your daughter!"

"I am not about to live up under your roof with your rules. Can't come in after ten, wash the dishes after you do your homework. I am too grown for that!"

"Kandy, there is one thing that you will learn in life. You will always abide by someone's rules, whether it is your parents', your job's, or the law of the land!"

"That is where you are wrong! I make my own rules and my own law! I am the sheriff!"

Suddenly, the telephone went dead, and Kandis stared into the speaker compartment of the phone.

"You want to hang up the phone on me? Huh? You never loved me! You— "

At that moment, everything in her condominium powered down.

"A power outage? Let me report this before my food spoils, and I have to call the power company to raise holy hell! They gonna get my power on!"

She stumbled over to her purse and picked up her cell phone. Then, she dialed her power company. An irritating message blared from her phone, "Message ATL-No Service!"

"I know I paid my cell phone bill!"

Suddenly, there was a clamorous noise at her front door. Kandis ran into her living room and saw the door explode off of its hinges. Several men dressed in black helmets and vests with the yellow letters ATF on their chests rushed in through her front door with their assault rifles extended.

"Get down! Get down!" shouted the men.

"No!" Kandis cried out.

One of the ATF agents tackled Kandis to the ground and bound her wrists behind her back with a pair of plastic twisty ties. They searched each room, confiscating stolen televisions, unauthorized credit cards, and other items. Then, they hauled Kandis away.

As the ATF agents hauled Kandis away to prison, Rasheed and Wolf drove north on Interstate 75 into the city of Atlanta. The orange sun was setting as light showers moved into the area. The two men were having a good conversation about music.

"Rasheed, you are new school," Wolf said as he drove the car, "You probably have some Soulja Boy in your CD player."

"To be honest, I am not that new school. I still like lyrists like Ludacris, T.I., Lil Wayne, and UGK."

"All from the south? No up north artists?"

"I still represent that Wu-Tang Clan!" Rasheed said as he formed a 'W' with his right hand.

"Wu-Tang Clan is one of my favorite rap groups. The artists you mentioned all have kept rap alive."

"The stories of struggle being told across beats attract people," Rasheed said. "Rap, hip hop, and gangster music can never die as long as there is the struggle."

"That is the great mystery of hip hop. Some believed it began in New York. Do you want to know what I believe?"

"What do you believe?" Rasheed asked.

"I believe it began in Egypt, in the cradle of civilization," Wolf said.

"Wolf," Rasheed laughed, "let me open the car door and push you out at eighty-five miles an hour, so you can get some sense knocked back into your head!"

"Seriously, just think about it. In present day, you work hard. After work, you go to the sports bar for a drink. Right?"

"Right, but there weren't any sports bars in Ancient Egypt."

"We don't know that yet, but more importantly, we know there was hard labor and hard times. I am talking about making bricks with no straw and firstborns being murdered! It can't get any harder than that!"

"That's pretty hard!" Rasheed said. "So, what's your point?"

"You can't tell me there wasn't a Jay-Z or Lil Wayne spitting lyrics to help people get through their day-to-day struggles!" Wolf exclaimed.

"I can dig it! I can dig it!"

"Not only were there rappers, Rasheed, but there were kings and queens whose skin color ranged from light brown to dark brown."

"Black people."

"Exactly," Wolf said. "We had a thriving civilization, perfected astrology, and agriculture."

"Then, we forgot who we were," Rasheed said.

"When you forget who you are," Wolf responded, "no one knows who you are."

"That is true to life," Rasheed answered.

"That is part of the reason why we are where we are today," Wolf said. "If black people could only remember who we were, then we would not promote the foolishness that is being promoted in our society today."

"I wish it was that easy, but there is always the crab in the barrel syndrome. I experienced that first hand when I started the record label."

"What happened?" Wolf asked.

"I dated my accountant, and she tried to forge my name on some false documents so that it looked like she was the CEO."

"That is crazy."

"Everything will be back on track next month," Rasheed said optimistically. "And yesterday, in Miami, I think I found a lead on my lost cousin."

"Your cousin has been missing?"

"She has been missing for a month and a half. Last night, I discovered that a group known as La Committee took her to Costa Rica."

"Are you sure that it was La Committee?" Wolf asked as a worried look came across his face.

"I am positive. The woman who was in the plane crash with me was held captive by El Hombre Guapo, but she escaped and bumped into me at my club last night."

"The news had reported that there was a suicide bombing at a club in Miami."

"We were chased across the bridge that connected Miami to Miami Beach," Rasheed explained. "We escaped to my private jet, but somehow La Committee contacted my pilot and ordered him to crash the plane!"

"You are Mr. Unbreakable! You survived a club fire, car chase, a plane crash, and a carjacking!"

"I know it all sounds farfetched, but I am telling the truth."

"I believe you. I need you to listen closely or else your friend is going to die."

"What do you mean? She is in a hospital. That's one of the safest places in the world!"

"La Committee has no boundaries. Even as we speak, I am quite sure that an assassin is headed to Jackson Memorial Hospital to kill your friend in order to protect the brotherhood."

"But how?"

"They have inserted a small chip inside her arm. This chip uses global positioning systems technology to track merchandise and people who are enslaved to the organization."

"Is that how El Hombre Guapo knew how to find us so quickly, and how they notified the pilot?"

"That is correct. When I was in Iraq, we came across a harem of women that were going to be shipped to Costa Rica to help with the drug trade. They were going to La Committee. One day after we rescued them, they were all brutally murdered."

"Do you know who is coming?" Rasheed asked.

"I don't know who he or she is, but I do know that this assassin is pretty good. We don't have that much time!"

"Let's go. Hopefully, we can save Keysha's life!"

They exited the interstate and took Peachtree Street toward the middle of the city where Jackson Memorial Hospital stood. Soon, Rasheed and Wolf parked in the parking deck next to a navy blue Crown Victoria.

"We need to hurry. I have a bad feeling," Rasheed said.

They rushed into the Jackson Memorial Hospital and went to the information kiosk where a red haired attendant greeted them, "Hello. How may I help you?"

"You have a patient by the name of Keysha Belle that was admitted today," Rasheed said.

"Are you family?" the attendant asked.

"Yes," Rasheed said with a straight face. "I am her brother, and this is our uncle."

"Good evening, ma'am," Wolf said.

"Same to you," the attendant replied as she quickly typed on the keys of her keyboard.

"Let's see. Ah ha! There she is. She is in room 225 on the second floor."

"Thanks," Rasheed said.

"No problem."

In silence, they walked briskly to the elevator. Only when the doors had closed did Wolf speak.

"Rasheed, my aunt is on that floor. There is one hallway in and one hallway out. If things get crazy, we may have to go through the ceiling."

"Okay."

"You go and get Keysha ready to move," Wolf instructed. "I am going to step into my aunt's room. I saw something in there that may be of some use."

The doors of the elevator opened, and they stepped out. The layout was just as Wolf had described. There was one nurse on duty at the kiosk and several rooms down the hallway. Rasheed went one way, and Wolf went the other. When Rasheed came to her room, he slowly opened the door.

"Keysha," Rasheed whispered, "I'm here."

There was not an answer, so he entered the room. Lying in the bed, fast asleep, was Keysha Belle. Rasheed walked over to the edge of the bed.

"My princess," Rasheed whispered as he placed his hands on her forehead and on the edge of her soft hair. "Keysha, I told you I would protect you. I'm here for you."

He leaned forward and kissed her on the lips. At that moment, Keysha opened her eyes and spoke to him as she yawned, "Hey, big head!"

"Keysha, you're awake!" Rasheed shouted.

"How could I stay asleep after feeling those soft lips? Give me another one!" Keysha said as she puckered her lips. They kissed again.

"Hmm, so sweet. So good," Rasheed said.

"They are all for you, so you can taste them anytime," Keysha replied. "Where am I?"

"You're in the hospital," Rasheed said as he walked to the closet and fished out a pair of jogging pants and a sweatshirt.

"Hospital? Oh, yeah, the plane crashed."

"Yes. Now, I need you to get dressed. We have to leave. La Committee is coming!"

"What? I thought that was over with."

"It isn't," Rasheed said. "There is no time to explain. Hurry!"

Keysha nodded her head. Rasheed turned his back as Keysha dressed. When she was finished, Keysha touched Rasheed on his shoulder and said, "I'm ready."

"Let's go," Rasheed said. "Give me your hand."

At that moment, Wolf came into the room with a portable defibrillator.

"Who are you?" Keysha gasped.

"He is my new security guard," Rasheed said. "His name is Wolf, and he has saved my life twice in less than twenty-four hours!"

"I've heard a lot about you, Keysha," Wolf said. "I need your cooperation."

"What is it that you need me to do?" Keysha asked.

"I am going to have to shock you with these two patches of the defibrillator. There is a possibility it will cause your heart to stop."

"O-okay," Keysha said uneasily.

"Do you remember having a small puncture wound on your arm or forearm when you were held captive?"

"Yes. Now that you mention it, I do remember. When I first

saw it, I thought they had injected me with heroin."

"Where is it?" Wolf asked.

"It is on my right arm. Right here," Keysha said as she rolled up her sleeve and pointed to a small wound on her right forearm.

"They injected a global positioning system into your arm," Wolf said. "That is how they have been able to track your every move."

"What is the shock therapy going to do?" Keysha asked.

"This blast of electricity will cause the chip to malfunction, but it could also kill you. Is this what you want?"

"What do you think?" Keysha asked as she looked from Wolf to Rasheed.

"It is your choice, Keysha," Rasheed said. "I will support your decision no matter what."

"If it will end the hunt, then, yes, this is what I want."

"Let's do it," Wolf replied.

Wolf turned the defibrillator on, and the device prompted him with its computerized voice, saying, "Place patch on designated area."

Wolf placed the patch on Keysha's arm, just over the scar.

"Stand back and press shock button," the defibrillator prompted.

"Rasheed, is there anything that you want to say before I press this button?" Wolf asked.

"There is," Rasheed said as he stepped forward and took Keysha's hand. "If this is our last moment together, I would like you to know that I love you. If this is not our last moment, I want you to know that I need you in my life!"

"Rasheed, you are amazing, and I am thankful that God sent you into my life. If I survive, I want to continue this life with you."

The two kissed, feeling more than just each other's lips. They felt each other's love, affection, and souls. They parted, and Wolf began the process.

"Rasheed, stand behind her and catch her if she faints."

"Gotcha."

"Now, Keysha, brace yourself," Wolf said. "You may feel a sharp sting."

"Go for it," Keysha said as she closed her eyes.

Wolf pressed the button and sent one burst of high voltage into Keysha's arm.

"Arrrgh!" Keysha screamed.

Wolf snatched the patch from her arm as she fell backwards into Rasheed's arms.

"Keysha! Keysha! Say something," Rasheed shouted.

Keysha moaned, "Did I just get tackled by an Atlanta Falcon defensive-end?"

"No, you just got zapped by a couple hundred volts," Rasheed said. "Can you stand up?"

"Yes, I can. Thanks for not killing me, Wolf."

"Anytime," Wolf replied.

"Thank you for loving me, Rasheed."

"Thank you for having me."

"Okay, I am a fan of this profusion of love, but we have to

go," Wolf said. "Keysha, they still know you are here!"

"Let's go!" Rasheed said.

He grabbed Keysha by the arm and walked into the hall, but Wolf lingered. They took two steps and paused as they saw the bloody kiosk.

"Good Lord!" Rasheed shouted. "The nurse is dead!"

"Oh, my God!" Keysha screamed. "It looks like her throat has been slit!"

"He's here!" Rasheed frantically whispered. "He's here!"

They heard the sound of footsteps. Rasheed pulled Keysha close to him as a man stepped from around the corner of the kiosk. The man had a square forehead and was dressed in a dark suit.

"Rasheed, I am scared," Keysha whispered.

"Who are you, and what do you want?" Rasheed yelled.

The man in the black suit aimed a chrome pistol at them and spoke in a cold, inhumane voice, "I am the Eliminator, and you have been eliminated!"

At that moment, the ceiling and Wolf fell on top of the assassin and knocked the pistol from his hand. He aggressively grasped the Eliminator by the neck and put him into a excruciating choke hold.

"Rasheed, get out of here!" Wolf ordered.

Rasheed grabbed Keysha by the arm and took to the stairs. As they disappeared, the Eliminator spoke in his intimidating voice.

"Are you finished massaging my neck, you little piss ant?"

"Now that you mention it, I think I will snap it," Wolf growled.

"We shall see. We shall see, my little piss ant."

The Eliminator pressed his palms against the ground and began to do a push-up with Wolf on his back. The Eliminator was strong.

"Soon, little piss ant, I will crush you!"

"N-not today," Wolf strained.

Despite Wolf choking him, the Eliminator struggled to a kneeling position. Wolf tightened the choke hold even more, causing a vein in his forehead to appear.

"Arrggh!" Wolf strained. "Why won't your neck break?"

"I am fortified, little piss ant. Now, I will crush you!"

The Eliminator began wildly swinging his elbows against Wolf's ribcage, knocking the air out of him and breaking the deadly choke hold.

"I will crush you, little piss ant!" the Eliminator yelled as he slapped Wolf with the back of his hand, knocking Wolf against a nearby wall.

"Ugh!" Wolf moaned.

"Little piss ant, see my sting!" the Eliminator said as he pulled out a fighter knife. "See how its blade thirsts for blood!"

"You call that a knife! Here's a knife!"

Wolf reached into his pocket and pulled out a scalpel he had picked up before climbing into the air conditioner vents.

"You make me laugh! I am an artist, and today I will paint a masterpiece with your blood!"

"Talk is cheap, sucka," Wolf said.

The Eliminator lunged at Wolf, slashing the knife sideways.

Wolf dodged the swing and kicked the Eliminator in the stomach. "Ugh!" the Eliminator cried out. He fell back and swung with a backhand swing. The tip of the sharp blade nicked Wolf across the chin. Wolf touched his chin then tasted his own blood.

"The last person who made me bleed is dead," Wolf said.

"Not only will I bleed you like a pig, I will break your legs one by one!"

"Enough talk! Time for you to die!"

Wolf swung a swift overhand right, and it smashed into the Eliminator's nose. He felt the bridge of the Eliminator's nose break.

"My n-nose! My nose!"

The Eliminator swung in retaliation, and his left hand pounded the side of Wolf's head. Then, he kicked Wolf in the ribs and elbowed him in the back. Wolf fell to the ground moaning in agony.

"Now, I will crush you. Head first!" the Eliminator threatened. He stomped forward to smash Wolf's head. Wolf, however, quickly shifted to the left as the Eliminator's dress shoe missed its target. Wolf rolled forward and slashed the Eliminator's Achilles' heel with the sharp scalpel. He collapsed to the ground, grasping his injured leg. All the Eliminator could do was scream. Wolf immediately put the knife to the Eliminator's throat and gave him an ultimatum.

"Call off the hit or die!"

"Little piss ant, there is no stopping an order by El Ojo!"

Wolf pressed the sharp blade into the Eliminator's throat and made a small incision. Warm blood squirted from the wound.

"I will cut you from ear to ear if you don't tell me what I want to know," Wolf threatened. "Where can I find this El Ojo?"

"Costa Rica, outside of San Jose!" the Eliminator said.

Suddenly, Wolf heard an audible ticking noise from the nurse's kiosk.

"What is that noise? Answer me!"

The Eliminator held up a small detonator that flashed and said, "I hope you like fireworks, piss ant!"

Wolf kicked the Eliminator in the back of the head, knocking him unconscious. Then he ran to the kiosk where he saw a bag. He quickly opened the bag and saw a black device loaded with explosives. A digital time clock was counting down.

"Thirty seconds!" Wolf yelled as he dashed to his aunt's room down the hall. Once he made it to her room, he opened the door and yelled, "Aunt Carolyn!"

25 seconds

Wolf saw his aunt's empty bed.

"Aunt Carolyn, where are you?!"

The closet door opened up and out stepped his aunt, speaking in her tiny voice, "Wolf, what's going on?"

"What are you doing in the closet?" Wolf inquired.

"I heard people running down the hallway," Aunt Carolyn said fearfully. "I thought it was them terrorists!"

"You are not far from the truth! We have to get out before the place goes boom!"

20 seconds

Wolf glanced at the clock on the wall. He knew that he didn't have much time.

"Aunt Carolyn, I need you to get on the bed. Trust me."

She climbed onto the bed, and Wolf pushed her bed into the hallway.

15 seconds

Wolf stopped as he quickly measured the distance to the elevator at the other end of the hallway.

"Too far. We are not going to make it."

"What are you talking about, baby?" Aunt Carolyn asked.

5 seconds

Wolf looked straight ahead and saw the large glass window.

"God be with us! Hang on, Aunt Carolyn!"

Wolf pushed the hospital bed as fast as he could.

3 seconds

Wolf leaped on the speeding hospital bed.

1 second

KABOOOM!

They crashed through the hospital window as the hospital exploded in a jet of orange flames. As Wolf and Aunt Carolyn crashed in the parking lot, Rasheed and Keysha came running from the ground level of the parking deck. Behind them, dressed in their gowns, were the patients of Jackson Memorial.

"Looks like you brought the network with you!" Wolf smiled.

"You know how we do!" Rasheed gleefully responded.

"Thank you for giving us a new life," Keysha said to Wolf.

"Don't thank me yet," Wolf said.

"Why do you say that?" Rasheed asked. "The chip is destroyed, and the hit man is dead, right?"

"Yes, but the person who issued the hit is still out there, and I presume he is in Costa Rica," Wolf said.

"That is where my cousin is. I would give anything to have her back."

"Then, I am going to Costa Rica to look for her and stop the person who is monitoring these chips," Wolf said.

"I can't ask you to go on some secret agent mission that might get you killed," Rasheed regretfully said. "I've lost one friend trying to play I-spy and I don't plan on losing another."

"I know the country and the people. I'm your best chance for finding her alive and stopping this menace."

Rasheed briefly thought it over. Then, he reached into his pocket. He handed Wolf his credit card and a picture of Gwen.

"Take this. You will recognize her by the English Ivy tattoo on her right hand. Use this credit card for whatever you need."

"I will. You had better leave from here," Wolf said. "After all, you are supposed to be in the hospital on the other side of town."

"You're right. Keysha, let's go. Be blessed, Wolf."

"You too, Rasheed."

9

As Rasheed and Keysha left the scene, the emergency sirens blared as the ambulance and police converged on the scene. Hundreds of miles away in Costa Rica, El Ojo saw the pulsating dot cease on his radar screen.

"The target has been eliminated. Monday, we will resume the slave and drug trade."

He sat back in his chair and stared at the ceiling as fantasies of domination ran through his demented mind.

Chapter 9
Solutions for a Resolution

While Wolf was giving a statement to the police, Kandis Wright sat in a metal chair at a chrome rectangular table within an interrogation room that was bordered in glass. Her hands were handcuffed and her feet were shackled. A tall black man dressed in a black suit and a light blue shirt walked into the room.

"Let me go!" Kandis shouted. "My ankles and wrists are hurting, you bastard!"

"Quiet down. Quiet down. I am Inspector Danny."

"Let me shackle you and handcuff your arms behind your back, and let me know how you feel!" Kandis shouted.

"I know that feeling. It hurts, but it is necessary. You see. Now, you belong to the state of Georgia."

"Shut up! I'm not a slave."

"No, but you are a criminal," the man said as he sat down across from Kandis and tossed a pack of cigarettes onto the table.

"Would you like a smoke?"

"Why don't you inhale that smoke that you are about to blow out of your butt!" Kandis rudely replied.

"Such a pretty face, such a foul mouth," Inspector Danny said as he lit a cigarette. "Just think what the ladies on D-Block are gonna think when they hear it!"

Kandis sighed.

"I'm just saying," Inspector Danny said as he inhaled, causing the tip of the cigarette to glow like amber. "In the belly of the beast, there are women who dress like women but act like dudes."

"That doesn't scare me," Kandis said.

"Do you know why you are here?" Danny asked as he blew the smoke in the air.

"To enjoy the view."

"You're pretty tough. It's a dude, I meant a woman, named Big Wendy. She likes 'em tough! Sometimes you can hear 'em kicking and screaming as she has her way with 'em."

"Your threats are useless!" Kandis snapped. "This is America, and I know my rights! You can't make me confess to something I didn't do!"

"Something that you didn't do?" Inspector Danny asked. "Are you sure you are innocent?"

"Yes, I am sure! What? You don't speak English?"

"Actually, I speak several languages," Inspector Danny said as he leaned back in his chair. "I speak credit card fraud, theft by receiving, identity theft, and criminal mastermind."

"Who do you think you are, accusing me of this and that?"

Inspector Danny took a drag from his cigarette. Kandis watched as the tip of the cigarette became a fiery orange.

"When I was little, my mother used to tell me a story about a tea kettle, a spoon, and some dirty dishes. Want to hear it?"

"Go to hell with your story!" Kandis shouted.

"Once upon a time, there was a tea kettle that sat on the stove, two dirty dishes that sat in the sink, and a spoon that sat in the tray with the other clean dishes."

"I am not in kindergarten, and this is not story time! Let me out of here!"

"One day, the heat was turned on beneath the kettle as it sat on the stove, and it began to scream as loud as it could. The sound was unbearable. Finally, someone heard it. Then, that person poured the hot water on the dirty dishes and washed them, making them clean."

"Let me out of here! I'm innocent!"

Inspector Danny took another drag of the cigarette and walked over to Kandis. He leaned forward and blew the smoke in her face. Kandis winced as the smoke stung her eyes.

"The moral of the story is come clean while you still can, Kandis. Someone is out there screaming, and we are listening."

"I don't know what you are talking about," Kandis said, turning her head away from Inspector Danny.

"Do stolen credit cards, big screen TVs, and the Jump Out Boys ring a bell?" Inspector Danny asked.

"None of it means anything to me!"

"Don't play with me, Kandis!" Inspector Danny yelled as he pounded his fists on the table. "The kettle is squealing, and those dirty dishes are about to be cleaned and put with the other clean dishes!"

Kandis dropped her head and became eerily silent.

"That beautiful daughter of yours is going to grow up without a mother because you are about to take the rap for some lowlife scumbags. You have one chance, Kandis. If you help me, I will see to it that you get less than six months. Afterwards, you will get a new life, new name, and another chance to better yourself."

Inspector Danny stood up and dropped his cigarette to the floor where he put it out with the toe of his shoe. He walked over to the door, turned around, and said, "Don't stay silent too long. Remember. That tea pot is singing. Soon, someone will pick it up."

Inspector Danny opened the door and walked out of the interrogation room, leaving Kandis with her thoughts. She just stared up at the ceiling. Things had changed from great to very bad in such a short period of time. She had to do something.

2

Inspector Danny walked into the surveillance room where Detective François watched Kandis from behind a two sided mirror. He gave Inspector Danny five as he stood beside him.

"Good work, inspector. I think you broke her."

"Maybe," Inspector Danny sighed. "She is a tough cookie to break."

"Do you see how she is tapping her feet and shaking her head?"

"She is tapping away, isn't she?"

"That is a telltale sign of extreme stress. She wants to make the right decision."

"One year ago, we put a tail on her at her favorite boutique and have captured her using several stolen credit cards," Inspector Danny said.

"Does she have a folder?" Detective Francois asked.

"She has a living document," Inspector Danny said as he placed a manila folder on the table that was filled with pertinent documents.

"This thing is huge!" Detective Francois said.

"She knows major players and runners who operate out of Miami, Atlanta, and New York. We have her with all of them."

"Excellent! This could be the break we needed to do a dragnet! If I were you, I would be getting my bags ready for that early vacation."

"Why is that?" Inspector Danny asked.

"Little Miss I Didn't Do Anything is starting to cry."

"Hook, line, and sinker!" Inspector Danny said with a smile. Then, he briskly walked out of the room and reentered the interrogation room.

"Kandis, I need to give you an update."

"W-what is it?"

"I just got word that time is up. We have statements from several of your accomplices. They say that you are the mastermind, supplier, and financial sponsor of this national crime syndicate. Do you know how much time that carries?"

Kandis looked at Inspector Danny with wide eyes.

"That is twenty-five years mandatory," Inspector Danny said as he turned around. "I am sorry. I wish you had cooperated from the beginning."

"No! No! It was Pressure! He led the Jump Out Boys!" Kandis cried out.

"The group that has been robbing sports bars across the area?" Inspector Danny asked.

"Yes! Yes! It was him!"

"What about the stolen credit cards?"

"I will give you what whatever you want! I will give you names, places, addresses, anything you want. Just please don't take my daughter away from me!"

"Let me see what I can do for you," Inspector Danny said.

He walked out of the room. Detective Francois was already in the hallway, ready to take over. The two men shook hands. Afterward, Detective Francois entered the room with a tape recorder to gather a confession.

3

As Detective Francois gathered a taped confession, Rasheed and Keysha stood on a curb, waiting for a taxicab as a light drizzle fell. It was a busy night, and no one was stopping for them. They had been waiting almost fifteen minutes, and they were starting to get wet.

"I never knew taxicab drivers in Atlanta were so busy," Rasheed said.

"There might be some type of convention going on," Keysha replied.

"Probably. If we don't catch a cab soon, this light drizzle is going to wash us away."

As another taxi passed, Keysha said, "That scrub had no intention of stopping."

"Hey, now, I used to be a scrub," Rasheed said.

"You? A scrub?"

"I was the poster child for scrubs!"

"I can't believe that!" Keysha exclaimed.

"Certified, stamped, and sealed," Rasheed said. "Where I am from, you didn't get a car at sixteen, eighteen, or twenty-one, so when my friend Tony got a car, we all got a car!"

Another taxi zipped by.

"I had a car at sixteen, but I still had a strict curfew, so I never really enjoyed it until I went to college."

"Even in college, I was a passenger," Rasheed laughed.

"Now you have cars and private jets! That's not scrub material. You went from zero to hero practically overnight!"

"You better believe it! When I signed the deal with the Atlanta FireHawks, boppers came out of bopperland in the droves! I literally had to fight them off with a stick!"

"That's hard to believe."

"Why is it?" Rasheed asked.

"Every man dreams of having women flock to his every need

and whim," Keysha said.

"Let me share something with you about the real world," Rasheed said. "Listen 'cause I want you to get this."

"Alright, give it to me straight," Keysha said as she crossed her arms.

"With more women comes more of a chance of contracting an STD! Not everyone is clean out there!"

"I see your point," Keysha said as she nodded her head. "The number of sexually transmitted diseases among minorities is staggering and breathtaking."

"The rate is dramatically increasing among our youth," Rasheed said. "Parents have to have a well-rounded conversation with their kids."

"I think that parents need to step it up. Kids are learning the wrong things from the wrong people. Wait, Rasheed, I think that one is coming near us!"

"Where?" Rasheed asked as he peered up the street.

"There."

"You're right! It is slowing down. Let's get in."

As the taxi cab neared, Rasheed held Keysha's hand. He was getting more and more used to that feeling. When the taxi stopped, Rasheed noticed the name of the taxicab service was Blanco and that they had a one eight hundred telephone number on the side of the door.

"Let me get the door for you, darling," Rasheed said.

"You are so sweet!" Keysha replied.

Rasheed opened the door for her and got in after her. As soon as they were inside the cab, Rasheed noticed the heavy smell of cigarette smoke. The driver was an older white man with a pompadour hairstyle. Separating the passengers from the driver was a clear protective wall.

"Hey, how are you this evening?" Rasheed asked politely.

The drive replied through a handheld intercom in a sarcastic tone, "Hay is for hosses, but I am fine as two-dollar wine! And, by the way, the name is Flint."

"Um, what's a hoss?" Keysha quietly whispered to Rasheed.

"You know dat thang the Lone Ranger rode on! A hoss!" Flint responded.

"You mean 'a horse'?" Keysha enunciated.

"Yah, a hoss is a hoss. So, where y'all going t'night?"

"Twenty-five, thirty-four Mallard Court in Jonesboro," Rasheed said.

"Whoa, Leroy! This ain't one of those busses that tour the city showing devastated flood areas, you know?"

Keysha frowned as she whispered to Rasheed, "This guy isn't wrapped too tight. We need to get out of here."

"I heard that!" Flint sharply stated. "I hear everything in this doggone cab! I got them good speakers and tweeters!"

"Um, Flint, are you alright?" Rasheed asked.

"Since the doctor slapped me on da right cheek!" he responded.

"Yeah, right," Rasheed said. "I know it is far out, but I am willing to pay top dollar."

"Are you on the run from da law?" Flint asked.

"No, our car died," Rasheed replied.

"Y'all look like criminals, savage animals of some sort! Unruly and such!"

"That's it!" Keysha exclaimed. "Let's go, Rasheed! We don't have to take this crap from this backwater racist!"

The drizzle became a hard rain.

"Hold on! Hold on!" Flint pleaded. "Before you get your stained undies in a knot and stand out there in the soaking rain and catch pneumonia, there is something you should know."

"Do we have a choice?" Rasheed asked as the rain thudded against the roof of the cab.

"There is a sci-fi convention in town tonight and that leaves only little ol' me to drive you around. Everybody else is booked to the door!"

"Then, drive us to our destination and keep your racist comments to yourself," Rasheed advised.

"Okay, Sambo!" Flint said. "Hey yah! Time to leave the stable!"

The taxicab pulled away from the curb. After three turns through the city, they cruised onto the freeway. As he drove south on the freeway, the rain lessened, and Flint started small talk by saying, "It is nice how the lights of the city shine at night."

"It sure is," Rasheed said.

"You know my father used to have a taxicab service until those towel-heads migrated here."

"Who do you think you are to call people names, Flint?" Keysha asked. "Are you a neo-Nazi or some Russian radical trying to keep his country from becoming a melting pot?"

"I am from the old country. My father is directly descended from the kings of old."

"Flint, we don't want to hear about your father or your rhetoric," Rasheed said. "Just get us home."

Flint disregarded both Keysha and Rasheed's remarks. He continued his tirade as he said, "Those towel heads don't even have to pay taxes for the first five years! Ain't that something?"

"Here we go again," Rasheed said as he rubbed his head.

"Towel heads and spicks. They stick together, but you mongrel people do the opposite."

"Who are you referring to as 'you mongrel people'?" Keysha angrily asked.

Flint chuckled, "You two African booty scratchers sitting in the back seat. Who else would I be referring to? I'm the only genuine symbol of white power in this here fine vessel!"

"Flint, I have a news flash for you," Rasheed said. "This is not 1960, and you will respect us! I promise you that!"

"What do black people know about respect?" Flint asked coldly.

"We know that respect is something that is earned!" Keysha angrily shouted.

"Being irate is a typical black person's reaction when challenged," Flint said. "It don't matter if the topic is race, politics, or war."

"You forgot about reparations," Rasheed said. "You racists never want to talk about repaying us for the evils you committed against our ancestors!"

"Why repay you for your ancestors?" Flint asked. "You were property then, and you are property now!

"Let's just end this before I come through this glass and put your head up your butt, so you can taste what you are talking!" Rasheed responded.

"There is no need to get mad, my dark horse! In the old days, segregation gave you pride. Black spook power is what I like to call it! We feared you!"

"Flint, I am warning you!" Rasheed angrily shouted.

"As long as we directly oppressed you, you were strong. Now that you have gained your rights, you are weaker than ever! You can't even keep your own black colleges open!"

"Did you even graduate from anyone's school?" Keysha asked. "Day care, elementary, middle, or even high school? Just pick one."

"He probably didn't graduate from any because he could not get past the fact that one plus one is two and not eleven!" Rasheed said.

"I'm smarter than you think," Flint said.

"Oh, yeah? Why is your counter not working?"

"Oh, it is working quite fine! Working like a charm!"

"I see what you are trying to do," Rasheed said. "You are going to make up some outrageous charge, but I am not paying it!"

"In my cab, you don't pay with money!" Flint replied.

"What do you pay with?" Rasheed asked.

"You pay with your fear!" Flint said as he held up a tape recorder. "When the grand wizard hears the terror in your voices, he will see that I have what it takes to be in the organization! White power!"

Flint swerved the taxicab in and out of the lanes. The tires squealed as he barely missed an SUV.

"You white bastard," Keysha shouted, "we are not participating in your sick class project!"

"That's it!" Rasheed yelled as he punched the glass that separated them from Flint.

"Ouch!" Rasheed shouted as he almost broke his hand.

"Heh! Heh!" Flint laughed. "You spooks are only good for entertainment! You make the worst doctors and lawyers but the best athletes!"

"At least we are not good at marrying our first cousins!" Keysha shouted.

"My cousin is beautiful, you spook!" Flint angrily replied. "A cousin makes a dozen, haven't you heard that?"

Rasheed popped his knuckles and yelled, "I can't wait to leave my fingerprints on your face!"

"Just because you don't see the Klan doesn't mean we don't exist!" Flint proudly said. "We put the white sheet on the inside with our white pride. We are in more corporations than computers!"

"Flint, let us out right now!" Rasheed angrily replied.

"My pleasure, Sambo."

The taxicab pulled onto the shoulder of exit 235 for Jonesboro. Rasheed and Keysha quickly exited the vehicle with their hearts racing in their chests. Flint rolled the window down a little and cried out as he sped off, "The South will rise again! White power!"

Before he could get back onto the interstate, Rasheed threw a rock at the car and broke his rear windshield. Flint extended his arm out the window and shot them the bird.

"I could have choked that dude until he was navy blue," Rasheed said.

"That guy is sick!" Keysha said. "If we don't wake up as a people, those types of people will try to bring the old days back."

"I know. I am sorry you had to experience that," Rasheed apologized.

"It is okay. Who knows, I probably saw it before but never so exaggerated and so blatant."

Rasheed glanced up ahead and saw a gas station. He turned to Keysha and said, "Come on. I know those people who own that gas station. They will get us home."

Rasheed and Keysha held hands as they walked to the gas station. They had been through so much in the last two days. Just how much more could they endure remained to be seen. Behind them, the rain moved closer to their side of town, and the temperature dropped even more.

While Rasheed and Keysha were walking to the gas station, Donna and Chanise were playing a popular wireless boxing game on their Nintendo Wii.

"Block! Block!" Donna coached.

Chanise held up her hands just below her chin as she imitated a boxer in a defensive stance, bobbing right and left. The avatar on the screen mimicked her actions.

"Like this, Grandma?" Chanise asked in her little voice.

"Yeah! Now, swing! Swing!" Donna coached.

"Uh! Uh!" Chanise grunted. "Take that! Take that, you bad guy!"

The avatar started to swing, and the opponent on the television screen suffered a barrage of punches then fell down with stars swirling around its head.

"The bad guy fell down, Grandma!"

"That's right! You knocked the bad guy down! Good job!"

"Yeah! I knocked him down! Pow! Pow!"

"Now, don't you go knocking people upside the head. Only do that to a mean person who tries to hurt you," Donna said.

"Okay. Can we play again?"

"No, it is night-night time," Donna said. "We have to go to church tomorrow."

"I like church! We get to sing a lot!" Chanise exclaimed.

"Then, go, say your prayers, and get ready for bed. I will be there to tuck you in in a few."

"I am a big girl! I can tuck myself in!"

"Okay, you do that," Donna said. "Show Grandma that you are a big girl!"

"Okay!"

Chanise ran to her bedroom as Donna turned off the appliances. There was a rumble of thunder as the rain started to fall. Donna peeked around the corner and watched Chanise say her prayers as she kneeled down at her bed.

"As I lay me down to sleep, I pray the Lord my soul to keep. Lord, please bless my Grandma and Ma Ma. When the morning light comes in, I pray the Lord makes Grandma, Ma Ma, and me a family again! Amen!"

Suddenly, the rotary telephone in the kitchen chimed.

"Who could this be at this time of night?" Donna muttered. "Better not be any telemarketers talking about how the warranty on my car is about to expire!"

She hurried to the kitchen and picked up the phone from the base that was attached to the wall. She answered the phone in her polite voice, almost smiling as she said, "Hello?"

"This a collect phone call from the Fulton County Correctional Facility," stated an automated message. "To accept charges, press one or simply stay on the line."

"What in the blazes? This has to be a joke!"

"To accept charges press one or simply stay on the line."

Donna pressed the number one key. At that moment, an unfamiliar voice came onto the line, but she could hear the relief in that voice as she said, "D-donna, it's you! Thank God you answered!"

"Who is this, and how do you know my name?

"This is Kandy, your daughter! I-I'm in jail!"

"God, not my daughter," Donna said as she leaned against the wall. "Please don't let my daughter be in jail!"

"D-Donna," Kandis sniffled. "I-I I am sorry for being so troublesome, so arrogant!"

"Kandy, what did you do?" Donna asked frantically. "How did you get sent to jail?"

"I-I made some bad choices, and they caught up with me."

"We all make bad choices, but were your choices so bad that you had to go to jail? My God! Where did I go wrong with you?"

"I made some real bad choices," Kandis admitted. "The condo in Atlanta, the nice cars, and basically my entire life there was a lie."

"I just feel like I let you down," Donna said.

"This was all my fault! All you ever did was try to help me. More than ever, I need you to do me a favor, please!"

"Sure! Sure! Anything. Just name it!"

"I need you to go to church and pray for me!" Kandis requested. "Then, on Monday morning, get me a lawyer! Can you do that for me?"

"Yes, I can do that," Donna said as she wiped away her tears. "I will get on it as soon as possible!"

Suddenly, an automated voice interrupted their conversation. "Twenty seconds remaining before termination."

"Kandy, I love you," Donna said. "Don't worry, Kandy. I am coming for you!"

"Thank you, Momma. I love you, too! You have been the best mother a child could ever ask for!"

The call ended, leaving Donna alone in her dimly lit kitchen with one thousand thoughts racing through her mind. However, there was one thought that stood out from the rest.

"The last time she called me Momma was when she was in grade school."

Donna hung up the phone and checked on Chanise. She was fast asleep in her bed just like the big girl she said she was. Then, Donna walked to her bedroom and opened up her Bible. The first verse Donna saw was Psalms 37:7. Donna read the verse aloud.

"Rest in the Lord and wait patiently for him: fret not thyself because of him who prospereth in his way, because of the man who bringeth wicked devices to pass."

Donna kneeled beside her bed and prayed for her daughter.

"Lord, your servant calls you. I have been young, and now I am old; yet, I have not seen the righteous forsaken or their children beg for bread."

Donna paused then wiped the tears from her face before she continued.

"Lord, you are merciful and your children are blessed. On this day, I ask that you guide our steps through these trying times and be with my daughter. I patiently wait for your spirit to move, and I rest in you. Amen. Amen. Amen."

Donna rose to her feet and prepared for bed. There was nothing else she could do for Kandis. Donna tied up her hair. Then, she fell asleep. Outside, the rain fell harder than ever.

In the meanwhile, a gray Mercedes pulled into Rasheed's driveway. Driving the car was a curly haired Italian man. In the backseat of the vehicle were Rasheed and Keysha.

"Thank you for the ride, Mr. Torceilini," Rasheed said.

"No problemeo, Mr. Rasheed. You helpa me with marketing by signing autographs at my gas station! Prego! Sales through roof!"

"Let me know if I can be of any further assistance," Rasheed replied.

"Ciao!" Mr. Torceilini said.

Rasheed closed the door of the Mercedes and stood by Keysha as the car exited the driveway. Rasheed turned to Keysha, stretched out his hands, and said, "Welcome to Casa de Locke."

"Your home looks wonderful! I love the Spanish arches!"

"Thanks. Come on. Let's go inside. It is cold out here, and the rain is almost here."

They walked up the steps to the front door. Rasheed unlocked the door and beckoned for Keysha to enter.

"After you, my lady."

"Are you always a gentleman?"

"Eight days a week, twenty-five hours a day."

As they entered the spacious foyer of the house, Keysha noticed the marble flooring, the crystal chandelier, and the winding staircase that led to the second floor. A portrait on the wall of a middle aged woman standing near a red car especially caught her attention.

"Rasheed, is this your mother?"

"Yes, we took this picture on her sixty-fourth birthday. Hindsight is twenty-twenty."

"Why do you say that?"

"This was the only picture we took that day. It was also her last picture before the cancer started to cause her health to fail."

"This portrait speaks volumes. She is so pretty and so happy."

"She was definitely happy that day. I had bought her an Ugly Stick fishing pole."

"What's that?"

"It is a fishing pole that has tremendous flexibility. You can bend the tip to the bottom without breaking it."

"The right tool for a fisherman," Keysha replied. "Rasheed, can I freshen up?"

"Yes, follow me upstairs," Rasheed said.

Keysha held her hand over chest and gasped in a joking manner, "Rasheed, I am not that type of girl!"

"Trust me. I would use a different set of skills if I was trying to get you in my bed. The bathroom is upstairs. I want to run you a hot bath."

"Then, I am that type of girl!" Keysha smiled.

She followed Rasheed up the winding stairs and down a hallway. He opened the door and entered a white tiled bathroom. On the far end of the room was a built-in jacuzzi that had a rose-colored marble finish and a separate glass shower. Rasheed began to run a hot bath for Keysha.

"The towels and bubble bath are in the cabinet near the sink," he said. "I will put some clean gym shorts and a t-shirt outside the door."

"Thank you, Rasheed."

"You're welcome. Enjoy."

Rasheed closed the door and walked down the hallway. Just as he passed his room, his stomach growled.

"Dang, I haven't had anything to eat all day! I bet Keysha is hungry, too."

Rasheed hurried downstairs and ran into the spacious kitchen. He opened up his stainless steel refrigerator, searching for something to cook quickly.

"Eggs, bacon, vegetables, juice, but nothing to cook immediately," Rasheed said. "Let's see what is up in the freezer."

Rasheed opened the freezer and saw frozen ground beef, pork chops, and chicken. He looked past the chicken and found a bag of frozen bow-tie chicken pasta that he had bought before going to Miami.

"Prepare in fifteen minutes," Rasheed read. "This is just what the doctor prescribed!"

Rasheed took the bag of pasta out of the refrigerator and turned the stove on a medium setting. Then, he poured the pasta into a flat saucepan and put a cover on the top. Rasheed walked over to his wine rack and chose a sparkling white wine to put on ice.

"Can't have a romantic dinner without candles."

Rasheed went to a nearby cabinet and took out two white plates that were trimmed in silver. He quickly set his glass dinner table and lit a scented candle. He took a step back and reviewed his handiwork. Once he was satisfied with the presentation, he ran upstairs to his room. Rasheed picked up a white Atlanta Fire-

Hawks t-shirt and a pair of mesh basketball shorts. Then, he placed them outside the bathroom door.

"Keysha, your clothes are outside the door."

"Thanks," Keysha replied from behind the door.

"Make yourself at home," Rasheed said. "I will be taking a shower."

"Okay," Keysha replied.

Rasheed walked down the hall and entered his restroom. In the meanwhile, Keysha sat in a tub full of bubbles, reflecting on the moment and her family.

"I have gone from prisoner to princess. This has to be unreal. I will go home Monday, but will the magic continue?"

Keysha bathed in the warm, scented water. When she let the water out of the tub, she also let all of her worries go down the drain. She dried off with a large orange towel and opened the door to pick up the clothes Rasheed had left for her. That was when she smelled the savory aroma and said, "Something smells delicious!"

She dressed quickly and exited the bathroom. As she neared the winding staircase, she could hear Rasheed singing in the shower.

"I hopped out of the bed and turned my swag on! Rasheed's getting money! I met a girl in Miami, and she is fine. Yeah, she fine! Oh!"

"That boy has lost his mind!" Keysha laughed. She walked down the stairs, following the enticing smell. Keysha entered a lavish dining room with a long, cherry wood table.

"All of my family and friends could sit at this table and still have elbow room."

She walked past another room. Then, she turned around to make sure she had seen what she saw. Keysha stared at the rows of bucket seats with cup holders, a popcorn machine in the right corner, and the large television screen embedded within the wall.

"Wow! This dude has a movie theater in his house!"

She continued to follow the smell. When she entered the spacious kitchen, Keysha experienced a shortness of breath. There was a large stainless steel refrigerator, a stove, and a pot rack that hung from the ceiling. This kitchen was a cook's dream.

"I could cook a feast up in here!" Keysha shouted. "Let's see what's cooking!"

She walked over to the stove where the pot was simmering. Keysha lifted the lid and inhaled.

"Mmmm, chicken pasta with bow-tie noodles! My favorite! How did Rasheed know?"

She picked up a nearby spoon and stirred the food. At that moment, Rasheed walked into the room dressed in black basketball shorts and a white tank top. Keysha dropped the spoon at the sight of his well rounded arms. She could even see his abdominal muscles pressing against his shirt.

"Are we having fun?" Rasheed asked.

"H-hi! I meant yes," Keysha stammered. "I-I was just checking on the food."

"Ten minutes here, and you already want to cook something," Rasheed said.

"I know, but it is in my nature. Louisianans love to cook."

"Well, you are my guest, and I am taking up the task," Rasheed said.

Keysha reached into a nearby trashcan and picked up the bag that held the pasta contents as she smiled, "Rasheed, this isn't cooking."

"You got me! I'm busted!" Rasheed laughed.

"But it is thoughtful, and I am thankful. By the smell, I think it is done."

"Then, let's eat up! You have a seat and relax while I serve you."

He placed a serving of chicken pasta on each plate.

"Thank you, Rasheed. It smells great!"

"You are welcome, mademoiselle. Hold that thought. I will be right back!"

Rasheed waltzed into the kitchen and took the wine bottle out of the freezer. Afterward, he waltzed back to the table and popped the bottle of wine. Then, he slowly poured it into their sparkling wine glasses.

"Are you trying to get me drunk and take advantage of me, Rasheed?"

"Trust me. The advantage is all yours."

"How do you figure?" Keysha asked.

"The fragrance, the long curly hair, and the straight teeth. How can I resist such temptation?"

"You have a way with words, Mr. Locke," Keysha said. "Could you please bless the food?"

"Sure."

Rasheed reached across the space and held Keysha's hands as he prayed, "Father God, thank you for this food today. Please bless the preparers and receivers of this food and transform it from a physical food to a spiritual food for the nourishment of our souls. Also, please bless those who are not fortunate enough to have meal. Thank you. Amen. Amen. Amen."

As they started to eat their pasta, the two began to make small talk about their beliefs.

"Rasheed, why do you say amen three times?" Keysha asked.

"Each one is for the Father, the Son, and the Holy Spirit."

"Duh! I am slow sometimes," Keysha replied.

"That's okay. I will speed you up! Do you go to church?"

"Yes, but I haven't been in a while," Keysha said. "When I was younger, I sang in the choir."

"Did y'all have the A & B section?"

"Yes, we did," Keysha laughed. "Believe it or not, I actually led some songs."

"I can tell you're talented," Rasheed said.

"Why do you say that?" Keysha asked.

"Because, at my church, if you can't sing, they are not ashamed to let you know!"

"Ha! Ha! Ha!" Keysha laughed.

"They will come and sit you down with Sister Allen if you are not in key!" Rasheed laughed.

Keysha ate a piece of chicken. Then, she continued after she wiped her mouth.

"There was no sugar coating at my church either!"

"I would never have the guts to get up and sing," Rasheed said.

"But you can get up and slam dunk in front of thousands?"

"That is a little backwards, huh?" Rasheed said.

"You said it; I didn't. Rasheed, what is your pet peeve, the thing that most gets up under your skin?"

"My biggest pet peeve is having people around me who think that money will solve all of their problems."

"I know exactly what you are talking about," Keysha said as she took another bite of her food.

"They can't do anything unless they have this amount of money in the bank," Rasheed said. "It makes me sick!"

"More money equals more problems."

"Exactly," Rasheed replied. Then, he ate some pasta.

"Talking about all of this real stuff makes me want to go to church tomorrow."

"What's stopping you?" Rasheed asked.

"There is only one thing stopping me. I don't have any clothes."

"That is an easy problem to solve," Rasheed said. "Shop-Mart opens at seven in the morning, and church starts at ten."

"Then, let's do it! Let's go to church!" Keysha said.

"Done," Rasheed said. "I have another question for you. When do you want to go home?"

"Monday. Are you coming?" Keysha asked enthusiastically.

"Do you want me to?"

"I would love for you to!"

"Then, I will come. Let's have a toast."

They lightly touched glasses.

"To us meeting on Valentine's Day. To love at first sight," Rasheed said.

"To us meeting on Valentine's Day. To love at first sight," Keysha repeated.

The two drank to their health, and they finished eating. Then, they went into the entertainment room and sat on a couch where Rasheed turned the eighty inch television screen on.

"What do you want to watch?" Rasheed asked. "I have hundreds of channels."

"The news. My dad is a First News Network freak. I bet that is what he is watching now."

"I like to watch the news, too. Let's see what is going on in Atlanta today."

Rasheed picked up the remote and turned his television to the local news station. The first thing they saw was an empty highway bordered by emergency vehicles and the news media. The camera was fixed on the damaged part of the cement wall.

"Wow! What is going on?" Keysha asked. "Did something bust through the wall on the interstate?"

"Ain't no telling," Rasheed answered. "Let me see what is on the other station Any Time News."

Rasheed changed the channel. At that moment, Dana Anderson appeared on the television where she was reporting live from the scene.

"This is Dana Anderson with 'Any Time News', reporting live from the scene where a fatal wreck has claimed the lives of two individuals and caused several wrecks on Interstate 285 and Interstate 85. The victims have been identified as husband Gary Campbell and wife Aisha Campbell."

"No!" Rasheed shouted.

"What's wrong? Do you know them, Rasheed?"

Rasheed rubbed his head in disbelief, "Gary is one of my best friends, and his wife was the woman I showed you after the club fire!"

"Oh, my God!" Keysha gasped.

Dana Anderson continued her live report as she walked over to a young white woman who was sipping a cup of coffee with a blanket draped around her shoulders as she sobbed.

"Sherry Atwater witnessed the entire event. Sherry, please share with us what you saw."

"I was like driving and like this car just passed me. Then, suddenly, a lady fell out of the car just before the car smashed through the wall."

"Did she jump out? Or did she fall out?"

"It…it looked like she jumped out, but why would she do that? Why?"

"That is what investigators are working on now. Stay tuned as we bring you more on this developing story."

As the rain came down hard outside, Rasheed turned off the television and looked at Keysha with wide eyes.

"I know why this happened."

"What are you saying, Rasheed? How would you know that?"

"A man can only take so much before he snaps. Aisha was beating Gary whenever she got drunk and had even hit him with a skillet."

"You're kidding me," Keysha said.

"No, I'm not. When I told him about what I had seen in Miami, he didn't even sound devastated."

"Sometimes after a person has been abused for a long time, he builds up a tolerance," Keysha rationalized. "Something must have caused him to go over the edge as they drove on the interstate."

"You're right. You're right. If he was that crazy, he would have done something at the airport when he had picked her up."

"Come on. Let's just lay here on the couch and listen to the rain."

Rasheed obeyed Keysha and laid his head on her lap. They laid there in silence, listening to the downpour. Soon, time became a blur. Before they knew it, sleep had claimed them.

As they lay on the couch, sleeping like little kids, an airplane flew the friendly skies, destined for Costa Rica. Sitting in the first class section was Wolf. Soon, he would be unleashed and would wreak havoc across the mainland.

Chapter 10
Love Is

Keysha woke up on Sunday morning, laying on the couch, all by her lonesome.

"Rasheed!"

There was no answer.

"Rasheed, where are you?"

She looked around and saw a note on the couch. She picked up the paper and read it to herself. As her sleepy eyes read and comprehended each word, she could hear Rasheed's deep voice narrating the letter:

Good morning, my love. Breakfast is in the kitchen. I am out jogging around the neighborhood and will return shortly. There is also a surprise for you upstairs in the restroom. I can't wait to see you!

Love,

Rasheed

"That boy is making me fall for him. Let me see what he cooked."

She walked out of the entertainment room and into the kitchen. On the glass table, where they had dined the night before, was a silver tray with a silver cover protecting its contents. Next to it was a pitcher of orange juice.

"Yum!" Keysha said, lifting the silver cover. "Pancakes, sausage, and three strips of bacon."

She sat down and ate her tasty breakfast. As she finished up her breakfast, Keysha saw the cordless phone on the side of the wall.

"I've got to hear her voice. I can't go another day without hearing it."

Keysha picked up the phone and dialed her house number back in Lafayette, Louisiana.

Ring!

Ring!

"Come on!" Keysha said impatiently.

Ring!

"Damn! No one is home!"

Just as she was about to hang up the phone, a clear, motherly voice answered, "Hello?"

It was the same voice that had yelled at her when she had done something wrong. It was the same voice that had congratulated her when she had performed well. The clear pleasant voice belonged to her mother, Mrs. Belle.

"Hello?" Mrs. Belle asked again.

Keysha's hand trembled and a lump formed in her throat as she began to suffer from a panic attack. Keysha tried to speak, but the lump in her throat kept her from speaking.

"Hello?" Mrs. Belle asked a third time.

"I think you have the wrong number!" Mrs. Belle said in a joyful voice. "Have a great day!"

"M-momma!" Keysha exclaimed, but it was too late. Mrs. Belle had already hung up the phone. Tears burst from Keysha's eyes as she hung up the phone and tried to catch her breath.

"Tomorrow…tomorrow can't come fast enough!"

Keysha hurried up the stairs to the restroom and saw a black and white dress, a toothbrush and toothpaste, and a bra with matching panties.

"A black and white dress like Mrs. Obama wore during the campaign! How did Rasheed pull this off?"

She tried on the clothes and found that they fit her perfectly. As she started brushing her teeth, Keysha heard the door chime as the downstairs door opened then closed.

"Keysha, I'm home," Rasheed called out.

She ran down the stairs without rinsing her mouth. Toothpaste foam covered her mouth. Rasheed laughed at the sight.

"Either you are glad to see me or you just got bit by a dog with rabies!"

"Oh, my God," Keysha laughed as she rushed back into the restroom where she washed her face.

By the time she was finished, Rasheed was standing in the bathroom doorway, sweat beading on his taut muscles.

"How was your morning?" Rasheed asked.

"It was fine. I slept hard!"

"It must have been a combination of the rain and the wine 'cause I slept hard, too."

"You were snoring like the little engine that could!" Keysha said.

"You're lying!" Rasheed laughed. "I don't snore!"

"Yes, you do!" Keysha said. "You almost sucked all of the air out of the room! You might want to get some strips for your nose!"

"Ha! I guess so," Rasheed conceded. "I hope that I didn't keep you up all night."

"No, I slept like a rock. I was just playing about the snoring!"

"You got me!" Rasheed said as he gave Keysha a love tap on the arm. "You had me going!"

"So tell me, Casanova, where did you get this authentic black and white dress?"

"Early this morning, I made a couple of phone calls to some friends who own boutiques and keep some inventory at their house due to the smash and grab robbers," Rasheed explained. "Does it fit?"

"It fits perfectly! How did you learn to size a woman up?" Keysha asked.

"One summer, I did customer service for an outlet store where most of the customers were women."

"Hmm, interesting."

"Our busiest time period was when daughters would come in to buy their mother a dress for Mother's Day."

"Oh, yeah," Keysha said in a somber voice as she looked down.

"Keysha, is everything alright?" Rasheed asked. "You have a troubled look on your face."

"Um…I, it's nothing," Keysha said.

"Come on, Keysha. You can talk to me."

"It's just," Keysha said as tears rolled down her eyes.

"I'm here for you, Keysha. Open up to me."

"I…I…huh…"

"Take your time," Rasheed warmly said. "You've been through a lot."

"I…I called back home to Lafayette while you were gone."

"And?" Rasheed asked.

"I am afraid to tell you because you are probably going think that I am crazy!" Keysha sobbed.

"Believe me. I know crazy when I see it," Rasheed said as he reached into the cabinet and gave her a washcloth.

"How do you know I am not crazy?" Keysha asked.

Rasheed smiled, showed his dimples, and said, "Your pupils have not dilated, and you are not baring fangs, so you are far from crazy!"

"Ha! Ha!" Keysha laughed. "That is what is making me fall

for you, Rasheed. You have a way of clearing up a dark sky."

"I try. When you are ready to talk to me, just know I will be here for you."

"I know. I am ready to tell you now."

"Okay, let's start over like nothing happened."

Keysha smiled and gave Rasheed a serious look as she picked up where they left off.

"I called home while you were gone."

"You called home?" Rasheed inquired. "Home as in Lafayette, Louisiana?"

"Yes. Are you mad?"

"No, of course not! I think it's great that you called!" Rasheed joyfully shouted. "What did your family say?"

"They said nothing! Nothing!"

"What do you mean? I am sure they said something!"

"They said nothing because I said nothing! I had a panic attack!"

"Keysha, listen to me," Rasheed said as he stepped forward and took Keysha's hand. "You have survived all of this. You're a winner."

"No, I'm a loser," Keysha wept.

"Why would you say something like that?"

"I should have never left home! Rasheed, I should have never left!"

Rasheed pulled Keysha close and held her in his strong arms as the stress broke her down.

"Keysha, it is okay. It's okay!"

"A-all I wanted was to move to a big city for better opportunities!"

"Keysha, there is nothing wrong with why you wanted to leave home. You wanted to better yourself."

"Rasheed, I turned my back on my family. I thought less of them because they wanted to work for the city or be teachers."

"Keysha, you were only chasing your dream," Rasheed said. "You didn't know your new job was going to lay people off, and you sure didn't know that there was a maniac kidnapping women!"

"Are you saying that it's not my fault?"

"Yes! That is exactly what I am saying. It is not your fault. I repeat. It is not your fault."

Keysha wrapped her arms around Rasheed's neck.

"Thank you, Rasheed, for everything! Thank you for believing in me!"

"You are always welcome. Now, let's get dressed."

"Yeah," Keysha said as she looked in Rasheed's eyes.

"Then, we will go to church. After service, we will catch the first thing flying to Lafayette!"

"Yay!"

"Let's hurry. Service starts in forty-five minutes. I will get the flight times and book our tickets."

Keysha passionately kissed Rasheed. Then, she said, "Thank you. I will be ready in a few."

Rasheed went to his room and showered while Keysha finished getting ready. After he showered, Rasheed accessed the

Swift Airlines website. Then, he booked a flight for two to Lafayette Airport and a rental car. In four hours, Keysha would be reunited with her family.

2

On the other side of town, Donna and Chanise had finished their breakfast of eggs and cheese, homemade biscuits, and grits. Now, they were getting dressed.

"Grandma, why does the wind blow?" Chanise asked.

"It has something to do with the change in temperature," Donna said.

"You mean like how it went from hot on Friday to cold on Saturday?" Chanise asked.

"Yes," she answered as she slipped Chanise's red and black dress on.

"Grandma, I haven't worn this dress before. Is it new?"

"Yes, it is for Valentine's Day because you are my valentine."

"What's a valentine?"

"A valentine is someone who is special," Donna explained. "If you ask someone you think is special to be your valentine, he or she will say yes."

Chanise crossed her arms and poked out her lip.

"I want to call Ma Ma and ask her to be my valentine!"

"Your mother is working on a special project for her job," Donna calmly replied as she held back her tears. "We can call her later."

"Okay."

"Now, go watch that video I bought you the other day while I get ready."

"You mean 'How to Count by Tens'?"

"Yes, that one."

Chanise went to her room and turned on her DVD player. She sat in her pink chair and watched her video.

"Ten, twenty, thirty," Chanise said as she counted her numbers along with the video.

As Chanise watched the video, Donna walked into the bathroom and quietly weeped for her family.

"Lord, be merciful! Remember us!" She said as she dried her eyes and looked in the mirror. Donna finished getting dressed for church. When she was done, she loaded Chanise into her car seat. She backed out of the garage and left for church. In a matter of minutes, they had reached Philadelphia Baptist Church in Locust Grove, Georgia. The church had been remodeled. The remodelers kept the traditional style of the interior with its stain glass windows but added a tidbit of contemporary style to the exterior by revisiting the overall look of the columns and steps. As they stepped out the car, they could hear the choir singing "This Little Light of Mine".

Donna and Chanise entered the church and saw Reverend Life standing up at the pulpit, pumping his arms and cheering the choir on. He was dressed in a black suit with a red tie. Donna and Chanise sat down on the third row and started to sing with the choir.

As the congregation continued to sing, Rasheed and Keysha

walked into the church. They sat in the second row, just in front of Donna. As the song died down, Reverend Life addressed his congregation in his powerful southern voice.

"Good morning, chuch!"

"Good morning," the congregation dryly replied.

"Let us try this again! Say it like the Lord is standing right here in the gap for you today! Good morning, chuch!"

"GOOD MORNING!" the congregation loudly replied.

Reverend Life straightened out his red tie as he addressed the church.

"Philadelphia, today we are going to mix it up! Shake it up! Yah!"

"Shake it up," the congregation cheered and clapped.

"Today, I am going to start the message first. Then, we are going to take the offering! Turn your Bibles to Matthew, Chapter 22, verses 36 through 40. Say 'amen' and stand up once you have found it!"

There was the sound of pages being turned as people flipped their Bibles to the appropriate chapter. Rasheed and Keysha stood and said 'amen' along with everyone else.

"Amen," the congregation acknowledged.

"The scripture reads as follows: Master, which is the great commandment in the law? And Jesus answered: Thou shalt love the Lord thy God with all thy heart, and with all thy soul, and with all thy mind!"

Reverend Life cleared his voice and continued, "This is the first and great commandment. The second is like unto. Thou shalt love thy neighbour as thyself. On these two commandments hang all the law and the prophets. Amen!"

"Amen!" acknowledged the congregation.

"You may be seated. May the reading of this word add a blessing to your lives and contribute to the edification of your soul."

Reverend Life looked out across the Congregation, at each person as they sat back down. Then, he spoke in a clear voice, "Today, my sermon is entitled "Love Is". Say it with me, chuch."

"Love is!" the congregation said.

"As I look out and about in the crowd," Reverend Life said as he pointed into the congregation, "I see some people who may know each other, may even live by each other, and have children that may even play with each other, but how many of you love each other?"

"Well," said a deacon with a powerful voice.

Rasheed leaned over and whispered to Keysha, "That is Reverend Life's right hand man. His name is Deacon Scott."

"That little man in the brown suit?" Keysha asked.

"Yes, but don't let the size fool you. His voice is powerful, and he is the real deal!"

Reverend Life continued to preach.

"The four letter word 'LOVE' is quite commonly used, sometimes confused, and often abused. We even have a holiday dedicated to love."

"Well!" Deacon Scott said again.

"Just yesterday, we celebrated that special day known to all as

Valentine's Day. On that particular day, men, women, and even children reach out to their loved ones. I once heard a person say, 'There is nothing better than to be loved by your valentine!'"

"Tell it! Tell it!" Deacon Scott shouted.

"Chuch, love is more than a word. No matter how you put it. Love is special, and it makes other people feel special! Think about how you feel when someone says, 'I love you' or asks 'Do you love me?' Feels good, don't it?"

"Yes," the congregation agreed.

"I love you, Rasheed," Keysha whispered.

"I love you, too," Rasheed softly replied.

Reverend Life continued, "Some of you probably were in the store last night, searching for chocolates, flowers, and balloons to make that person feel special!"

A murmur ran through the crowd. Clearly, there were many individuals who could relate to Reverend Life. Keysha scooted closer to Rasheed and lightly placed her hand on his as she listened to Reverend Life.

"Think back to when you were a child, and your mother had to wipe your nose or clean you because you had messed yourself. She did not do it because she was getting paid; she did it because of love! Love is!"

"Tell it! Tell it!" Deacon Scott said.

"When your father went to work with his shirt all clean and came home after the sun had gone down with his shirt stained with sweat and grime, he did not do it because he had to but because of love. Love is!"

"Tell it! Tell it!" Deacon Scott erupted as he waved his hand in the air.

"Friends in Christ, I shared with you the scripture. I share this with you because you cannot fully love your neighbor if you can't love your God with all your heart!"

"Preach!" shouted Deacon Scott as he stood up, clapping his hands.

"It's a two way street, chuch!" Reverend Life said. "You have to love your neighbor if you are gonna love God!"

"Preach! Preach!" Deacon Scott shouted.

Reverend Life began to let a little growl be heard in his powerful voice as he continued, "Today, um, Philadelphia! I want you to know that loving God with all your heart will take you a long way!"

"Tell it! Tell it!"

"Um...that's the first commandment. Similar to it is the second commandment. Love your neighbor as you would love yourself...hmm! God, thank you for letting me feel your holy spirit!"

"Tell it! Tell it!"

Rasheed glanced over at the mother board, dressed in their white suits with their large Sunday hats. They were all rocking from side to side.

"Love! Hmm. Love Is! Love is the key. If you ain't got love, you ain't got nothing!"

"That's right!" cried a woman on the mother board.

"Chuch, God wants your talents, your intelligent ideas, and

most of all, your will!"

"That's what I am talking 'bout!" Keysha said.

"Chuch, when God brings you out of the valley of the shadow of death, you can't act like you did that all by yourself! You have to give Him the glory because He did it out of love! Love is!"

"Talk to em', reverend!" Rasheed shouted as he stood up.

"God, the doors of the chuch are open! Philadelphia, let the doors of the chuch open!"

The ushers opened the doors.

"Philadelphia, love is! Hmm! Love is!"

Donna wiped her eyes. It was becoming harder and harder to hold the tears back.

"Love is not jealous, and it does not boast. It suffers long and is not easily provoked. It does not think evil, but it bears all things, believes all things, and hopes all things. It endures to the end!"

"Tell it! Tell it!" Deacon Scott yelled.

"If someone around you ain't loving you….hmm… love them anyway, so said the Lord. Luke! Chapter six! Verse twenty-seven! Bless them that curse you and pray for them that use you!"

"Thank you, Jesus!" Keysha shouted.

Reverend Life walked from the pulpit and crouched low to the ground.

"I've been down and low. I've been down so low that I could slide under a rock and not be seen!"

"Tell it! Tell it!" shouted Deacon Scott.

"I've been so high that I could sit on an eagle's nest!"

"Yes, Lord," Donna shouted.

"Through all the celebrations and the tribulations, negatives, positives, and rigmarole, the love of the Lord brought me through!"

"Yes, He did!" Keysha said.

"Hmm! Philadelphia! Hmm! Love is! Love is…God! Don't let today pass 'cause we don't know which day will be our last! Aahhh!"

The church applauded as the music began to be played. Reverend Life twirled around, yelling into the microphone. Keysha was in tears, and Rasheed comforted her.

"It's okay. It's okay."

"I just miss them so much! I miss my mom! I miss my dad! I miss my sisters!"

"Then, let's not wait any longer," Rasheed said. "Let's catch an earlier flight."

"No, let's wait. I need this."

Rasheed nodded his head. Reverend Life stood before the congregation and extended an invitation to Christ.

"Is there anyone who wishes to join the chuch today? Come! Today could be your last chance!"

Donna stood up and walked toward Reverend Life as tears streamed down her face.

"Welcome, Sista Wright!" Reverend Life said as he hugged Donna.

The congregation applauded. Reverend Life let the clapping die down. Then, he spoke into the microphone, "Sister Wright, what brings you to the threshold? If I am not mistaken, you are already a fine member of this chuch!"

"Sister Wright? She looks so familiar. Could it be?" Rasheed said.

"I have been a member of the church for ten years, Reverend Life. Church, I need to solicit your prayers for my daughter."

"I remember her," Reverend Life said. "Is she okay?"

"No, my daughter is in jail and asked me to pray for her. Now, I am asking you, church, to join me in prayer."

Reverend Life beckoned for a member of the mother board to bring a chair. Rasheed leaned over and whispered to Keysha.

"I know that woman."

"Who is she?" Keysha asked.

"The mother of the person who tried to steal my company with fake documents!"

"What?" Keysha exclaimed.

"Yeah, we were dating for a while when I caught her redhanded, but I did not press charges. I guess her crimes finally caught up with her."

"Look how distraught her mother looks. She is tore up from the floor up!"

At that moment, the little girl who had been sitting behind them ran into the aisle and to Donna. Reverend Life looked surprised.

"Hello, little one."

"This is my granddaughter Chanise," Donna said.

"Why are you crying, Grandma?" Chanise asked. "Are we

still going to be able to call Ma Ma?"

"I'm sorry, baby! I am so sorry," Donna cried.

Reverend Life patted Donna on the shoulder as she hugged Chanise.

"Donna, I want to assure you that you have done the most appropriate thing. Chuch, hold your neighbor's hand and bow your heads. Let us pray."

Reverend Life reached down and held Chanise's hand as he prayed.

"Etertnal Father God, God of Abraham and Isaac, God of Shadrach, Meshach, and Abednego, hear our prayer."

"Yes, Lord," said the congregation.

"Today, your child has come before the chuch and is asking for your favor and your mercy."

"Yes, Lord."

"Donna's daughter, Kandis Wright, is behind bars, labeled a prisoner of the state, but today we call her a child of God and ask that you improve her situation."

"Yes, Lord."

"Break her bonds! Remove her from the pit, Jesus! As our prayer goes up, Lord, let your blessings come down! Strengthen this family for the days to come and bring them out of the wilderness and into the land of milk and honey! Amen! Amen! Amen!"

"Amen!" responded the congregation.

At that moment, Rasheed stood up and walked to Reverend Life. Some people noticed him from the news. Various whispers could be heard as they said, "It's Mr. Unbreakable! It's him!

He's here!"

"My name is Rasheed Locke, and I have a testimony, Reverend Life. May I?"

"Please share it."

Rasheed took the microphone.

"First, I want everyone to know that I am alive and well."

There was a round of applause.

"In the past forty-eight hours, I have survived suicide bombers, a plane crash, and a carjacking! God is good!"

"All the time," responded the congregation.

"In the midst of it all, I found unconditional love for myself, for another, and for God. My testimony is that love is powerful and that it flourishes during the hardest of times!"

"Amen," Reverend Life agreed.

"I ask that the congregation pray for my family as well. My cousin has been missing for almost a month and a half. I pray that she is found alive."

"Amen," replied the congregation.

Rasheed looked down at Donna.

"I also would like to extend my help to the Wright family. Mrs. Wright, we met a long time ago. I was your daughter's previous employer and ex-boyfriend until the incident."

Donna looked up at Rasheed in astonishment, "Rasheed? Rasheed?"

"Yes, ma'am."

Donna shook his hand.

"My daughter did some terrible things to you."

"That is fine, but more importantly, take this card. These lawyers can probably help with Kandis' case. Tell them you are a friend of mine."

Rasheed reached into his pocket and pulled out a card that was titled Charles & Steve Esquire.

"T-thank you," Donna said.

"No, thank you. Tell Kandis I forgive her, and I hope that everything works out for her."

"O-okay," Donna replied.

Rasheed walked back to where Keysha sat as Reverend Life addressed the congregation.

"Thank you, Donna, for your request. Thank you, Rasheed, for your testimony. Now, let us take up an offering. All of the proceeds will go towards assisting the Wright family. Deacon Scott, I am going to need you to lead the prayer."

There was a loud applause. The ushers came forward and passed along an offering tray. When it came to Rasheed, he dropped in a thousand dollar check. After the collection plate had passed, Rasheed whispered to Keysha, "We have a flight to catch."

She nodded her head. As Deacon Scott prayed over the offering in his deep majestic voice, Rasheed and Keysha eased out of the church. They hurried down the steps and hopped into their car. They exited the church grounds and drove north to the Atlanta Airport in silence. Rasheed cherished the moment as he rode with this beautiful woman on his passenger side. This was a life-changing moment, and he was cherished every second of it.

Chapter 11
No Place Like Home

Rasheed parked his car in parking lot A at the Atlanta Airport. He took his duffle bag out of the car and looked at Keysha as reality set in.

"Keysha, this is it."

"I know. I can't believe it is about to happen. At least we are going to make it happen together."

"Well, let's do it before we freeze together."

The couple walked across the parking lot as the cold wind gusted against them. Shortly after, they entered the airport and walked to the attendant at the Swift Airlines kiosk.

"Good afternoon. How may I help you?" the attendant asked.

"I have reservations for two for a three o'clock flight to Lafayette, Louisiana but would like to see if there is anything flying sooner."

"Okay, let's see. What is your name?"

"Rasheed Locke."

After typing in some information into her computer, the attendant looked back up. There was a regretful look on her face.

"I am sorry, but, when you made your reservations, we were experiencing a glitch in the system. I have one seat available for 1 pm and two seats available for 3:30 pm."

Rasheed turned back to Keysha and gave her the bad news. Then he asked, "Do you want to leave at 1 pm by yourself or do you want to leave together at 3:30 pm? What do you want to do?"

"Rasheed, I can't choose!" Keysha cried out. "I want to be with you, but I want to see my family!"

"You have to choose. If you can't, then I will choose for you."

"Hmm!" Keysha pouted.

"Keysha, don't poke your lip out at me!"

The attendant at the kiosk studied the couple and thought that they were a perfect item.

"That is so sweet! Are you two engaged?" the attendant asked.

"No," Keysha blushed.

"Well, you should be," the attendant said. "You two are a perfect match!"

"She hasn't seen her family in a while, and I am just trying to get her home," Rasheed explained.

"Oh! Happy tears!" the attendant said. "I am going to put you both on a flight together."

"I thought you said the flights were booked," Rasheed said.

"They are, but I can work it out."

"Why are you doing this?" Keysha asked.

"I rarely see people in love like you two. I can feel it and almost touch it! Hopefully, I will have the privilege to be in love like that one day."

"I can't argue with that," Rasheed said.

The attendant keyed in some more information. Moments later, two tickets printed, and Rasheed checked in his bag after paying for the tickets.

"Thank you," Rasheed said.

"You are welcome, Mr. Locke. Enjoy your flight."

Keysha and Rasheed held hands as they filed in behind the other passengers in the check point line. Keysha noticed the people in front of her had their tickets out plus an ID card.

"Rasheed?"

"Yeah. What's up, love?" Rasheed asked.

"I-I don't have a picture ID. They are not going to let me on the plane."

Quickly, Rasheed thought about how they could avoid that part of the security check. He reached into his pocket and fished out a piece of gum.

"Pull your bangs in front of your face and chew on this."

"Huh?" Keysha asked.

"Trust me," Rasheed whispered. "Act young. Act careless."

Keysha started chewing the gum and played with her curly hair as they approached the middle aged female attendant who sat on a stool, checking each passenger's ID and ticket. They walked up to the attendant, and Rasheed handed the two tickets and picture ID to the attendant.

"Good afternoon," Rasheed said.

"Hello," the attendant dryly replied. "I need her ID."

"My daughter is underage."

"Underage? Where at? Certainly not with those hips!"

Rasheed leaned forward and whispered to the attendant.

"She is almost fifteen. You should see her mother. She is an Amazon. She is from Sweden and plays volleyball."

The female flight attendant glared at Keysha with critical, disbelieving eyes.

"She even wears a size eleven shoe," Rasheed whispered to the flight attendant.

"Good gibbity goo!" the woman said as she looked down at Keysha's feet. "Go on! Go 'head!"

"Thank you," Rasheed said.

They walked past the attendant and through another checkpoint. Then, they caught the escalator to the train. As they boarded the train, Keysha pulled her hair back.

"What did you say to that lady?"

"I told her you were my fourteen year old daughter."

"Rasheed, you're crazy!"

"That's what they keep telling me, but I don't believe them."

"Concourse C is the next stop," advised the computerized voice.

The train stopped, and everyone disembarked. Rasheed led Keysha to Concourse C where they sat in front of a glass window. They could see planes landing and taking off.

"Rasheed, I have to warn you about my father."

"What about?" Rasheed asked fearfully.

"He is nice, but he likes to play jokes on people. Nasty jokes."

"Nasty jokes? Like what?"

"He chased me and my sisters around one day with a large bull frog that sits in our water fountain outside, and he likes to keep a machine that makes farting noises!"

"Ha! Ha! Ha!" Rasheed laughed. "I thought you were 'bout to say something outlandish!"

"There's something else I need to warn you about," Keysha said in a more serious tone.

"What's that?" Rasheed asked.

"It's just that your world is very different from mine."

"What is that supposed to mean?"

"Rasheed," Keysha replied, "I could put six of my houses into your house and still have room!"

"And your point is?"

"I am poor! Okay? There! I said it! I don't mean dirt poor, but we have had more hard times than the average family!"

"So you think that I may be turned off by the type of house you live in or the neighborhood you are from?"

"Yes! They call my neighborhood Fruity Town because you can get dope on any corner!"

"Look into my eyes and listen to the words that come out of my mouth," Rasheed said, caressing Keysha's soft hand.

"I'm listening," Keysha said. She peered into Rasheed's

brown eyes and felt all of the tension in her body go away.

"I love you. I appreciate where you come from and everything that defines you. There is only one of you."

"T-thank you. I love you, too!"

The two hugged and passionately kissed. At that moment, a man walked past, shaking his head and talking to himself.

"Gosh, how could they have a glitch in the system? How can they not have my tickets? I ordered them months in advance! Now, I have to catch the 3:30 flight!"

Keysha looked at Rasheed smiled. They both knew that the flight attendant had pulled some strings to get them on the same earlier flight. Even though the man seemed distraught, they knew he would be fine. Suddenly, the attendant at the kiosk made an announcement.

"Ladies and gentleman, Flight 725 is ready to board. Now boarding Sections A thru B."

"This is it. Are you ready?" Rasheed asked.

"I am scared, Rasheed."

"Love always overcomes fear. I am here with you."

Rasheed took Keysha by the hand as they stood in line. The attendant took their tickets and processed them. Then, hand in hand, they walked down the walkway. When they made it to the airplane, the flight attendant greeted them, "Good afternoon!"

"Good afternoon!" Keysha and Rasheed replied.

They walked down the aisle and found their seats. After all the passengers were settled, the flight attendant greeted the passengers over the intercom.

"Good afternoon, ladies and gentlemen. Welcome aboard Flight 725 to Lafayette, Louisiana. My name is Lisa Goode, and I am your senior flight attendant."

Keysha tuned Lisa Goode out and whispered to Rasheed, "I am going to take a nap."

"I think I will, too," Rasheed said.

They both tuned the flight attendant out as she advised about the exits and emergency procedures. Shortly after, the engines began to whirr as the plane started to make its way toward the runway. When the airplane was in position, the whirring of the engines became a crescendo. Then, the airplane burst down the runway at a magnificent speed and lifted off. Keysha Belle was on her way home.

2

As they were taking off from Atlanta Airport, Wolf was putting his bag in the back of a small, yellow cab. The afternoon sun was hot and blazing in San Jose, Costa Rica.

"¿Habla Ingles?" Wolf asked.

"Sí, señor," the cab driver responded.

"Bueno. Take me to El Hotel del Sol, northeast of downtown."

"No problemo. That is near the jungle?"

"Correct."

The dark haired cabdriver nodded his head and sped through the streets. Wolf noticed that there were no addresses on the buildings as they passed.

"Señor, I do not see any addresses on the buildings," Wolf

said.

"Addresses? What is 'addresses'?" the cab driver asked.

"You know, um, street numbers."

"Ah! Street numbers. No street numbers in San Jose. We do things the old way."

"You still use landmarks to navigate."

"Sí, señor."

They passed the crowded downtown district of El Pueblo. Wolf marveled at the numerous people going to and fro, the various restaurants, bars, and music clubs.

"I see that San Jose has embraced tourism well."

"Sí, but don't let the good taste fool you. Nobody want to see the bad side."

"Bad side? Everything looks nice from here," Wolf replied. "Crowded, but nice."

"Looks can be deceiving, señor. Bad people everywhere. This is the home of La Committee. Their palace sits on that hill."

Wolf raised his eyebrows as the cab driver pointed his finger. On a nearby green hill that overlooked the downtown district and the jungle was a white palace.

"Nice home."

"Head honcho of La Committee resides there. They kidnap our women and sell drugs to our kids. Bad people! Very bad!"

"Why don't the police do something?" Wolf inquired.

"Polícia no more," the cab driver said. "The ones with the most money is polícia now."

The cab driver turned onto a narrow street, exiting the downtown district. In a couple of minutes, the rusty cab pulled up at a wooden shack that sat on the edge of the lush green jungle. A yellow sign with orange words protruded from the side of the building. The sign read as follows: El Hotel del Sol.

Wolf got out the vehicle and paid the cabdriver twenty dollars. Then, he walked into the building. He walked down a short hallway to the front desk where a slick haired man smoking a long thin cigarette greeted him. Behind him was a wall with four keys hanging on a board.

"¿Como estás? My name is Senga."

"I need a room," Wolf replied dryly.

"You are in luck, my friend! We have several rooms available."

"Room 235, please."

"Um. I am sorry, but we only have ten rooms and four are available. None of them are 235."

"Is the manager available?"

"I am—"

Wolf interrupted Senga and cut directly to the chase, "Look. Call Keifer. He knows me."

"I don't know a Kiefer."

Wolf reached across the desk and grabbed the man by the collar.

"You don't listen too well, do you? I said call Keifer. I didn't ask if you knew Keifer."

"O-okay, and then what?"

"Tell him that Wolf wants room 235."

"O-okay. Can you let me go now?'

Wolf released Senga. The mentioning of the name had startled Senga. Not many people knew his boss's real name. He picked up a nearby phone and made the phone call. There was a brief moment of whispering. Then, Senga reached into a drawer and pulled out a golden key.

"I apologize for any inconvenience. Keifer sends his greetings."

"I accept your apologizes. Tell Keifer I am much obliged."

"He also says if you need anything to let me know. I was a prisoner during la Resistencia. I am honored to serve the person who freed us!"

"Gracias. Is The Millionaire Next Door the book everyone is reading this month?"

"No. The Art of War is the book of the month."

Wolf was about to walk away when he turned and asked Senga another question.

"Senga, do you like fireworks?"

"Who doesn't?" Senga smiled. "Bang! Bang! Boom!"

"There is going to be a good show tonight. Don't miss it."

Wolf walked up the stairs and to the end of the hallway where he found a bookshelf. He searched the books that were lined up and found The Art of War. Wolf slightly tugged on the spine of the book. The bookshelf slid to the side and revealed a steel door. Wolf inserted the key into the lock and turned it. He could feel the tumblers giving way and unlocking the door. The door creaked open, and Wolf walked inside.

301

"I love it! Just what the doctor ordered!"

There was a bed, a lamp, and a nightstand with a Holy Bible on top. Instead of a dresser and television being positioned on the nearby wall, there was a wall of machine guns, automatic pistols with silencers, grenades, and other items used to wage a war and to demolish an enemy stronghold.

3

The sound of the pilot speaking over the intercom awoke Rasheed.

"Thank you for your patience, ladies and gentlemen. I apologize for any inconvenience."

"Keysha, what is wrong?" Rasheed asked as he glanced at her and noticed the scowl on her face.

"There is bad weather in Louisiana, so we are going to have to layover in Biloxi," Keysha said. She was very disappointed.

"Man," Rasheed said in frustration. "If it ain't one thing, then it's another!"

Suddenly, the pilot came back on over the intercom and said, "Greetings, passengers of Flight 725! Because of this inconvenience, we have arranged for a charter bus to take you to a nearby casino."

"Have you ever been to a casino?" Rasheed asked Keisha.

"No. I've never had money to throw away like that!"

"Well, then, the game you will want to play is blackjack. All you have to do is count the cards!"

"Rasheed, that is like asking me to speak Greek. I can't play cards to save my life better yet to win some money!"

"Then, you might want to watch me," Rasheed said. "I am a professional!"

The pilot spoke over the intercom again.

"Ladies and gentlemen, we are about to start the decent. Please fasten your seatbelts."

Rasheed could feel the pressure in his ears as they started to descend from their high altitude. They passed through a cloud. Then, Rasheed saw the beautifully lit city of Biloxi, Mississippi, the crown jewel of southern gambling. In minutes, they had landed on the runway where a charter bus awaited them. After they had landed, the flight attendant, Lisa Goode, passed out pagers with a small red light and explained what they were for.

"Listen up, ladies and gentlemen. These pagers will start to flash once it is time to return to the bus! Enjoy!"

The passengers hurried off the plane and to the awaiting bus. When everyone was aboard, the charter bus drove down the runway. In a few minutes, they had pulled up at a casino that sat on a waterway bordered by palm trees.

"Wow! This is beautiful!" Keysha exclaimed.

"Wait 'til you see the inside!" Rasheed said. "Let's get some moolah, baby!"

Rasheed opened the glass doors of the casino, and Keysha walked inside. There were numerous machines where people sat, pulling levers and other games where a person dealt cards. Rasheed took her by the hand and led her to a blackjack table.

"Twenty-one is the game! Making money is my thang! Dealer, cut me in like a piece of cheese on a double cheeseburger!"

"The cut is one thousand dollars," the dealer said.

"Then, let there be light! Let's do it!" Rasheed said as he pulled out his credit card and slapped it on the table.

"Very well," the dealer said.

He slid a couple of chips towards Rasheed. Keysha tugged at Rasheed's sleeve like a little kid and asked, "Before you get started, can you spot me some money?"

"Here take two hundred," Rasheed said as he counted out some money. "Good luck."

"Thanks. I will be right over there at the slot machines."

"No problem. I love you."

"I love you, too," Keysha replied.

Keysha walked away as Rasheed rubbed his hands. She walked to and fro, searching for a machine to sit at, but there seemed to be just too many, so she tried a process of elimination.

"Bubble gum, bubble gum in a dish, how many pieces do you wish? One, two, three!"

She sat down at the twenty-five cent slot machine. A waitress quickly walked over to her.

"Hi, what would you like to drink?"

"Can I get a rum and coke?" Keysha asked.

"Sure. Do you need change?"

"Yes. Can you give me twenty in quarters?"

"Certainly."

Keysha handed her a one hundred dollar bill. The waitress

fished into the belt that hung from her side and pulled out eighty dollars in twenties and twenty dollars in quarters.

"I will return shortly with your drink," the waitress said.

"Um, ma'am, do you know how to play this machine?" Keysha asked.

"You basically want each slot to line up in a specific combination. The cherry, banana, grapes combination is the jackpot, and it looks like it is up to ten million! Any other combination is worthless."

"Jumpin' Jehosophat!" Keysha exclaimed. "It is all or nothing!"

"Basically," the waitress responded.

"Thank you for your time! Hurry back with that drink. I'm going to need it."

Keysha enthusiastically unrolled the quarters and began to feed the machine.

"Come here, money! Come to mommy!"

Keysha pulled the lever.

Cherry, Banana, Hammer

"Doggone your soul!"

The waitress returned with her drink. Keysha sipped the drink as she put in another quarter and pulled the lever.

Grapes, Hammer, Car

"Dang it!"

Keysha glanced over at the blackjack table and saw Rasheed rubbing his head. The stack of chips was now down to a few. She put in another quarter.

Grapes, Hammer, Lips

Frustration began to set in each time a ridiculous combination appeared that did not result in a reward. She went through another twenty like wind through a tunnel. Before she knew it, Keysha had devoured five rum and cokes and was down to her last quarter.

"Why...Why...Why?" Keysha asked in a pitiful voice.

The quarter gleamed at her inquiry.

"I's married nah," Keysha said to the quarter. "Hah! Hah! Hah!"

Rasheed walked over to her and massaged her shoulders.

"Looks like someone has had too much to drink! You are talking to your money!"

"Who me?" Keysha snickered in a drunken way. "Those girlie drinks couldn't get me! I'm a souljah in da army!"

Suddenly, the pager went off.

"This thing is buzzing," Rasheed said as he held the pager. "We have to get back to the bus."

"One more. One more for ol' time's sake! Let me send him home to his family."

"Ain't nothing to it but to do it," Rasheed said.

Keysha put the quarter into the machine and pulled the lever. Everything moved in slow motion as the dials turned.

Cherry

Rasheed leaned forward as the slot came to a stop.

Banana

The third slot rolled, and Keysha braced herself.

Grapes

Keysha sat stunned as alarms blared and confetti fell from the ceiling. Rasheed jumped around celebrating as he threw his hands in the air. The pager flew from his hand and smashed against the ground.

"Jackpot! My baby hit the jackpot! Yeah! Yeah!"

"I hit the jackpot?" Keysha asked softly. "I hit the jackpot?"

"You hit the jackpot!" Rasheed shouted as he kissed Keysha. "Ten Million smackaroos! Keysha, you just won ten million dollars!"

Keysha looked around with wide eyes and jumped around, yelling, "I hit the jackpot! I hit the jackpot!"

People began to push and shove each other, trying to see the winner of the ten million dollar jackpot. A man stepped on another man's shoes, causing a fight to break out.

"You stepped on my shoes!"

"Those pieces of cowhide ain't shoes!"

"A wise guy, huh? I know what to do with a wise guy!"

"They knuckin'," Rasheed said, pulling Keysha out of harm's way as the fight broke out.

"Get off Jimmy!" someone yelled as he leaped into the fight.

"Let Larry go!" another person cried out.

The fight escalated into an all out brawl as other people joined in the fray. Within seconds, the supervisor of the casino and his security team were on the scene, restoring order, calm, and peace.

"Miss, if you don't mind," the supervisor said in his southern dialect, "can y'all please come with us? It is for your own good!

People done got rowdy in here."

The supervisor quickly escorted Keysha and Rasheed to the back office of the casino where he sat down at a computer and addressed them.

"My name is Vincent, and you are?"

"Keysha Belle, and this is Rasheed Locke."

"Nice to meet y'all! Keysha Belle. That is such a lovely name."

"Appreciate it."

"Well," Vincent said, "Keysha Belle, to make a long story short. I would like to congratulate you on winning the ten million dollar jackpot. Your name will be placed on the Wall of Millionaires, and the machine will be named after you!"

"Oh, my!" Keysha gasped in excitement.

Vincent quickly typed her name into his database and pressed print. Behind him a certified check for ten million dollars printed on a watermarked check.

"This is yours! Well earned!" Vincent said.

He handed her the check and a pair of keys.

"What are the keys for?" Keysha asked.

"The winner of the jackpot always gets a little extra to go along with the money. Waiting for you outside is a new car. All I need you to do is sign this waiver that states you have received your earnings."

Keysha signed her name on the waiver and shook Vincent's hand. Then, Rasheed asked, "Vincent, is there a backdoor we can go out of? Someone may try us. You know what I'm saying?"

"Of course. Follow me."

Keysha and Rasheed followed the representative of the casino through a side door. Then, they walked down a long hallway to the back door. As they exited the casino, Rasheed saw that the bus had left already.

"How far is it to Lafayette?" Rasheed asked.

"At least three hours from here," Keysha replied.

"Toss me the keys, and let's ride!"

Keysha tossed him the keys, and he pressed the unlock button on the keypad. There was a chirp from the front row where a large SUV blocked their view. They walked around the corner for a better angle.

"Press it again," Keysha requested.

The tail lights of a black Porsche SUV that was trimmed in chrome flashed.

"Oh, my God! I didn't even know they made a Porsche truck!"

"It was made just for you," Rasheed said as he opened the door. "Your carriage, my lady!"

"Thank you, kind sir!"

She hopped inside feeling like a princess. Rasheed followed suit, then backed the car up and pulled out of the parking lot of the casino. Their next stop would be Lafayette, Louisiana.

It was nightfall in the jungle surrounding San Jose, Costa

Rica. Frogs and other night animals chirped as tourists walked to and fro, from one bar to the next. High above the vibrant town was the palace of La Committee. Surrounding the palace was a ten foot stone wall. The white palace was as quiet as a cemetery.

Two guards, Cardonza and Amierez, stood at attention at the entrance to the white palace. They wore green camouflage with belts of bullets crisscrossing their chests. They each held machine guns. They had been trained to kill with no mercy.

That night, as a party raged on below them, they whispered about the emerging nightlife of San Jose.

"The party is loud, ay, Cardonza?" Amierez asked.

Cardonza looked down and spat on the ground.

"Sí, Amierez! Tourists! Such scum!"

Suddenly, a knife was hurled through the air. The knife stabbed Amierez in the throat, preventing him from screaming. Rushing from the jungle was a man dressed, like the two guards, in camouflage. The commando was Wolf.

He grasped Amierez by the neck and snapped it. Then, he quietly dragged him into the jungle while Cardonza continued to talk, oblivious to what was occurring.

"The scum Americans and Europeans trash our streets while civil Costa Ricans serve them! Pathetic! Amierez, do you know what we should do?"

There was no answer.

"Amierez? Don't you hear me talking to you?"

Cardonza turned to acknowledge his friend, but there was no one there. He smiled, laughed aloud, and said, "Amierez! I told you not to eat those raisins! Ha! Ha!"

At that moment, a noose slowly descended from the wall above him. As it slid under Cardonza's chin, a dry voice whispered from above, "I see you like to hang around."

"What the —"

The nose tightened, causing Cardonza to drop his machine gun. Cardonza reached for the knife that was attached to his waist, but the noose tightened more. The rope cut into his skin. He struggled as he grasped the rope. The rope tightened again. He was raised from his feet. He kicked and struggled, but it was too late. Cardonza's neck snapped. Once he was dead, the rope lowered him to the ground and into the bushes. Wolf slid down the wall and into the shadows where he looked through a pair of night vision binoculars.

"All perimeter guards eliminated," Wolf said. "Let's see where everyone else is?"

He clicked on a button, and the optic view changed to display body temperature. In the right wing of the palace, there were numerous orange objects. He panned to the left wing. There was one orange object. Wolf licked his lips and whispered, "El Ojo de la Committee."

He rose to his feet and sprinted across the courtyard. Wolf knew that he had the element of surprise on his side, but he could not want to underestimate his opponent. Revenge was a dish best served cold.

Inside the palace, El Ojo sat at his desk and turned on the one hundred-inch television screen to First News Network. The anchor woman, Monica Drake, appeared on the television screen. A "breaking news" caption hovered over her head.

"Hmm, more drama in Atlanta," El Ojo said. "They must have discovered the bodies or what was left of them! At times, the Eliminator can be messy!"

"Good evening! This is Monica Drake! We have late breaking news! Rasheed Locke, the pilot of the plane that crashed in the Chattahoochee River, is not at the hospital. His female acquaintance is missing as well!"

El Ojo smiled, exposing his brown rotting teeth, and said, "Flawless victory!"

Monica Drake continued, "However, there have been numerous reports of people seeing them around the city!"

"Impossible!" El Ojo shouted.

"Witnesses saw them rescuing people moments before Jackson Memorial Hospital exploded in flames. Others saw them at a gas station in Clayton County, and we are now receiving reports that they were recently seen at a casino in Biloxi, Mississippi!"

El Ojo slammed his feeble fist on the desktop and screamed, "The Eliminator has failed! He has failed La Committee!"

Suddenly, the electricity in the palace went out. El Ojo sat calmly in the darkness, waiting for the generator to kick-in. He picked up his radio and chirped his technician, saying, "Amierez, the generator is off line! Get it fixed! Amierez, do you read me?"

There was no reply.

"Cardonza, answer me! The generator is off line. Get it fixed, now!"

"It won't be fixed," a calm voice said in the darkness. "Because there is no one to fix it."

El Ojo wheeled around. His heart pounded wildly in his feeble chest.

"Who are you?"

Like the eyes of a demon, two infrared dots appeared on his chest.

"My identity is not important!"

"Whoever you are, you are finished!" El Ojo yelled. "I will peel your skin off your body while you are alive and dip you into a vat of acid!"

"Go ahead. Make your move."

El Ojo pressed a button beneath his desk, but nothing happened. No alarms blared.

"Something is wrong. This can't be!"

"No one will answer you, El Ojo. Your help has been sent to the upper room!"

"But I-I have over fifty guards!"

"Fifty-seven to be exact. I counted them as I tossed them into the bushes."

El Ojo's heart fluttered as he realized that this was the end. At that moment, the emergency flood lights came on in the hallway. El Ojo stared at a man with black and green paint streaked across his face. His bare arms were massive. Protecting his chest was a green armored vest with grenades. Two pistols with infrared laser beams were in his hands.

"Who...who are you?"

"The name is Wolf, but, more importantly, where is your private plane, and where are the women?"

"Señor Wolf, you will not get away with this shameful robbery!"

Wolf aimed his left pistol at the large television screen and fired.

"I beg to differ!" Wolf said. "Now, get up and do what I say before I shoot you one piece at a time!"

Wolf pointed the red beams at El Ojo's pelvic area. El Ojo got the message. He got up from his chair and hobbled toward the door. Wolf gave him plenty of distance and followed him down the hallway. They came to a door that led to the back yard.

"The plane is out there!" El Ojo said.

Wolf looked out of the window. The private plane was there.

"Good. Now, take me to the women!"

They made a left and walked down a corridor until they came to a door that required fingerprint and eye recognition.

"Open the door!"

El Ojo reluctantly put his first finger onto the pad and looked into a small opening. A green laser scanned his finger and eye. Then, the door opened. Packaging several different drugs were twenty-five naked women. They looked famished and starved. Their ribs and sternums showed. Wolf held up a picture and yelled, "Gwen Harris! Gwen Harris! Show yourself!"

A young black woman looked up from her work. It had been

so long since she had heard her name spoken with concern, care, or compassion.

"Gwen Harris! Gwen Harris! Your cousin Rasheed has sent me!"

Gwen snapped out of her trance and responded in a tearful voice, "I am here! Oh, my God! I'm right here!"

Wolf spotted the woman and nodded his head.

"Good! Are there any more prisoners anywhere else in this palace?"

"No, some died of hunger, and others just killed themselves," Gwen said.

"Gwen," Wolf delegated, "take the other women and get yourselves some clothes. Then, meet me in the backyard in two minutes! We are going home!"

"Yeah! Yeah!" cheered the women.

They rushed out of the room, leaving Wolf and El Ojo alone. Wolf stepped back and stood in the doorway as he stared at the feeble old man. He licked his lips. Then, he quoted a verse of scripture, "Old wicked idolater, thus said the Lord: And I will set my face against them. They shall go out from one fire, and another fire shall devour them and ye shall know I am the Lord!"

"A street-preacher!" El Ojo laughed. "You will go to hell before me!"

Wolf reached into his backpack and extracted an explosive. He attached it to the wall.

"You worship money and drugs. You place people in chains," Wolf said. "An end has come. The end has come."

"Without evil, the world is nothing!" El Ojo shouted. "Nothing, Señor Wolf! Evil is necessary for this world to survive!"

"Today, your evil ends," Wolf said.

Wolf closed the door and placed another explosive on the outside of the door. He hurried to the door that led to the backyard. He tossed the backpack of explosives down the hall and ran down the steps and into the backyard. He rushed to the plane as Gwen stuck her head out of the cabin.

"Over here!" Gwen shouted.

"Here I come," Wolf cried.

He ran over to the plane and dashed up the steps. Then, he pressed the button to close the stairs and sat in the pilot seat. The engines of the plane whirred as he steered the nose towards the runway. Then, he picked up the intercom and addressed his passengers.

"This is Wolf. I would like to thank you for flying Freedom Airlines. Our next stop will be the United States."

"Yeah!" cheered his female passengers.

Wolf waited until the cheers died down. Then, he continued, "Fasten your seatbelts. For your enjoyment, there will be fireworks as we take off!"

He clicked the red button of his remote detonator. The bombs he had placed along the wall and inside the palace began to rapidly countdown.

El Ojo collapsed to the ground as he reiterated the catechism of La Committee.

"May the angels welcome me to heaven or hell!"

Wolf's plane took off and thirty seconds later, the palace exploded.

The people partying in the streets of San Jose cheered at the sound of the explosion. Standing in the midst of a crowd was Senga, the front desk clerk. He looked up at the fiery explosion and waved his hand.

"Farewell, Wolf! Until we meet again, whether in this world or the next!"

Senga walked into a nearby bar. He wanted to be the first to toast to the destruction of La Committee.

It was a stormy night in Lafayette, Louisiana. The thunder boomed, and the lightning flashed as the rain fell in sheets. At the Belle residence, the house was as silent as the bottom of a deeply dug well. It was uncanny.

A tall man with dark brown skin stood at the bottom of a flight of steps dressed in a tank top and pair of black shorts with a red dragon imprinted on each side. He stared up the steps to the upstairs portion of the home where his daughter had once slept. The man was Keysha's father, and his name was Rice.

On this stormy night, Rice stood at the bottom of his steps and called out to his wife as she walked around upstairs, "What are you doing up there, Cher?"

A beautiful voice responded to him. The voice belonged to Keysha's mother, and her name was Gail.

"Nothing. Just cleaning up the room. It has a little dust on the dresser."

"Hmm," Rice said as he leaned against the wall and rubbed his bald head.

It was getting harder and harder to deal with the fact that Keysha was never coming home. They had no idea where she was. They did not know if she was alive, dead, or even worse.

Rice walked back into the kitchen. He was supposed to be cooking, but, for some strange reason, his appetite had vanished.

At that moment, there was a loud knock at the door.

"Who is it?" asked Rice.

"Your daughter Candace."

"Go away!" Rice playfully responded before he opened the door.

"You know you miss me," Candace said joyfully as she walked into the house.

"If I miss you, why are you here?"

"Yeah! Yeah!" Candace giggled.

Rice sat down on the burgundy leather couch in the living room and turned his big screen television to First News Network. Candace came in the room and sat down beside her father.

"Where is Mom?" Candace asked.

"Upstairs, cleaning your sister's room."

"Is Mom gonna be okay?" Candace asked as a troubled look came over her face.

"Let her deal with it how she deals with it. I don't ask if you alright when you deal with it the way you deal with it."

"Look, cher! What do y'all have to eat?"

"Air and farts," Rice replied.

"You're so nasty!" Candace laughed.

She walked into the kitchen. Rice smiled as she walked away. He was glad that his youngest daughter had stopped by to see him and his wife. Once Candace made it into the kitchen, she saw that everything was clean, but there was no food.

"Y'all don't like to cook no more, I see."

"We don't eat as much as you," Rice nonchalantly replied.

"Nikki should be over here soon. I just got of the phone with her."

"Then, you all can make some shrimp fettuccini. Look in the refrigerator."

At that moment, another knock came at the door.

"If you ain't Jesus, then stay outside!" Rice said.

The door opened, and Rice's second eldest daughter, Nikki, walked in. She removed the plastic bag that covered her black shoulder-length hair and said, "It is raining cats and dogs outside, Daddy!"

"Then, why are you coming in?" Rice asked with a smirk on his face.

"Shut up, you!" Nikki smiled. "Where is Candace?"

"In the kitchen, making shrimp fettuccini. She need yo' help."

"Okay. Let me get in there before she poisons us all!"

Nikki walked to the kitchen where Candace was. It was these comical remarks that had nurtured the family's strong bonds that had been weakened by Keysha's unexpected absence. Rice leaned back and turned the volume up on the television as Monica Drake reported for First News Network.

"This is Monica Drake with First News Network. We have late breaking news in Lafayette, Louisiana."

"Come see!" Rice shouted. "Come see! Lafayette is on the news!"

"An unmarked private plane has just landed at De Gaulle Airport. The passengers are twenty-five women who have been missing for months! Here is some footage from a local news station!"

"Everyone, come here now!" Rice shouted. "Good God! Look! Them women look bad!"

Soon, everyone had crowded into the living room to watch the footage of the women being assisted. Gail pulled her long silver hair back into ponytail as she leaned on Rice.

"What is it, Rice?" Gail asked.

"Them women were kidnapped!"

"Rice, do you think Key…" Gail started. Then, she broke down crying.

Rice held his wife as his daughters drew closer to them. At that moment, there was another knock at the door.

"Who could that be during this type of weather?" Nikki asked. "Candace, get the door."

"You're closer, Cher."

"Somebody, just get the door before they beat it down!" Rice said.

"I've got it," Gail said weakly.

She walked over to the door and grasped the golden door hand. She turned it to the right and swung it open. What she saw made her fall back into a nearby recliner.

"Merciful Mary! Gracious Lord! It is you! It is you!"

Everyone looked at Gail as tears streamed down her face.

"Mom, what is wrong?" Nikki asked.

"There!" Gail said as she pointed. "She is here! Merciful Mary! She has come back to us!"

The screen door opened, and Keysha stepped into the room, drenched from head to toe. Candace and Nikki rushed to her and hugged her.

"You're here! You're here!" Candace shouted.

"Thank you, God! I can't believe it!" Nikki cried.

Rice stood up from his seat, dumbfounded. He stumbled over to his wife and held her as they both cried.

"Our baby has come home, Rice," Gail cried.

"I-I-I-know," Rice cried. "Thank God!"

Candace and Nikki finally let go of Keysha. Then, Keysha stooped down and laid her head on her mother's lap. No one noticed Rasheed, standing behind her in the doorway. He held his peace. Suddenly, his cell phone vibrated, and he answered it.

"Hello?"

"Rasheed, are you near a television?"

"Yes. Who is this?" Rasheed asked.

"This is Wolf. Put it on First News Network ASAP!"

"Wolf—"

"Just do it!" Wolf urged.

Rasheed walked across the living room and looked at the television. Monica Drake was standing there speaking in her microphone.

"People, we have one of the victims of an organized crime family known as La Committee. She has been missing for almost two months now. Please tell us your name."

The cameraman panned to the left, and Gwen came into view. Rasheed's heart dropped to his knees as he heard his cousin speak.

"My name is Gwen Harris. I am from Atlanta, Georgia, and my cousin Rasheed Locke has been looking for me! Rasheed, wherever you are, please come pick me up! I am ready to go home to my momma!"

Rasheed slowly put the cell phone back to his ear.

"Wolf, I will be there in ten minutes."

"See you soon, Rasheed," Wolf said as he hung up the phone.

Finally, Rice and the rest of his family noticed the man in their house. Rice stood up and looked upon the man with great regard.

"Keysha, I have to go," Rasheed said. "Wolf, found my cousin! She was just on television. She's at the airport!"

"We are coming with you!" Keysha said.

"Let's go! You drive!"

Rasheed handed Keysha the car keys. Everyone dashed to the vehicle and piled into Keysha's new car. As she drove to the airport, Rice spoke from the back seat, "I am sorry, dude, but I didn't even ask your name."

"I am Rasheed Locke."

"Everyone calls me Rice. My wife and I would like to thank you for bringing back my baby girl."

"Thank you for your help," Mrs. Belle said. "You may call me Gail."

"You're welcome."

Rice smiled as he joked with Rasheed.

"Now, I am going to need you to give me something on the power bill because Keysha is going to be messing with the heater every night!"

"Be quiet, you!" Keysha laughed.

"Keysha, this is a nice car. What kind is it?" Gail asked.

"It is a Porsche."

"I didn't even know that they made a truck," Gail replied. "How long have you had it, Rasheed?"

"Actually, it is Keysha's. Tell them what happened, baby."

"To make a long story short. We stopped in Biloxi, and I won the jackpot! I got this car and ten million dollars!"

"My God! We are in heaven!" Rice said.

"Be quiet, you!" Gail said. "Keysha, you are a millionaire!"

"Correction, we are millionaires! I am going to set my family straight!"

"That's my big sister right there, Cher!" Candace said.

"I want you all to start packing tonight because tomorrow we are going house shopping, just like that!" Keysha said.

Keysha turned left onto the expressway. Soon, they saw the exit for De Gaulle Airport. She slowed her speed as they came to a police barricade. An officer dressed in an orange slicker walked over to the driver's side of the SUV. Keysha rolled down the window.

"I am sorry, but we can only let family members and media pass," the officer said.

"We are family!" Keysha said.

"Then, go down and make a right. The people are in the waiting area of the airport."

Keysha drove off and pulled up in the parking lot near a rectangle-shaped building. Rasheed leaped out of the SUV and ran into the airport. He stood in the lobby and yelled aloud, "Gwen, where are you?"

"Rasheed! Over here!" she called from down the hall.

Standing near baggage claim were Gwen and Wolf. Rasheed rushed over and tightly hugged his cousin.

"I thought you were dead!" Rasheed said.

"I thought I was, too! I thought that no one was ever coming to save me!"

Rasheed and Gwen held each other and cried as Keysha and her family walked up. Rasheed let Gwen go. Then, he hugged Wolf.

"You are truly a godsend, my brother!"

"No, that is you, Mr. Locke, and I believe this is yours. I hope I didn't spend that much."

He gave the credit card back to Rasheed.

"That is water under the bridge," Rasheed said. "This moment is priceless!"

"Rasheed, you believed in me and gave me another chance when I was dressed in rags. I am just honored to be a part of this reunion!"

"I still need you as head of my security team," Rasheed said.

"I think I can swing that," Wolf said.

Rasheed turned to Keysha. He walked over and kneeled before her. In turn, everyone in the airport turned their attention to Keysha and Rasheed.

"Rasheed, what are you doing?" Keysha asked.

"I am taking this to the next level. I want to know if you will marry me, for better or for worse."

Keysha sobbed as she answered, "Y-yes! Y-yes! I will marry you for better or for worse!"

"Crawfish boil tomorrow at noon at the Heyman Park! Everyone is invited!" Rice shouted.

Rasheed rose to his feet and passionately kissed Keysha as their family and friends stood around them. A month and a half after she had gone missing, Keysha had found the true love of her life. Six months later, Rasheed and Keysha exchanged vows before a host of their friends and family at a cathedral in Lafayette. They have now begun the greatest adventure ever as husband and wife.

7

Thousands of miles away in a Costa Rican hospital, a severely burned man was wrapped in gauze from head to toe. Only his eyes and stringy white hair were visible. The nurse walked into the room and checked the settings on his ventilator.

"You are lucky that we got to you in time," the nurse said. "We will rebuild you, El Ojo. La Committee will be stronger than ever! I am the Brown Recluse, and I will not fail!"

The nurse walked out of the room and closed the door. She had work to do. Restructuring the crime syndicate would take more than beauty and brains. It would take killing.

The End...For Now

G.S.CREWS

www.ingramcontent.com/pod-product-compliance
Lightning Source LLC
LaVergne TN
LVHW041606070426
835507LV00008B/163